'This book provides inspiring and various interpretations of manabi crossing East-West boundaries, in theory and in practice. For those who are interested in 'learning' in East Asian and global contexts, this book is a must-read.'
Ruyu Hung, *Distinguished Professor, National Chiayi University, Taiwan*

'The subject of "Manabi" is nearly unknown in the western educational discourse. It opens up an opportunity to develop a greater appreciation for traditional Japanese educational theory and educational practice and their historical roots. The authors show us how Buddhist culture of ZEN influenced teaching concepts in school. The "didactic" of the book is grounded in a comparison between Western and Japanese concepts of learning and Bildung, which facilitates access to understanding Japanese ideas of learning and development.'
Uwe Uhlendorff, *Professor, Dortmund University, Germany*

Manabi and Japanese Schooling

Manabi and Japanese Schooling: Beyond Learning in the Era of Globalisation considers the theory and practices behind the Japanese concept of Manabi, particularly as the progressive concept of learning in the globalised world. It seeks to provide educational visions of Manabi as an alternative concept of learning in the era of post-globalisation.

The authors derive different perspectives in Manabi from Eastern philosophy, clarifying and comparing with learning and Bildung to give alternative educational discourses. It considers the idea of Confucius and Taoism and studies the practice of Minna, characterising it as a cooperative and peaceful problem-solving method. Addressing the trend of 'learnification' and its contribution to educational reform, it explores the impacts, conflicts, and difficulties of introducing learner-centred education into East Asian educational settings as well as the potential of Manabi as an effective tool for all types of learning.

Expertly written and researched, this book includes a foreword by Gert Biesta and is a valuable resource for researchers, academics, and postgraduate students in the field of educational philosophy, educational theory, and Eastern philosophy.

Masamichi Ueno is Professor of Education at Sophia University, Japan.

Yasunori Kashiwagi is Professor of Early Childhood Care and Education at Chiba Keizai College, Japan.

Kayo Fujii is Associate Professor of Education at Yokohama National University, Japan.

Tomoya Saito is Professor of Education at Kokugakuin University, Japan.

Taku Murayama is Associate Professor of Special Needs Education at Tokyo Gakugei University, Japan.

Theorizing Education Series
Series Editors
Gert Biesta
Maynooth University, Ireland & University of Edinburgh, UK
Stefano Oliverio
University of Naples "Federico II", Italy

Theorizing Education brings together innovative work from a wide range of contexts and traditions which explicitly focuses on the roles of theory in educational research and educational practice. The series includes contextual and socio-historical analyses of existing traditions of theory and theorizing, exemplary use of theory, and empirical work where theory has been used in innovative ways. The distinctive focus for the series is the engagement with educational questions, articulating what explicitly educational function the work of particular forms of theorizing supports.

Inoperative Learning
A Radical Rewriting of Educational Potentialities
Tyson E. Lewis

Religious Education and the Public Sphere
Patricia Hannam

Art as Unlearning
Towards a Mannerist Pedagogy
John Baldacchino

Education in the Age of the Screen
Possibilities and Transformations in Technology
Edited by Nancy Vansieleghem, Joris Vlieghe and Manuel Zahn

Manabi and Japanese Schooling
Beyond Learning in the Era of Globalisation
Masamichi Ueno, Yasunori Kashiwagi, Kayo Fujii, Tomoya Saito and Taku Murayama

For more information about this series, please visit: www.routledge.com/Theorizing-Education/book-series/THEOED

Manabi and Japanese Schooling

Beyond Learning in the Era of Globalisation

Masamichi Ueno, Yasunori Kashiwagi, Kayo Fujii, Tomoya Saito and Taku Murayama

LONDON AND NEW YORK

First published 2020 by Routledge

2 Park Square, Milton Park, Abingdon, Oxon OX14 4RN
605 Third Avenue, New York, NY 10017

Routledge is an imprint of the Taylor & Francis Group, an informa business

First issued in paperback 2021

Copyright © 2020 Masamichi Ueno, Yasunori Kashiwagi, Kayo Fujii, Tomoya Saito and Taku Murayama

The right of Masamichi Ueno, Yasunori Kashiwagi, Kayo Fujii, Tomoya Saito and Taku Murayama to be identified as authors of this work has been asserted by them in accordance with sections 77 and 78 of the Copyright, Designs and Patents Act 1988.

All rights reserved. No part of this book may be reprinted or reproduced or utilised in any form or by any electronic, mechanical, or other means, now known or hereafter invented, including photocopying and recording, or in any information storage or retrieval system, without permission in writing from the publishers.

Notice:
Product or corporate names may be trademarks or registered trademarks, and are used only for identification and explanation without intent to infringe.

Publisher's Note

The publisher has gone to great lengths to ensure the quality of this reprint but points out that some imperfections in the original copies may be apparent.

British Library Cataloguing-in-Publication Data
A catalogue record for this book is available from the British Library

Library of Congress Cataloging-in-Publication Data
A catalog record for this book has been requested

ISBN: 978-0-8153-5467-3 (hbk)
ISBN: 978-1-03-217300-9 (pbk)
DOI: 10.4324/9781351132190

Typeset in Bembo
by Apex CoVantage, LLC

Contents

Foreword: Manabi beyond learning ix
GERT BIESTA
Acknowledgements xii
List of authors xiii

Introduction 1

PART I
The concept of Manabi 7

1 The thought of Manabi: learning in the age of globalisation reconsidered 9
MASAMICHI UENO

2 The analysis of Manabi: learning towards Nothingness and Selflessness 37
YASUNORI KASHIWAGI

3 Body and mind in Manabi: focusing on Kata and Shūyō 69
TOMOYA SAITO

PART II
Practices of Manabi 87

4 The resonance of Minna's voice in Japanese schooling 89
KAYO FUJII

5 Inclusiveness in/of Manabi 103
TAKU MURAYAMA

6	**Practices of Manabi in school**	125
	YASUNORI KASHIWAGI	

Conclusion	140

Index	144

Foreword
Manabi beyond learning

Gert Biesta

The ongoing globalisation of educational discourse, policy, and practice, 'supported' by the spread of the English language as the main medium of communication across a wide range of linguistic, cultural, political, social, and historical differences, seems to suggest that education is more or less the same 'thing' everywhere and that, where differences still exist, it will mainly be a matter of time before they have caught up with the global 'consensus.' While this may look like a satisfactory situation from the point of view of native speakers of the English language, it feels less so for those working in different languages and traditions, particularly traditions that have not just different educational practices but also different concepts to make sense, understand, and act within such practices. The key issue here is that of *translation*, and the main point is that the language of 'teaching and learning,' which has become ubiquitous in the English-speaking world, is not a neutral conduit in which all words and concepts from other languages can easily be translated. Rather, the language of 'teaching and learning' is itself a very specific, historically and culturally situated way of speaking 'in' and 'about' education – which also means that the word 'education' cannot be considered as neutral and as innocent as it may appear to some.

All this is partly a question of words but also of underlying concepts and conceptual structures. For example, whereas in English there is the word 'education,' the German tradition has at least two concepts, namely *Bildung* and *Erziehung*, indicating a way of engaging with the 'reality' of education that is quite different from what is possible with the single word 'education.' There are similar issues with the German words *Didaktik* and *Pädagogik*, which, although they have equivalents in the English language – 'didactics' and 'pedagogy,' respectively – actually contain quite different meanings from how 'didactics' and 'pedagogy' are commonly understood. And finally, all this is not just a matter of words, concepts, and language but also impacts on the social organisation of the field where, for example, in the English-speaking world 'education studies' is generally configured as a multidisciplinary applied field of study, whereas in the German-speaking world and countries influenced by Germanic traditions, 'education' has established itself as an academic discipline in its own right (see Biesta, 2011).

These issues begin to show the unique contribution that the current book is seeking to make but also highlight some of the difficulties in achieving what the chapters in this book seek to achieve. Whereas the conversation between the English-speaking world and the German-speaking world has developed a little over time – the word *Bildung* has, for example, become quite well known in English-speaking circles – there is far less known about words, concepts, and traditions from other languages and cultures. One thing that the current book seeks to do, therefore, is to gain for its readers an insight into a unique Japanese concept – Manabi – and the unique practices that are associated with this idea. This, in itself, is already an important contribution to educational scholarship, precisely because it challenges the hegemony and alleged neutrality of the way education is being discussed in the English language. More than thinking of this exercise in terms of anthropological curiosity – that is, it may be 'nice' to know something about Japanese education – this book actually raises fundamental questions about what the 'field' of education is 'about' and who has the right to name and claim it.

What makes all this difficult, however, is that this book is written in English and therefore at least has the difficulty of finding English words and phrases to articulate something that at a very fundamental level cannot be articulated – or at least not articulated perfectly – in the English language. This is one reason why the authors of the book have used a phrase from the title of my 2006 book *Beyond Learning* (Biesta, 2006), in order to indicate that, even where they do argue that the term *Manabi* can be translated as 'learning,' this translation is actually not entirely accurate. This at least means that there is more to 'Manabi' than learning and may even mean that to understand what Manabi is about, readers should suspend their ideas about learning and open themselves to ways of understanding and doing education that go well beyond everything they thought they knew about learning and about education more generally. In this regard the encounter with the chapters in this book may perhaps best be approached as an exercise in defamiliarization: leaving one's common perceptions and assumptions behind in order to find something different, unfamiliar, new, difficult to pin down but nonetheless of crucial importance for anyone with an interest in the theory and practice of education.

This is, however, not the only 'intention' in the book and not the only way in which the authors of this book pose a challenge to its readers. They also explain that, from a Japanese perspective, Manabi may be perceived as an old-fashioned idea and practice, that is, as something that should be replaced by more contemporary ideas, particularly – as previously alluded to – contemporary ideas that seem to constitute the 'global consensus' about education. If that global consensus is all about learners and their learning, and if this is the horizon towards which some may want to see Japanese education go, the case for Manabi also goes 'beyond learning' in this way as the authors make a case for the progressive meaning of a conservative idea – referring to a trope I have explored in relation to the status of teaching in the contemporary 'global consensus' (see Biesta, 2017).

This book is therefore not just an important contribution to educational scholarship because it provides readers in the English-speaking world with insights in a Japanese educational concept and practice. It is also important – and perhaps this is even the more important contribution the book makes – because it challenges commonly held assumptions about what education is and how it should be understood and in this regard has the potential to open up the 'global consensus' to what is beyond it and in a sense cannot be contained by the theories and concepts that make up this consensus.

Bibliography

Biesta, G. J. J. (2006) *Beyond Learning: Democratic Education for a Human Future,* Boulder, CO., Paradigm Publishers.

Biesta, G. J. J. (2011) "Disciplines and Theory in the Academic Study of Education: A Comparative Analysis of the Anglo-American and Continental Construction of the Field," *Pedagogy, Culture and Society,* 19(2), 175–192.

Biesta, G. J. J. (2017) *The Rediscovery of Teaching,* London/New York, Routledge.

Acknowledgements

This book is about Manabi and Japanese schooling. The ideas presented in this book stem from our experiences in exploring ways to present Japanese thought and educational practices in a globalised world. We grappled with two questions: Can Manabi give an alternative perspective to the theory of learning in Western discourse, and if so, how will it produce different educational practices in schools? Is it possible to discuss Manabi in terms of the progressive approach to education? We suggest that the concept of learning and its practices in Japan have unique connotations that cannot be interpreted fully by its Western counterpart.

In this study, we have been encouraged by many researchers, colleagues, teachers, educators, and students. We would like to express our deepest gratitude to Professor Gert Biesta and Stefano Olivelio for providing many inspiring discussions about the topic and for giving us a wonderful opportunity to include our research in Routledge's Theorizing Education series. We would also like to extend special thanks to Professor Uwe Uhlendorff and Professor Yasuo Imai for their fruitful suggestions and cooperation. In addition, we appreciate the unwavering assistance given by Routledge, particularly by editors Emilie Coin, Will Bateman, Ann-Kathrin Klein, Joshi Swapnil, and Christopher Mathews in completing this project.

List of authors

Masamichi Ueno is Professor of Education at Sophia University, Japan. He has previously served as a professor at Daito Bunka University, a visiting associate professor at the University of British Columbia, a visiting scholar at the University of Luxembourg, and a visiting professor at the University of Jinan. He currently works as a visiting professor at Shandong Normal University and Northwest University, China, and is president of the Institute of East Asian Education. He is the author of *The Publicness of Schools and Democracy* (University of Tokyo Press, 2010), *Education for Democracy* (University of Tokyo Press, 2013), and *Democratic Education and the Public Sphere: Towards John Dewey's Theory of Aesthetic Experience* (Routledge, 2016).

Yasunori Kashiwagi is Professor of Early Childhood Care and Education at Chiba Keizai College, Japan. He is the author of *Babyklappe and Women in Need* (Kitaohji Shobo, 2013), *The Praktike of Manabi* (Ikkei Shobo, 2015), and *Gazing at the Nameless Mothers and Babies* (with T. Hasuda, Kitaohji Shobo, 2016). In addition, his works include 'Child-Rearing Support and *Babyklappe* of SterniPark: The New Anonymous Support for Mothers and Their Children in Germany' (*Research on Early Childhood Care and Education in Japan*, 52[3], 2014) and 'The Early Childhood Education of Jürgen Moysich before *Babyklappe*: Anti-authoritarian Education and Education after Auschwitz in Germany' (*Research on Early Childhood Care and Education in Japan*, 56[3], 2018).

Tomoya Saito is Professor of Education at Kokugakuin University, Japan. He is the author of '"Shuyo" in Learning Methods of KINOSHITA Takeji in 1920s: Autonomy and Collaboration, Moral Judgement, Body' (*The Journal of Kokugakuin University*, CX, 2009), 'Shuyo in Gaku-shu of SAWAYANAGI Masataro' (*The Journal of Kokugakuin University* CX(II), 2011), and 'Seinen no jiritsu ni okeru "Kyōyō" to "Kyōyō shugi"' ('Seinen no jiritsu to kyōiku bunka,' 61st *Bulletin of the Noma Education Laboratory*, 2019).

Kayo Fujii is Associate Professor of Education at Yokohama National University, Japan. She is the author of 'Possibilities of Communicative Action in Educational Relationship: Towards Human Self-Formation Theory of Reciprocal Recognition' (*Studies in the Philosophy of Education* [88], 2003), 'History of Educational Thought as Critical Research' (*Forum on Modern Education* [18], 2009), 'Discourse Ethics and Knowledge of Moral' (*Forum on Modern Education* [24], 2015), 'Experience of Recognition and Autonomy: Focus on Recognition Theory of A. Honneth' (*Journal of YNUSE*, 3, 2016), and *Ninngennkeisei and Recognition* (with L. Wigger and J. Yamana, Kitaohji Shobo, 2014).

Taku Murayama is Associate Professor of Special Needs Education at Tokyo Gakugei University, Japan, Visiting Associate Professor at the Open University of Japan, Visiting Research Fellow of the Institute of East Asian Education, and Visiting Researcher at the Institute of Teacher Education of Waseda University. He has previously served as Lecturer at Tokyo City University. He is a member of the executive board and secretary general of the Japanese Society for Special Needs Education, and secretary general of the UK–Japan Education Forum. He is the author of 'Key Issues of Health Literacy' (*The Journal of East Asian Educational Research* Issue No. 2, 2016), 'Japanese Teacher Education for Special Needs Education' (*Forum* [3], 2017), and co-author of *Special Needs Education* (The Open University of Japan Press, 2019).

Introduction

What is the translation of the term 'learning' in your native language? Does learning in your country have unique theories and practices? Will an attempt to express learning in your language have any different suggestions as to the forms of learning that are discussed in today's globalised education?

For most readers of this book, this might be the first time you have encountered the words *Manabi* (学び) or *Gakushu* (学習). It might even give readers a strange or mysterious feeling to see this book entitled *Manabi and Japanese Schooling*. Though *Manabi* is a term frequently used as a translation of notions of 'learning' in English, *Lernen* in German, and *Xue* (学) and *Xuexi* (学习) in Chinese, it is an educational concept that partly corresponds to these notions but partly does not. Manabi contains exceptionally important thoughts that were used widely in the classics of Confucianism (儒教), Buddhism (仏教), and Taoism (道教), and it is also a frequently used term in present-day Japanese schools and academic discourse meaning 'learning' – yet there is a dearth of English research and books that focus on the word *Manabi*. What, then, is Manabi? What is unique about Japanese Manabi, and what is different about learning based on East Asian thought as compared with learning philosophies in the West? How can we better understand the practice of teaching and learning in Japanese schools?

The aim of this book is to consider Japanese philosophy and practices of Manabi that might provide an alternative perspective to understand 'learning' in the era of globalisation. Manabi is not entirely identical to learning, and the whole point of this book is first of all to show what is special about Manabi that goes beyond rather prevalent notions of learning and secondly to show what is progressive about Japanese education. The discourses of 'learning' and 'learner-centred education' have become increasingly influential, and 'active learning,' 'problem-solving learning,' 'project-based learning,' 'twenty-first-century learning,' and 'competency-based learning' have been extensively prevalent in educational theories and practices. In addition, because students in East Asia, particularly in Japan, China, South Korea, Hong Kong, Taiwan, and Singapore, are known for getting extremely high scores in tests such as those offered by the Program for International Student Assessment (PISA) of the Organisation for Economic Co-operation and Development (OECD) and by Trends in International Mathematics and Science Study (TIMSS) of the International Association for the Evaluation of Educational Achievement (IEA), international student testing has become the driving force behind global curriculum standards and educational practices.

In this movement, the theory of learning seems more and more to stress self-centred activity in which learners become centres of educational processes and outcomes. Learning is understood as the acquisition, improvement, or expansion of learners' knowledge, skills, comprehensions, application, analysis, productivity, synthesis, dispositions, habits, and values through interacting with and adapting to the environment. Even when we think of learning in terms of socio-cultural and constructive approaches that are seen as innovative – leading to the expansion of students' creativity, generic skills, critical judgement, reflective thinking, and social responsibility – their practices are likely to be connected to an active Self that would demand acquisition and application of various skills, comprehensions, and abilities through interaction. Though learning, driven by active, inquisitive, reflective, communicative, collaborative, and problem-solving practices and processes, has already become widespread in Japanese education, we continue to use traditional Asian philosophies and practices of learning as Manabi that cannot entirely be explained by the Western ideas of 'learning' or 'education' in English or *Bildung* in German.

The main issue is that while the discourse of learning is attractive and has contributed tremendously towards the transformation of classrooms in which teachers had previously transmitted knowledge by merely reading the textbook aloud with students sitting still and taking notes that had been written on a blackboard, studies on learning have been standardised to the narrow field represented by learning science and has marginalised different perspectives of learning that have different historical and theoretical backgrounds. The reason we use the word *Manabi* instead of 'learning' is that mainstream discourse on learning seems to disregard such diverse understandings of learning, despite the current information and technology age in which social and cultural interactions are spreading to the whole world. More specifically, since much emphasis is placed on Western definitions of learning, which is accelerated by global standards in education, it has failed to consider East Asian thought on learning, which might include different connotations for the West.

This book suggests that Japanese schools embrace a unique theory and an outstanding set of educational practices called Manabi that derives from East Asian thoughts such as Nothingness (無, *Mu*), Selflessness (無我, *Muga*), Emptiness (空, *Kuu*), Silencing (沈黙, *Chinmoku*), No-mind-ness (無心, *Mushin*), and so on. Japanese Manabi is the entire practice that transcends the limitations of dualistic worldviews between the Self and others, mind and body, language and non-language, logos and pathos, and consciousness and unconsciousness and that creates authentic education and enriches human relationships with everyone through practices such as 'self-formation without a self,' 'learning without learning,' and 'teaching without words.' The concept of Manabi is of paramount significance in modern Japanese education as well as in the pre-modern era. It is not too much to say that Manabi is embedded in many aspects of current school practices. For instance, educators are encouraged to teach Selflessness rather than how to build an active Self; to unite body and mind through *Kata* (型) and *Shūyō* (修養) rather than to see them as separate; to be recognised as part of a collective voice, a voice of *Minna* (みんな), which means 'everyone' or 'all,' rather than to be recognised as an individual voice; and to encourage inclusive education rather than being exclusive.

Despite the fact that studying the uniqueness of Manabi, which is deeply embedded in East Asian culture and traditions, is strategically experimental, it is noteworthy that it arouses an antithetical and contradictory relationship with the concept of learning in both the West and the East. While Manabi may provide an alternative or more progressive approach to education in the West, it reminds many Japanese of a traditional and conservative approach that is a relic of pre-modern society. For the West, the relationship of 'Manabi' to 'learning' might include it standing as an alternative, one exemplified by the relationship of 'futon' to 'bed,' 'tatami' to 'carpets,' 'kimono' to 'clothes,' 'sushi' to 'sandwiches,' 'green tea' or 'macha' to 'coffee and tea.' On the one hand, Manabi as discussed in this book would present an alternative perspective to Western ideas of learning, which is founded on modern philosophies of education; on the other hand, Manabi should be examined for those of its theories that retain traditional meanings in Japan – concepts that historically were used for authoritarian and militaristic training.

We intend to study Manabi and Japanese schooling as a progressive concept of 'learning' in a globalised world. What is missing in this argument is a consideration of the meanings of 'traditional' and 'progressive,' which have significantly different connotations in the West and the East. Japanese modern education in the post–World War II era has redefined learning by introducing the Western ideas of human rights (人権) and democracy (民主主義), which contributed to implement 'the right to learn' (学習権) in the Japanese Constitution (日本国憲法). The so-called new education movement, connected with 'learner-centred' or 'child-centred' education, tends to deny the theories of Nothingness, Selflessness, Emptiness, and Silencing. Faced with the globalisation of the twenty-first century, the concept of learning has been narrowly standardised, together with our knowledge-based economy and our many information and technological innovations. Thus, alternative meanings of 'learning' that have different social, cultural, and historical backgrounds are likely to be swept away.

In this book, many educational practices that are used every day in Japanese schoolrooms will be discussed, including time for cleaning (掃除, *Souji*), instruction during school lunches (給食, *Kyushoku*), toothbrush guidance, sports festivals (運動会, *Undokai*), cultural festivals (文化祭, *Bunkasai*), chorus competitions, excursions, field trips, entrance ceremonies (入学式, *Nyugaku-shiki*), and graduation ceremonies (卒業式, *Sotsugyo-shiki*). Cleaning time and lunchtime instruction, during which children are educated as 'the whole child,' are already known internationally and have been incorporated into several countries. Foreigners may be surprised to learn that in many schools in Japan, students are not allowed to talk to one other during cleaning time and lunchtime in order to keep students concentrating on their activities without distraction. In most kindergartens and elementary schools, the teacher and students take care of the classroom's many plants, fish, insects, birds, and animals, a practice that is particularly related to our embedded attitudes of reverence for and appreciation of nature. There is a growing interest in the Japanese educational model based on the East Asian system, which cannot be reduced to the Western model. Such a Japanese model is partly incorporated into the educational system in other Asian countries.

However, if Manabi is a response to the concept of learning in the West, it would not be enough to introduce the Japanese curriculum or educational methods such as cleaning and lunchtime instruction or sports festivals called *Undokai*. What we should consider is that Japanese and East Asian philosophies that have been constructed throughout history and have constituted the foundation of our educational practices are located outside the concept of learning in the Western perspective. One of the main ambitions of the book is to show how Manabi is about theorising and practising education in ways that are quite different from how, in some parts of the work, education has been reduce to the standardised concept of learning. In this sense, the discussion of Manabi and Japanese schooling is truly experimental and could open the world to a number of alternative methods of learning in the era of post-globalisation.

In Chapter 1, Ueno explores the concept of Manabi through East Asian philosophy and Japanese history. Manabi is related to the Chinese words *Xuexi* and *Xue*, which were used in ancient China by Confucius and Lao Tzu. However, their understandings of the word form a contrast to one another: Confucianism emphasised the importance of moral ideas such as *Ren* (仁, *Jin*) and *Xiao* (孝, *Kou*), which demand benevolent love and filial piety thorough self-control, while Taoism insisted that we will find *Tao*, which means 'way,' 'path,' or 'road' (道), by 'quitting learning' and 'doing nothing,' which will lead to Nothingness, Selflessness, Emptiness, No-mind-ness, and 'teaching without words.' These views on learning have had a huge influence on Japanese education for long time. In this chapter, the thought of Manabi, which might provide an alternative approach to learning, will be considered.

Chapter 2 analyses the structure of Manabi from the perspective of Japanese traditional thought and practices: Nothingness, Selflessness, Silencing, *Shugyō* ('training', 修行), and *Seken* ('world' or 'society', 世間). Using the Japanese word *Manabi*, Kashiwagi will analyse Japanese learning progressively by defining an alternative perspective on learning. Analysing Japanese learning positively without using the prefix *non-*, the structure of Manabi – the structure of Japanese learning – is articulated, a reconstructed learning model is established, and its possible application in (post-)global society and education will be discussed.

Chapter 3 discusses traditional methods of Manabi in terms of the relationship between body and mind. While the West, following Descartes, has tended to explain it as a mind–body dualism, it is explained as mind–body monism (or 'bodymind') in the East. Saito shows that at the centre of traditional Manabi in Japan was mind–body monism in the sense of 'changes in the body changing the state of the mind, and vice versa.' Keeping this in mind will help the reader understand the characteristic methods of Manabi, involving *Kata*, *Keiko* (稽古), *Shugyō*, and *Shūyō*. The relationship between the teacher and the learner in Manabi, which is called the *Shi-tei kankei* (師弟関係), is also studied.

Chapter 4 examines Japanese Manabi and schooling by studying the word *Minna* and the Japanese conception of the self. Minna means 'everyone' and 'all' and is a term used by teachers, students, and parents in Japanese schools. Minna is frequently used in ordinary school activities and creates a unique learning environment as Manabi. Fujii will propose that Manabi is a living art in our unpredictable and unprecedented world coping with globalisation.

Chapter 5 analyses a case study that uses a specialised practice of Manabi in which Japanese teachers and students regard Manabi as being inclusive of others through collaborative and reciprocal situations. Murayama focuses on social change for inclusion, including literacy for children with hearing impairments, language as both a barrier to and a medium for communication, and the case study of an art project and workshop in which literacy and art are the requisite tools that make it possible for disabled students to learn and participate in Manabi activities, even though these same tools may also cause alienation from the learning community in regular classes.

Chapter 6 introduces typical school activities in Japan such as Nyugaku-shiki, Sotsugyo-shiki, Souji, Kyushoku, Shiiku (飼育活動), Undo-kai, and Bukatsu (部活). Those activities support Japanese learning as Manabi (in this case, roughly equivalent to the German Lernen, 'learning') in school. Kashiwagi will show that there are a variety of activities reflecting the effects of Manabi and that such practices help children develop Manabi in schools.

Part 1

The concept of Manabi

Chapter 1

The thought of Manabi
Learning in the age of globalisation reconsidered

Masamichi Ueno

Introduction

The thought and practice of Japanese *Manabi* (学び) and *Gakushu* (学習), which derive from an East Asian historical and cultural background, offer the possibility of opening a different and progressive approach to 'learner-centred education,' which is being promoted in the era of educational standardisation and globalisation. Manabi and Gakushu have been used as words equivalent to the translation of 'learning' in English and *Lernen* in German, but Manabi contains connotations that cannot fully be expressed by the Western concepts of learning, *Lernen*, and so on. The concept of Manabi is infused with culture and traditions that are particular to East Asia including Confucianism (儒教), Buddhism (仏教), and Taoism (道教, Daoism), and it has a meaning that cannot entirely be explained by the concepts of learning and *Bildung* in Western languages.

Tao (道, Dao, Michi), which underlies the philosophies of Confucianism, Buddhism, and Taoism and means 'a way,' 'a path,' or 'a road,' also occupies a significant position in Manabi. For example, *Manabi* is a word derived from the term *Manebi* (真似び). The term *Ma* (真) refers to 'authenticity' or 'truth,' and *ne* (似) means 'emulation' or 'imitation.' *Manebi* suggests a way (Tao) of emulation until one becomes a master in the learning process. That is, it is a path for emulating the authenticity of both the master and the world. In Chinese tradition, the Four Books and the Five Classics of Confucianism (四書五経) are authoritative texts. The Four Books are comprised of *The Great Learning* (大学), *The Doctrine of the Mean* (中庸), *Confucian Analects* (論語), and *The Works of Mencius* (孟子), while the Five Classics are *The Book of Poetry* (詩経), *The Book of Documents* (書経), *The Book of Rites* (礼記), *The Book of Changes* (易経, usually known as the *I Ching*), and *The Spring and Autumn Annals* (春秋). In Japan, writing and imitating the classics (臨書, *Rinsho*) and reading the text aloud (素読, *Sodoku*) are seen as the basis of learning.

In this chapter, I will discuss the thought of Japanese Manabi in East Asia, which might provide an alternative approach to 'learning,' having been influenced predominantly by educational globalisation and standardisation. In this vein, Manabi occasionally reminds us of the conservative end of education that has contributed to the revival of authoritarian nationalism in Japan, but what has been missing in educational research is the reconsideration of Manabi in terms of a progressive framework. The main question here is how to connect Manabi's East Asian philosophy to a progressive interpretation of learning.

Rethinking learning in the age of globalisation: is Manabi an alternative?

Faced with a globalised, post-industrial society, educational reforms in East Asian countries have made a fundamental shift towards the development of academic achievement based on global standards. The advancement of a knowledge-based society, an information society, a multicultural society, and an environmentally sustainable society facilitates professionalisation, multifaceted approaches, specialisation, and cross-disciplinary cooperation. Globalisation and technological innovation have intertwined the issues and challenges of politics, economics, and education, while accelerating the political and educational uncertainty, instability, and risk of society. The twenty-first century is also known as the Asian Century with an expectation of dramatic developments in the social and economic fields. Students' subjective, collaborative learning and competencies are emphasised, and education, learning, and school innovation are highly promoted. Despite the fact that a global standardisation of academic achievement is developing that will extend beyond national boundaries in a knowledge-based society in East Asia, it also has a tendency to strengthen authoritarian nationalism in education by emphasising traditional culture and patriotism.

East Asian countries have addressed common educational issues at various levels while maintaining different political systems and social backgrounds and having a diversity of cultures and traditions. Discussed as hallmarks of East Asian education have been excessive examination competition, uniform education, and control-oriented education in the 'compressed modernisation' that is rooted in 'East Asian-type education' (Sato, 2000, 2016); 'faith in effort,' which is found in a 'Japan-type education system' or an 'East Asian examination-type society' (Tsuneyoshi, 2008); or the 'Japan model (J-model)' (Cummings, 1997), which creates a strong link between economic growth and scholastic development. Among them, Japan, China, Korea, Taiwan, and Hong Kong SAR have gotten high scores in students' international academic assessments, such as the Program for International Student Assessment (PISA) of the Organisation for Economic Co-operation and Development (OECD) and the Trends in International Mathematics and Science Study (TIMSS) of the International Association for the Evaluation of Educational Achievement (IEA). Additionally, it has been discussed widely that fierce examination competition and the entrance examination system remain only in East Asia. On the other hand, it has been confirmed that students in East Asia give low scores in student surveys when asked whether they found meaning and motivation in learning and whether there are interactive processes and dialogues in everyday classroom practices.

In such situations, the trend of educational reforms in East Asian countries is in promoting changes from old approaches to learning – based on the transmission and passive acquisition of deterministic knowledge – to a more progressive schooling in which students learn to be more active, collaborative, and creative through practicing 'learner-centred education.' Since the 1990s, East Asian countries have been pushing forward with strong educational reforms, fostering reforms in such areas as school organisations, textbooks and curricula, admissions systems, and teacher training. Each country has tried to change the so-called 'cramming' system of education and its overemphasis on exams and competition and has pushed its school and curriculum policies on the basis of the concept of students' 'learning.' Accelerated by OECD's PISA 'literacy' and ATC21 (Assessment and Teaching of 21st Century Skills), the movement of 'learner-centred education,' 'competency-based-curriculum,' 'active learning,' and 'project-based learning' has been a driving force in Japanese educational reform.

In Japanese curriculum reform, teaching 'zest for living' (生きる力, *ikiru chikara*) has become the slogan since the late 1990s, along with the shift of the views on academics from the mere acquisition of deterministic knowledge and skills to the inclusion of students' interests, motivation, ability to think, judgement, modes of expression, problem-solving abilities, and communication and social skills. A shift occurred from teaching to learning as Manabi, and it came to open a new era for education in accordance with the trend of learner-centred education. In recent years, the movement has been confirmed as an aspect of 'active learning'; it could also be characterised as 'proactive learning,' 'interactive learning,' and 'deep learning.' In line with the movement towards the formation of a globalised standardisation of academic competencies, a number of skills that help people participate in a sustainable society have become highly valued: twenty-first-century skills, broad-based skills and knowledge, autonomy and subjectivity, problem-solving skills, interpersonal relationships, collaboration and communication skills, and social skills.

In East Asia, it is also true that there has been a traditional way of learning that cannot necessarily be reduced to the Western concept of learning that is prevalent in the current educational contexts of globalisation and standardisation in a knowledge-based society. Specifically, East Asia has not only achieved the exchange of the thoughts and culture of Confucianism, Buddhism, and Taoism (Daoism) but has also shared the sense of values and culture it has held since the ancient era. In East Asia, there is a long tradition of thinking and practicing Manabi, with an abundance of wisdom that cannot be fully grasped by the concept of learning in English or *Lernen* in German.

Regardless of the fact that Manabi in Japanese education partly attempts to harmonise with the learning of knowledge, skills, and competencies in the globalised educational settings, it might cause conflicts with a relatively recent trend that focuses so much on the concept of learning. Biesta (2017) criticises this as 'the "learnification" of education,' which means to 'express much if not all there is to say about education in terms of a language of learning,' and in that situation, the teacher is seen 'as a facilitator of learning.' In Japanese educational studies, the words 'learning' and 'Manabi' are prevalent and are applied to recent curricular and educational policies. In addition, both concepts are likely to be accepted as having the same meaning, but as the idea behind Manabi includes the historical and cultural background of East Asia, it might indicate a somewhat different viewpoint on learning. The crucial point is that Japanese Manabi should not be interpreted as the revival of authoritarian conservatism but should be considered from the perspective of progressive arguments.

In addition to this, the ideas of the 'literacy' and 'competency' approaches, as represented by OECD's PISA, recently received criticism is that they tend to measure the academic skills of students without considering the many differences in cultural and historical backgrounds. It is pointed out that Japanese schooling is embedded with different values and approaches. For instance, schools in Japan have been recognised for practicing *Tokkatsu* (特活, 'special activities') such as homeroom activities, student meetings, cleaning, and many school events such as *Undokai* (運動会, 'sports festivals') (Tsuneyoshi, 2008; Tsuneyoshi et al., 2016), and 'holistic learning' or 'holistic Manabi,' which is integrated into subject learning, student guidance, and club activities (Benesse Corporation, 2017). To understand Japanese education, it is more effective to think of it from the progressive perspective of learning based on East Asian culture and philosophy.

An introduction to Manabi's thought

We think that Manabi is an exceptionally important concept that originated in Japan, and, as I have suggested elsewhere (Ueno, 2018; Ueno et al., 2018), it has almost equal significance to other Japanese ideas that have permeated the Western world: Teaism, advocated by Kakuzo Okakura (岡倉覚三) in *The Book of Tea* (1906); the idea of Zen (禅), introduced by Daisetz Teitaro Suzuki's (鈴木大拙) books such as *Essays in Zen Buddhism* (1927, 1933, 1934) and *Zen and Japanese Culture* (1938); and *Bushido* (武士道), as discussed in Inazo Nitobe's *Bushido: The Soul of Japan* (新渡戸稲造) (1900). The word 'Zen' derives from the Sanskrit word *dhyāna* that is frequently understood in terms of 'absorption' and a 'meditative state' based on ascetic practices rather than as an object of faith. The concepts of Zen and Tao as a Way are combined with the notions of Nothingness (無) and Emptiness (空). Such ideas certainly affected the concept of Japanese Manabi. Though the theories of Okakura, Suzuki, and Nitobe in the early twentieth century should not easily be identified with Manabi, their perspectives give us illuminating views on Manabi that open the possibility of a progressive and alternative approach to education derived from a globalised standardisation of learning.

Okakura is a thinker who contributed to the development of the Japanese concept of art in the late nineteenth and early twentieth centuries. Okakura (1906) described Teaism as follows: In the taste of tea there is 'a subtle charm' that is irresistible and makes for idealisation. Westerners might be inclined to mingle the fragrance of its thought with aroma. Tea does not have 'the arrogance of wine, the self-consciousness of coffee, nor the simpering innocence of cocoa.' Teaism is 'the art of concealing beauty that you may discover it, of suggesting what you dare not reveal.' Teaism is 'a cult' that adores the beautiful among the sordid facts of everyday existence and is essentially 'a worship of the Imperfect,' 'a tender attempt to accomplish something possible in this impossible thing we know as life.'

At the foundation of Okakura's Teaism lies Taoism (Daoism) and Zen, which are concerned with the concept of the Tao, Nothingness, Emptiness, vacuum, and being incomplete. Okakura insisted that Tao literally means 'a Path.' It has been translated as 'the Way, the Absolute, the Law, Nature, Supreme Reason, the Mode.' These interpretations are not incorrect. In Okakura's introduction, he quotes Lao Tzu (老子) as saying:

> There is a thing which is all-containing, which was born before the existence of Heaven and Earth. How silent! How solitary! It stands alone and changes not. It revolves without danger to itself and is the mother of the universe. I do not know its name and so call it the Path. With reluctance I call it the Infinite. Infinity is the Fleeting, the Fleeting is the Vanishing, the Vanishing is the Reverting.

Thus, the Tao is 'in the Passage rather than the Path,' 'the spirit of Cosmic Change,' and 'the Great Transition.' The Tao is subjectively 'the Mood of the Universe' and 'its Absolute is the Relative.'

According to Okakura, Lao Tzu claimed that 'only in vacuum lay the truly essential.' Lao Tzu argued that the reality of a room was to be found in the vacant space enclosed by the roof and the walls, not in the roof and walls themselves, and the usefulness of a water pitcher dwelt in the emptiness where water might be put, not in the form of the pitcher or the material of which it was made. In Okakura's perspective, 'vacuum is all potent because [it is] all containing.' Motion becomes possible only in a vacuum. 'One who could make of himself a vacuum into which others might freely enter would become master of all situations.' The whole can dominate the part. Okakura believed that Taoism had an enormous influence on all theories of Japanese actions such as fencing, wrestling, and jiu-jitsu. In jiu-jitsu, one seeks to draw out and exhaust the enemy's strength by non-resistance – vacuum – while preserving one's own strength in order to win. This view can also be applied to artworks. In the theory of art, vacuum and unsaid things matter since 'in leaving something unsaid the beholder is given a chance to complete the idea and thus a great masterpiece irresistibly rivets your attention until you seem to become actually a part of it.' A vacuum is there for the appreciators to enter and take the full measure of the artist's aesthetic emotion.

Okubo's study (2015) on Okakura's Teaism clarifies that it can be expressed as 'aesthetics of the imperfection.' 'Being incomplete' means that 'an infinite possibility is opened towards completion,' while 'being completed' suggests that we cannot expect 'room for further change and development.' The tea room, where the tea ceremony is extremely spare and gives the impression that through empty and vacant space the flower of the season is well decorated, the scroll is placed; a once-in-a-lifetime opportunity of the master and the guest can be achieved; and 'the possibility which can contain various things' can be opened. That is to say, the essence of Oriental art is not that 'the artist enforces the self-expression' but that 'it reaches the state of oneself and others by making oneself empty, attracting the others and extracting a free conception.' Therefore, unlike Western modern paintings, where artists' self-expression fills the canvas, Oriental ink paintings are reminiscent of a variety of natural possibilities and natural colours by restricting colour and leaving margins on the screen. Nothingness and Emptiness matter in orienting towards an infinite possibility and completion.

It is also important to note that Okakura, who believes that 'Asia is one,' thinks of Taoism and Zen as seen in Teaism as being 'the true spirit of Eastern democracy.' *The Book of Tea* was published in 1906 when Japan moved towards Westernisation and modernisation by establishing the emperor system. Indeed, at this time, Japan was seen as a member of a civilised state due to its victory in the Sino-Japanese War of 1894–1895. However, Okakura criticised such a view in an ironic way. He wrote that the average Westerner regards Japan as 'barbarous' while Japan indulged in 'the gentle arts of peace' and that 'he calls her civilised since she began to commit wholesale slaughter on Manchurian battlefields.' Okakura further criticised the Western view: 'fain would we remain barbarians, if our claim to civilisation were to be based on the gruesome glory of war. Fain would we await the time when due respect shall be paid to our art and ideals.'

Zen, which is closely related to Tao as a Way, was deeply studied by Suzuki who defined it as perfect *Satori* (悟り), that is, beyond logical interpretation of the world and outside the limits of language. Suzuki (2005) expounds that Zen is 'a form of Buddhism' developed in the early T'ang Dynasty in China in the eighth century, though it started with the coming of Bodhidharma (菩提達磨) to China from southern India in the early sixth century. Its teaching is the same as the teaching of Mahayana Buddhism, and Zen wants us to see directly into 'the spirit of Buddha,' which is *Prajñā* (般若) and *Karunā* (大悲). In Sanskrit that could be translated as 'transcendental wisdom' and 'love.' Suzuki stated that Zen awakens Prajñā by revolting against the 'unconditioned surrender to the intellect' under 'the thick clouds of Ignorance and Karma.' The expression of 'intellection' is done through logic and words, but Zen disdains logic and remains 'speechless' when it needs to express itself, since 'the worth of the intellect' comes after 'the essence of things is grasped.'

Suzuki asserts that in the Prajñā school of Buddhism, 'Śūnyatā is Tathatā and Tathatā is Śūnyatā; Śūnyatā, Emptiness, is the world of the Absolute, and Tathatā, Suchness, is the world of particulars.' Emptiness in its absolute sense is not reached by 'the analytical process of reasoning' but is 'a statement of intuition or perception.' The mind directs its attention inwardly by going out of Emptiness and returning to it instead of going outwardly towards intellect. Suzuki considers 'passivity' important since it opens absolute inclusiveness that can accommodate things with innocence and non-resistance, whereas if there is something, it would block and resist other things to enter. Suzuki calls this *Mushin* (無心, 'No-mind-ness').

Carl Jung (1964: xiv) wrote in the Foreword of Suzuki's *An Introduction to Zen Buddhism* that Satori is 'a breakthrough of a consciousness limited to the ego-form in the form of the non-ego-like self.' Thus, Zen reverses the ordinary course of knowledge by upholding intuition against intellection, since intuition is the more direct way to reach the Truth. Erich Fromm (2013), who analysed the relationship between Zen Buddhism and psychoanalysis as formulated by Sigmund Freud, stated that the aim of Zen is 'enlightenment: the immediate, unreflected grasp of reality, without affective contamination and intellectualisation, the realisation of the relation of myself to the Universe.' It is an experience of a 'repletion of the pre-intellectual, immediate grasp of the child, but on a new level, that of the full development of man's reason, objectivity, individuality.' While the experience of 'immediacy and oneness' lies before 'the experience of alienation and the subject–object split, the enlightenment experience lies after it.' Likewise, the aim of Freud's psychoanalysis is to make the unconscious conscious and to replace 'Id by Ego.' Fromm argued that 'well-being' is 'the state of having arrived at the full development of reason,' which is not a merely intellectual judgement but the means to grasp 'truth' by 'letting things be,' in Heidegger's term. Well-being is possible only to the degree of overcoming 'narcissism' – to the degree that 'one is open, responsive, sensitive, awake, empty (in the Zen sense).' It is a state of overcoming 'separateness and alienation, to arrive at the experience of oneness with all that exists.'

In the 1920s, German philosopher Eugen Herrigel visited Japan and encountered through Japanese archery the thoughts of Buddhism and Zen, which constituted the essence of Japanese culture. His archery master taught him the No-mind-ness of Mushin. According to Herrigel (2018), the master said it is necessary for the archer to become 'an unmoved centre' and thus become 'the supreme and ultimate miracle: art becomes artless, shooting becomes not-shooting, a shooting without bow and arrow; the teacher becomes a pupil again, the Master a beginner, the end a beginning, and the beginning perfection.'

The master explained that the more obstinately you try to learn how to hit the target, the less you will succeed and that only by letting go of yourself, with nothing planned, striven for, desired, or expected – purposeless and egoless (無我) – are you to able to master the art of archery. In Japanese educational practices, being purposeless and egoless – in which students let go of themselves while studying or performing other activities, including cleaning, and become 'truly spiritual' in equanimity – is highly encouraged. It is not learning itself but a way of learning that erases your learning purpose, ego, desires, and expectations.

Nitobe (2008) described Bushido as the soul of Japan. Bushido literally means 'the way of warriors' and refers to the ethical codes of conduct and honour that dictated the samurai way of life. Instead of having religious doctrines as seen in Western countries, Nitobe said that Bushido embodied the concepts of justice, courage, benevolence, chivalry, truthfulness, and loyalty.

For Nitobe, Japanese people cannot share 'the admiration of the Europeans for their roses' because roses lack 'the simplicity' of Japan's cherry blossoms. He contrasts the rose's 'showy colours and heavy odours,' its thorns hidden beneath the sweetness, its tenaciousness in clinging to life and refusing to drop its petals, with the cherry blossom, which 'carries no dagger or poison under its beauty, ever ready to depart life at the call of nature' and whose colours and light fragrance are delicate and refreshing.

Nitobe also talked about Japan's 'canons of politeness' and how awkward Westerners feel because of its deferential behaviour. In the United States, when you give a gift, you sing its praises to the recipient, saying in essence, 'This is an excellent gift: If it were not excellent, I would not dare give it to you – it would be an insult to give you anything less.' In Japan, people think, 'You are a wonderful person, and no gift is good enough for you. Please accept this poor gift not for its intrinsic value, but as a token of my good will – it would be an insult to your worth to call even the best gift good enough for you.' Despite the fact that Nitobe's view on Bushido has been harshly criticised by Japanese scholars because it was associated with the nationalistic ideology of the emperor system and militarism and was used to reframe death and self-sacrifice during World War II as a means of purification for the nation, it also disseminated East Asian thought and values to the international community in the early twentieth century.

The more inspiring thing is that, in 1919, Nitobe (2007: 215–222) developed the concept of democracy as *Heimindo* (平民道, 'way of the common man'), which is 'the extension' of Bushido. At the time, Nitobe participated in the Taisho democracy movement (大正デモクラシー) by becoming a member of Reimeikai (黎明会). During the Taisho democracy era in the 1910s and 1920s, a movement began to institute universal suffrage; the freedoms of speech, assembly, and association; and gender equality and to bring an end to the social discrimination experienced by Buraku (an outcast group at the bottom of the traditional Japanese social order). Sakuzo Yoshino (吉野作造) was one of the leaders who advocated democratic ideas. Nitobe's notion of democracy as Heimindo was affected by John Dewey, who was a good friend of Nitobe – while Dewey was visiting Japan in 1919, he even stayed at Nitobe's home. The two had studied in the same college of Johns Hopkins University, and while they never actually met while they were at Johns Hopkins, Nitobe's brother, who was also a graduate of Johns Hopkins, had attended the same seminar as Dewey.

Dewey's educational theory of democracy is 'a way of living together' by the 'common man,' which appears to have a meaning similar to that of Nitobe's democracy-as-Heimindo, since *Heimin* (平民) indicates 'common man,' and *Do* (道), which is also used in Bushido's *do*, is Tao (道), meaning 'Way.' Tao and Do are written as the same character (道), and its meaning comes close to Dewey's theory of 'democracy as a way of life' in that it pursues the way common men should live. Dewey (1939) wrote that 'democracy is a way of life controlled by a working faith in the possibilities of human nature.' When Nitobe's idea of Bushido, which had Confucianism as its origin, was developed into his concept of Heimindo, it was mediated by exchanges with Dewey, who was a leading advocate of democratic education.

We should stress again that Manabi itself is not identical to Teaism, Zen, or Bushido and that the theories of Okakura, Suzuki, and Nitobe were partly used to enhance Japanese militarism and the nationalism of the emperor system during World War II. However, Japanese Manabi also incorporates East Asian values and cultures that could not be grasped fully by the concept of learning in the Western perspective. The Japanese learning style of Manabi includes ideas that link to the practice of Tao as a Way that includes Nothingness, Emptiness, vacuum, being incomplete, No-mind-ness, purposelessness, egolessness, and benevolence. Manabi provides a progressive approach to education when we look at the learner-centred education occurring in the face of the globalisation and standardisation in the twenty-first century, in that it is not the learning itself but rather a way to live and learn through eliminating the purpose for learning, as well as ego, desires, and expectations. Even more interesting is the fact that these concepts are associated with democracy and are connected to Western thought and efforts to modernise Japanese society.

Theories of learning in Confucianism and Taoism

The words *Manabi* (学び) and *Gakushu* (学習) correspond to the Chinese words *Xue* (学) and *Xuexi* (学习). The word *Xue* was used in the classics of Confucianism and Taoism. However, the thought of Confucianism and Taoism indicates different attitudes towards learning. *The Analects of Confucius* was not written by Confucius (孔子) himself but are the contents of his recorded dialogues with his disciples. It was edited about 2,500 years ago and had a profound effect on the constitution of politics, society, and culture in East Asia. Confucianism is thought to have flowed to Japan through the kingdom of Baekje of southwest Korea in the early sixth century.

In the Edo period (1603–1867), Confucianism was widely read and spread to the samurai class and to the people after the Neo-Confucianism of *Shushigaku* (朱子学), developed by Zhu Xi (朱熹), was adopted by the Tokugawa Shogunate as an official guiding philosophy for controlling people. Tsujimoto (2018) wrote that Confucianism was 'the intellectual foundation' during the Edo period, and all the intellectual activities occurred within 'the conceptual framework and specific terminology of Confucianism.' Taoism was also introduced to Japan in the Nara period in the eighth century, and it spread widely in the Edo period.

Confucius (1999) advocates the concept of society by emphasising 'learning' (学, 學, *Xue*). In Chapter 1 of *Analects*, Confucius said, 'Is it not pleasure to learn and to practice what is learned time and again? Is it not delightful to have friends coming from afar?' (子曰。學而時習之。不亦説乎。有朋自遠方来、不亦楽乎。) (1:1). And in Chapter 2, Confucius said, 'If one learns from others but does not think, one will be bewildered. If, on the other hand, one thinks but does not learn from others, one will be in peril' (子曰、学而不思則罔、思而不学則殆。) (2:15). Learning (Xue) constitutes one of the central concepts in *Analects*, and it is concerned with practices that could be applicable to daily life. One is taught to think by oneself instead of merely accumulating knowledge learned from others, including teachers and books; one is also taught to learn from others in order not to think in isolation. The main point of Confucius's theory of intelligence lies in the fact that he did not separate thinking and learning but connected them one to the other by 'developing new ideas based on study of the past, learning from the past' (温故而知新) (2:11); he also mentioned that 'to know it is not as good as to love it, and to love it is not as good as to take delight in it' (6:18).

In Chapter 16, Confucius (1999) said, 'Those who are born with knowledge are the highest. Next come those who learn through study. Next come those who learn through hard work. Those who work hard and still do not learn are the lowest of the people' (16:9). In Chapter 17 (17:8), he taught:

> One who loves benevolence but not learning leads to a foolish ignorance. One who loves knowing but not learning leads to a lack of principle. One who loves faithfulness but not learning leads to rudeness. One who loves uprightness but not learning leads to violence. One who loves firmness but not learning leads to extravagant conduct.

Furthermore, moral principles such as *Ren* in Chinese or *Jin* in Japanese (仁, 'benevolence,' 'humaneness') and *Xiao* or *Kou* (孝, 'filial piety') are preached, while benevolent compassion and kindness to the others by directing oneself and controlling one's feelings and desires through *Li* (礼, *Rei*) are encouraged.

One the other hand, Taoism reveals a different view of learning. Lao Tzu (2001, 2016) said in Chapter 20, 'If you quit learning, there will be no worries' (絶學無憂). Lao Tzu also stated in Chapter 48:

> The more you learn, the more you get knowledge. The more you pursue Tao, the more you reduce your knowledge. Reducing your knowledge again and again, you finally reach the stage of 'doing nothing.' Once you have reached the state of doing nothing, nothing is left undone. You even can get the world if you practice the principle of 'there-is-nothing-to-do.'

If you adhere to the principle of 'there-is-something-to-do,' you can never get it (爲學日益、爲道日損。損之又損、以至於無爲。無爲而無不爲。取天下常以無事。及其有事、不足以取天下。).

What is suggested here is that, through quitting learning (學, *Xue*), we could reach the state of Tao, 'doing nothing and taking things as they come' (無爲自然), 'abandoning artifice and just being oneself,' and 'being ignorant and disinterested' (無知無欲). It aims to eliminate artificial learning and to lead to Tao as a Way with purity by quitting learning that is forced from the outside. In terms of positively affirming doing nothing and ignorance, Taoism is explicitly distinct from Confucianism, which values learning based on Ren and Xiao. The point is that Confucianism and Taoism, both of which had a great influence on East Asia, show conflicting views on the educational philosophy of learning.

Reinterpretation of education in Japanese Confucianism

During the Edo period from the early seventeenth century to the mid-nineteenth century, the Tokugawa Shogunate accepted Neo-Confucianism as a guiding philosophy. Learning Confucianism through memory and recitation of the Confucian texts was supremely important throughout the era. In China and Korea, it became a requirement to study Zhu Xi's commentaries in order to get a position in government through the civil service examination. According to Tucker (2008), Neo-Confucianism viewed learning as the 'basic method of self-cultivation' that helps one fully realise one's morally good human nature. In Japan, Jinsai Itō (伊藤仁斎) and Sorai Ogyū (荻生徂徠) endorsed Zhu Xi's teaching that learning basically involved 'the process of emulation.' Jinsai assumed that calligraphy would be the model of learning because in learning to write, a teacher presents the example to a student and a student will emulate it. Sustaining this effort throughout the process would require comprehension and the ability by the student to thoughtfully complete the task that has been learned. Neo-Confucianism also emphasised learning the ancient classics and historical literature, especially the *Four Books* and Zhu Xi's commentaries.

Tsujimoto (2018) notes that the fundamental method for learning Confucianism was conducted through *Sodoku* (素読), which means 'phonetic recitation' – memorising the classics by repeatedly reading them aloud. Sodoku was practiced 'on a one-on-one basis as opposed to uniform class instruction.' The teacher and a student sat in front of each other, and the text was read. If a student failed to recite the text properly, he or she needed to continue to practice it at home since 'perfect memorisation' was required in Sodoku. As a result, Confucianism became the most prevalent during the Edo period.

Even after the Meiji Restoration era, beginning in the late 1860s, Confucianism played an influential role in educational philosophy, despite the fact that Japan oriented its direction towards modernisation through introducing

Western models of the nation-state, including political organisations and societal structures. In the educational field, it is interesting to see the concept of learning (Manabi, Xue) in East Asia by comparing it with the concept of 'education,' which has been translated as 教育 (*Kyōiku* in Japanese and *Jiaoyu* in Chinese). This widely used word now means education in Japan, China, and Korea, though it was hardly used until the nineteenth century, and scholars struggled to find the precise word for translating the term 'education' (see Ueno, 2018).

It is Ota (2016: 30–42) who argues that the translation of 'education' as Kyōiku is a mistake. He states in *Shuowen Jiezi* (説文解字, *Analytical Dictionary of Chinese Characters*), written in the early second century, that *Kyō* or *Jiao* (教, 'teaching') of Kyōiku or Jiaoyu (教育, 'education') means that 'the upper-class person teaches the lower-class people, and the lower-class people learn from the upper-class person.' This was used by successive political powers as a 'ruling principle' within Confucianism. According to Ota, it is completely different from the word 'education,' which originally derives from the Latin *educare*, meaning 'bring up' and 'lead out,' and was added to the understanding of human rights and democracy in the process of modernisation in the West. Confucianism, unlike the teachings of Lao Tzu and Chuang Tzu (荘子), valued the 'wisdom of advanced social governance,' and it was accepted as a 'basic construction of the state in modern Japan.' According to Ota, the Kyōiku (教育) as a translation for education, which is also used in China and Korea, is an export from 'modern' Japan, and it was a 'mistake' to follow the flow of the East Asian cultural sphere based on 'the spirit of Confucianism.'

As previously mentioned, the term 教育 (*Kyōiku, Jiaoyu*) as a translation of 'education' was not generally used in East Asia, including Japan until the mid-nineteenth century. When Japan encountered Western civilisation and underwent modernisation in the Meiji Restoration (明治維新) period of the 1870s, the word *Kyōiku* was reintroduced. The process in which 'education' is translated into *Kyōiku* in Japan is described in detail by Tajima (2016). According to his research, the term 教育 (*Kyōiku*) originally meant 'indoctrination,' which is enumerated as one of the three pleasures that an educated man (君子, *junzi*) enjoys in Mencius's (孟子) philosophy, and its meaning as founded on Confucianism was different from its use in translated form in the late Edo and Restoration periods of the mid-nineteenth century. Intellectuals at the end of the Edo period had translated the word 'education' into Kyōiku, but even then, this translation was not stable and consistent. For instance, when Masanao Nakamura (中村正直) published the translation of *Self-Help* by Samuel Smiles in 1871, he used not only *Kyōiku* (教育) but also *Kyōyo* (教養), which usually means 'culture,' 'cultivation,' or 'liberal arts.' When James Curtis Hepburn published the first edition of *A Japanese and English Dictionary: With an English and Japanese Index* in 1867, he did not use the word *Kyōiku* (教育) in the Japanese–English section, and in the English–Japanese section, 'educate' was translated into other words such as *shitateru, oshiyeru, shikomu*, and so on. The word *Kyōiku* as the translation of 'education' appeared for the first time when the second edition of the dictionary was released in 1872.

Furthermore, Tajima (2016: 3–5) also argues that the word *Kyōiku* is not found in *An Encouragement of Learning* (1872) by Yukichi Fukuzawa (福沢諭吉), who played a prominent role in the modernisation and Westernisation of Japan in the late nineteenth century, nor could it be found in the Educational System Order (学制, *Gakusei*) proclaimed by the Grand Council of the State in 1872, which attempted to establish the first public educational system in the Meiji period (1868–1912). *Kyōiku* as a translation for 'education' was adopted in the Education Order (教育令, *Kyōikurei*) that was promulgated as a replacement of the Educational System Order in September 1979. It was the Movement for Liberty and People's Rights called Jiyu Minken Undo (自由民権運動) that triggered discussion about *Kyōiku* as the word for education.

Fujimaro Tanaka (田中不二麿), who promulgated the Education Order, criticised the too-centralised educational system in Japan and attempted to transform it into a more community-based system by acknowledging the 'educational freedom and autonomy' he experienced during his visit to the United States. The Meirokusha (明六社) group, established by Arinori Mori (森有礼), Fukuzawa, Nakamura, Amane Nishi (西周), Shuhei Mitsukuri (箕作秋坪), and others, whose intention was to 'promote civilisation and enlightenment' through introducing Western concepts of science, logic, and rationally organised government, contributed to spreading the new concept of Kyōiku as a translation of education. Mori, the first Minister of Education, enacted the School Ordinance (学校令, *Gakkorei*) in 1886 and appropriated the Chinese character of 教育 (*Kyōiku*) for 'the modern concept of education,' which goes back to the birth of civil society in Western Europe.

On the other hand, Nagazane Motoda (元田永孚), a conservative scholar of Confucianism, asserted that education should aim to cultivate 'the virtues of humanity, justice, loyalty to their masters, and filial piety' (仁義忠孝ノ心). After a severe feud between the radicals and the conservatives, the latter group gradually increased their influence. As a result, in the Imperial Rescript on Education (教育ニ関スル勅語, *Kyōiku ni Kansuru Chokugo*) in 1890, profoundly influenced by Confucianism, 'the source of education' was understood as building *Kokutai* (国体, the Constitution of the Empire of Japan) by cultivating 'subjects' under the emperor system in which the virtues of loyalty (義) and filial piety (孝) became essential.

The crucial point is that Japan not only proceeded to modernise the educational system through Westernisation but also aimed to combine it with the classical values that derive from East Asian traditions. Confucian theory has had a predominant impact on Japanese education throughout its history, although the terms *Kyōiku* and *Jiaoyu* were not prevalently used to represent education in Japan and China until the mid-nineteenth century. Confucian theories of learning and education came to be reconciled with their Western counterpart in a particular way that deviates from the original meaning of *educare* in Latin and from the modern Western concept of education, which originated from the ideas of human rights and democracy.

Encounter between Confucius and Dewey in learner-centred education

As we have noted, East Asian views of learning – Manabi and Xue – might include different and progressive meanings that cannot entirely be captured in the Western theory of learning. More specifically, one of the predominant educational trends in the era of globalisation and standardisation is expressed as 'the "learnification" of education' (Biesta, 2017). Biesta argues that 'the "learnification" of educational discourse has marginalised a number of key educational questions, particularly regarding the purposes of teaching and of education more widely.' In his perspective, 'the rise of the language and logic of learning' has transformed 'the teacher from a "sage on the stage" to a "guide on the side" – to a facilitator of learning' and even to 'a "peer at the rear".' Though it is undeniable that this movement might risk sweeping away diversity in educational research, it might open an opportunity to reconceptualise 'learner-centred education' that might contain different historical and cultural backgrounds as seen in the concepts of Manabi and Xue.

Following Emmanuel Levinas's perspective, Biesta argues that the foundation of 'learnification' lies in 'the egological worldview,' that is, in 'the way of thinking that starts from the [assumption of the existence of the] self as self-sufficient ego or consciousness, in order *then* to thematise everything that is "outside the subject".' He characterises this imaginary by citing, for example, the function of robot vacuum cleaners, since they can perform their task autonomously and can become more efficient through adapting to their environment in an intelligent way. Biesta calls these 'intelligent adaptive system[s]' in that they can learn without 'intervention from the outside.' Likewise, learners are expected to learn autonomously and efficiently by adapting to the given environment without needing the experience of being taught by others. Through this discussion, Biesta's intention is not to revive 'traditional' or 'authoritarian forms of teaching.' Instead, he attempts to seek 'the third option' that reconstructs 'our understanding of teaching and the teacher along progressive lines.'

In order to find an alternative meaning of learning that could be grasped differently from standardised curriculum, Manabi suggested a more progressive approach to 'learner-centred education'; it should be noted, however, that current research has found similarities as well as differences between East Asian educational thought and its Western counterpart. For instance, researchers noted the similarities between so-called Confucian democracy and John Dewey's theory of democracy and progressivism, though Confucianism was already expressed as having 'quite democratic theories' in Nitobe's *Bushido: The Soul of Japan* (2008), which inspires our study of connecting East Asian thought to the Western idea of democracy. Okakura also suggested that Teaism is 'the true spirit of Eastern democracy.' While Dewey was staying in China after visiting Japan in 1919, he was often called the Second Confucius; he was first referred to this way by the then-president of Beijing University, Cai Yuanpei (蔡元培). Interestingly enough, Dewey (1916) writes in *Democracy and Education* that 'a democracy is more than a form of government; it is primarily a mode of associated living, of conjoint communicated experience.'

The educational encounter between Confucius and Dewey has two aspects. First, it addresses the issue of how we should consider a democratic constitution of our society and community. Tan (2004) states that 'the current encounter' between Dewey and Confucianism would be more reciprocal; that is, while both see 'the person as social,' Confucius's theory of 'authoritative personhood' (仁, *Ren*) stresses the role of community more than Dewey's notion of liberalism, which emphasises individual choice. In addition, while both value working on all aspects of human interaction and connecting feeling to thinking in building communities, Confucius emphasises the aesthetic in ritual practice (禮, *Li*), while Dewey underscores thinking in 'cooperative inquiry.' The difference will give rise to a philosophical distinction in which Confucius pursues 'government *for* the people' but not 'government *by* the people,' whereas Dewey sees the connection between the two as being more important.

Second, it raises the question of how we should think about learning in learner-centred education. According to Tan (2004: 47–49), Confucius thinks that 'learning is the first step in self-cultivation, the first move in ethical progress, and it must continue without ceasing to sustain ethical living.' The question, 'What is to be done?' can only be answered with, 'A combination of learning (學, *Xue*) and thinking (思, *Si*),' which is close to Dewey's theory of intelligence, using past experience to shape and transform future experience, though Confucius sometimes speaks of *Si* in contrast to 'learning.' In spite of the similarities between Dewey's and Confucius's views of the thinking and acting process required for ethical life, we should not exaggerate their correlations too much. Dewey's theory of inquiry draws on the scientific method, which was not available in early Confucianism. In addition, Dewey's philosophy scrutinises 'ends and means, both instrumental and constitutive,' which early Confucian texts do not have. Third, both regard 'customs and traditions' as being important, but Dewey stresses deviation from them in the emergence of individual minds, while Confucius stresses continuity with the past.

Thus, the encounter between Confucianism and Dewey might provide a different perspective to education that is represented by the standardised definition of learning. As long as its emphasis is laid on Ren, Li, Xue, and Si, it is not premised on 'the egological worldview' and the 'intelligent adaptive system' of education that Biesta criticises. Biesta denies the view because it starts from and returns to 'self' as 'self-sufficient ego' and 'consciousness.' However, the Deweyan reinterpretation of Confucian democracy would transform the idea of learning in educational globalisation and standardisation into a slightly different form of 'learner-centred education,' though we also have to take into account the fact that Confucianism was used to enhance Japanese militarism and nationalism under the emperor system, which emphasised the virtues of loyalty and filial piety.

Dewey and Taoism: learning by doing or doing nothing?

A more radical perspective can be drawn when we compare Dewey's progressivism with Taoism because, interestingly enough, both pursue a Way or Tao (道, *Dao*) that is concerned with the theory of learning. As mentioned, whereas Dewey focuses on 'democracy as a way of life,' which he combined with the idea of learning by doing, the Tao of Taoism focuses on 'quitting learning' and doing nothing. How should we think about the relationship between the democratic way of life in Dewey and Tao in Taoism? Are there any tensions and conflicts between Dewey's thought and Lao Tzu's thought on learning, since the former is often related to 'active learning,' 'problem-solving,' and being 'child-centred,' whereas the latter encourages us to 'cast off learning,' to 'do nothing,' to 'reduce knowledge,' and to 'be ignorant'? Nothingness, Emptiness, vacuum, being incomplete, No-mind-ness, purposelessness, and egolessness are located at the centre in Taoism. In this sense, it is not a theory of learning that starts with and returns to the self as being self-sufficient or the seat of consciousness, but is a philosophy of eliminating self, ego, and consciousness and of reaching the state of doing nothing.

In Confucianism, Tao is also the highest ideal, which becomes a model for human life and is the standard and discipline of our action. Tao in Confucianism is practiced through the respect of morals, such as *Li* in Chinese or *Rei* in Japanese (礼), *Yi* or *Gi* (義), *Ren* or *Jin* (仁), *Xiao* or *Kou* (孝). The ideal in Confucianism is that self-improvement attained by learning (学, *Xue*) spreads to the house, the nation, and the whole world. It is for this reason that Li and Rei of Confucianism tended to be used as and connected with a strict class system and a feudal system. In fact, in the process of Japanese modernisation, Confucianism was widely adopted as the principle of education and social governance in controlling the people. In opposition to Confucianism, the Tao that Lao Tzu extolled refers to the fundamental principle of the universe and the creation of all things, which generate the basis and existence of everything. As the foundation of all things, Tao is beyond description and cannot be expressed in any other form than that it is 'nothing.'

Lao Tzu rejects the Confucian practice of Li (ritual rites and propriety) due to its too formalistic attitude of a Way. Lao Tzu's criticism is also directed at the concept of Xue that is aimed at self-improvement. In Chapter 21, Lao Tzu (2001, 2016) stated:

> Tao as a thing is utterly obscure and indefinite. Utterly obscure and indefinite, yet it presents an image. Utterly Indefinite and obscure, yet it embodies

substance. Utterly profound and dark, yet it embodies essence. The essence is supremely genuine. Within itself it contains a truth. From ancient times to now, its name has never left. Thereby, it comprises the beginnings of all things. How do I know the initial state of all things? Precisely by means of Tao.

In Chapter 40, he says, 'The movement of Tao is to return. The working of Tao is so weak. Myriad things and creatures under heaven were born out of Being; this Being was born out of Nothingness.' What is important here is that Nothingness is that which goes beyond the limitation of language, description, and existence; it is a state from which all things are born, and all possibilities can be generated, because it is Nothingness, not Being, that can encompass everything.

Lao Tzu also thinks that tenderness, gentleness, fragility, and weakness reflect the liveliness of all beings and offer the blessings and possibilities of encompassing everything due to their supple flexibility. In Chapter 76, Lao Tzu (2001, 2016) says:

> A man is born gentle and weak, but when dead, he is hard and stiff. Grass and trees are tender and fragile while alive, but once dead, they are dry and stiff. Thus, the hard and stiff are the companions of death. The tender and weak are companions of life. . . . The strong and big end by being cast down, whereas the tender and weak end by occupying a higher place.

In Chapter 8, Lao Tzu observes, 'The highest goodness is like water. Water benefits myriad things, yet never contends with anything. And it settles in low places loathed by all men. Therefore, water is closest to Tao.' Being tender, gentle, weak, and fragile should not be considered as something we should eliminate and overcome. Lao Tzu observes that the hard and stiff will fail and that the gentle and weak will occupy higher places – something that can be seen in nature, in trees, green plants, and water.

The Japanese traditional paintings of Ukiyo-e (浮世絵), represented by Hokusai Katsushika (葛飾北斎), had a huge influence on the phenomenon of Japonisme in Impressionism and Post-Impressionism in Western countries in the nineteenth century. Artists such as Edger Degas, Claude Monet, Pierre-Auguste Renoir, Paul Gauguin, and Vincent van Gogh took inspiration from Japonisme, which absorbed the creative essence of art forms that were quite unfamiliar to them. According to *Hokusai and Japonisme* (2017), when Western artists depict still life, they draw cut flowers and plants arranged in vases that have been cut off from nature. It is meant to give the 'Christian message of *memento mori* – do not forget that death awaits all.' In Japanese Ukiyo-e paintings, contrary to traditional Western paintings, 'flowers are rooted in the ground and reach up towards the sky,' and 'at times they are blown by the wind, at times butterflies flit by, resting on their leaves.'

It could be said that in traditional Western paintings, there was a hierarchy of genres reflecting Christian beliefs that positioned God as the pinnacle. Within this hierarchy, historical paintings – drawing scenes from the Bible and classical literature – were ranked as the highest in importance; portraits came next, then genre scenes, landscapes, and finally still life images because it was believed that humans were the greatest among 'God's creation,' and so plant motifs were relegated to a low-ranking still life genre. Taoism not only affected Hokusai's essence of art, but his Ukiyo-e reflected the liveliness of tender and gentle views of nature. In this way, the elegantly curving lines of plants and flowers were also incorporated into the Art Nouveau movement by the Nancy School of artists in France.

But how should we interpret and practice Lao Tzu's idea of the Tao as a Way of 'quitting learning' and doing nothing? Is it desirable to cast off learning, which apparently takes a view opposite to Dewey's educational view of learning by doing? Learning by doing involves a theory of experiential education extensively practiced in the progressive education movement in the United States in the early twentieth century. Learning by doing requires active and relevant participation of the students in social and community life, instead of the mere transmission of knowledge and its passive reception in a classroom. Such views on education reflect Dewey's understanding of 'democracy as a way of living together' or 'democracy as a way of life.'

Dewey (1897: 87) declared:

> I believe that education, therefore, is a process of living and not a preparation for future living. . . . I believe that the school must represent present life – life as real and vital to the child as that which he carries on in the home, in the neighbourhood, or on the playground. . . . I believe that the school, as an institution, should simplify existing social life; should reduce it, as it were, to an embryonic form.

In Dewey's view, learning should not be understood as 'an accumulated and transmitted body of knowledge' but should be acknowledged as 'the acts of apprehending, understanding, and retaining in and for subsequent use' (Dewey, 1931). The schools would provide 'an opportunity to travel the road to learning' (Dewey, 1923) that occurs when students could connect knowing to the real and vital world through an experience of life by reducing it to 'an embryonic form' instead of by increasing and accumulating knowledge.

Learning for Lao Tzu contains an explicit denial of learning and the elimination of knowledge. According to Lao Tzu (2001, 2016), the practice of reducing knowledge and doing nothing leads to Tao as a Way. Through this, nothing is left undone. In Chapter 37, it is said that 'Tao is permanently doing nothing, yet it leaves nothing undone.' It is important to note that this does not mean we do not do anything at all but implies that we should not pursue something artificially made, nor should we have the intention and will to achieve something forced from the outside. Namely, Lao Tzu tried to eliminate the purposes and reduce the knowledge that human beings are likely to have, such as winning against a competitor, attaining an artificially and externally constructed goal, and fulfilling and exhibiting a desire for honour. Additionally, reducing knowledge indicates that it is important to doubt established knowledge by rethinking, reconsidering, and recreating the information, since being suspicious about artificially made values and knowledge that is forced on one from the outside will help to overturn wrong messages and prejudices.

Despite the similarity between Dewey's and Taoism's pursuit of 'learning' and 'doing,' Dewey's theory is more concerned with common man's 'life' and 'living,' which constitute democracy and education, whereas the Tao in Taoism leads to the fundamental principle of the universe generating and encompassing all things. While Dewey's idea is based on a humanistic and democratic understanding of our life that is defined as 'a mode of associated living, of conjoint communicated experience,' Taoism is oriented towards the cosmological view of the essential source of everything that is supremely genuine and indefinite and that presents truth and substance. It is linked with theories of Nothingness, Emptiness, and No-mind-ness, which would reconstruct the idea of learning into a way to unite with the universe through eliminating externally constituted purposes and deterministic knowledge.

Cast off learning: teaching without words

One of the characteristics of learning in East Asia is a suspicious attitude towards the certainty of using language; this is known as 'teaching without words' (不言之教) in Taoism. Lao Tzu (2001, 2016) said in Chapter 56: 'One who knows does not talk, one who talks does not know. Keep your mouth closed. Shut your senses. Blunt your sharpness. Untangle your knots. Soften your glare. Be at one with dust. This is the state of primal indistinction.' In Chapter 81, he writes, 'Truthful words are not beautifully adorned. Adorned words are not truthful. He who is really good does not talk much. He who talks much is not really good. He who really knows does not display wide knowledge. He who displays wide knowledge does not really know.'

Toshihiko Izutsu (井筒俊彦, 1991) writes that there is a strong suspicion about language in Zen Buddhism. In Zen practice, it is thought that language cannot display and explain existence fully. This is the reason Zen emphasises Satori through intuitive awakening, without depending on words and letters. Contrary to Zen, Izutsu insists that Heidegger, who said that 'language is the house of Being,' showed 'a deep trust in language,' though his focus is not on an ordinary and non-creative language but rather freshly, vibrantly, and creatively used language as seen in the poems of Friedrich Hölderlin. Since Zen's suspicious attitude about language is directed to 'an ordinary and conventional language,' Heidegger's thesis might be 'an expression of a more positive way of Zen's thoughts.'

The thought of Tao as a Way to 'quit learning' and 'do nothing,' which is one of the fundamental roots of Manabi practice in Japan, seems to include conflicting views on education compared with learning by doing and learner-centred education. However, Dewey's suggestion about connecting and knowing the real and vital world refers to reducing knowledge artificially made or externally forced, though Dewey did not explicitly mention doing nothing. Dewey's theory of 'primary experience' and 'direct experience' – or, more specifically, a theory of 'pure experience' as elaborated by William James whose philosophy had a profound effect on Dewey's pragmatism – draws near to the concept of Nothingness. Indeed, Kitaro Nishida (西田幾多郎), a philosopher who was devoted to building a notion of Nothingness, also refers to James's philosophy in that it undermines the distinctive dualism between mind and body, knower and known, and subject and object.

Sōseki Natsume (夏目漱石), a novelist and scholar in the Meiji period, also discusses Lao Tzu's harsh criticism of learning in terms of the theory of Nothingness. According to Natsume (2004), Lao Tzu's standpoint follows the cosmological principle of 'from nothing comes nothing,' which completely denies Confucian theories of Ren (仁), Yi (義), Li (禮), and Zhi (智). Natsume assumes that Lao Tzu rejected myriads of 'doings,' such as learning, observing, and knowing, and encouraged a return to behaving like 'an infant' who is tender and unites with nature. Lao Tzu's perspective of 'teaching without words,' Natsume writes, has views in common with William Wordsworth's poems ('A Poet, one who loves the brooks/Far better than the sages' books' and 'The child is father of the man;/And I could wish my days to be/Bound each to each by natural piety'), though Lao Tzu seems to be more radical. Natsume illustrates Lao Tzu's theory of moral education as shown in Figure 1.1.

Regardless of the apparently unbridgeable differences that are laid between learning by doing and doing nothing, they should not be considered as an either/or question that we need to choose between in educational settings. The theory of learning by doing proposes that learning should not be separated

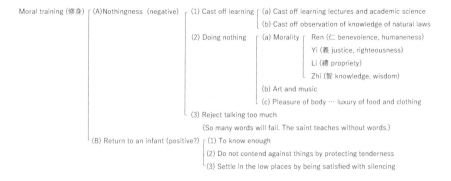

Figure 1.1 Lao Tzu's theory of moral education

from doing and that knowing something should be deeply rooted in our fundamental experiences when implementing it into educational practices. In fact, Dewey's theories of 'democracy as a way of life' and a 'reconstruction of experience' connote more positive expressions of doing nothing in that his theory of 'primary experience' is that of a precognitive experience out of which emerges perceptive, reflective, and inquisitive attitudes to the world and cannot be expounded entirely by descriptive language due to its pre-reflective nature. The idea of primary experience appears to come close to Nothingness, since it unveils an underlying state that is prior to the distinction between knowing and known, between subjective and objective polarity.

Taoism suggests that we should 'quit learning' and direct our attention to the practice of 'teaching without words.' While we are involved in doing nothing in Manabi, showing our genuine and sincere attitude is encouraged rather than communicating and displaying knowledge too much, since our commitment to learn and perform other activities is what reveals our sincerity and authenticity without speaking any lies or prevaricating. More precisely, a form of learning that is motivated by artificially made or externally forced purposes, honours, values, desires, and expectations should be rejected. Manabi also values tenderness, gentleness, fragility, and weakness, which are positioned as valuable in contrast to being hard and unbending, which might prevent responding with suppleness and encompassing all things. In Taoism, Tao is a Way that leads to the fundamental principle of the universe and the creation of everything that cannot be expressed in any way other than in Nothingness and Emptiness.

Manabi as authentic education: 'what is' is 'what is not'

As mentioned, Manabi was originally derived from *Manebi* (真似び), which means 'imitation,' 'emulation,' or 'modelling.' The Chinese character *Ma* (真) means 'truth,' 'reality,' or 'authenticity' imparted by the master, while *ne* (似) is 'imitation,' 'emulation,' or 'similarity.' From this, we can infer that Manabi is accomplished through Manebi, in which students or followers imitate and practice the skills and knowledge already perfected by their masters. Manabi and Manebi are closely related, linked with the practice of imitating the way a master acts or completes tasks in authentic ways. Imitation is the inevitable process through which followers master skills, much as an infant imitates a parent. Indeed, we can see that infants acquire language by imitating what their parents or other adults say, indicating that they engage in a learning process that takes place through the emulation of the authenticity embodied by the master.

Sato (2000) indicates that the focus of classroom lessons should be placed more on Manabi and that Manabi should be used to describe situations where there is interaction with objects, others, and yourself, as part of a community. In Manabi (学び), it is important to note that the Chinese character 学 was originally 學, though the latter is rarely used now. The character 學 was inspirational.

The upper part (乂) means children's (learners') interactions with ancestors in the areas of academies, art, and culture, which is the foundation of human's recognition and knowledge, while the lower part (乂) represents interaction with others, which constitutes society. This means that Manabi is accomplished by involvement in academics, art, and culture, spheres traditionally cultivated by the ancestors, while interaction involves other people, including friends and classmates. The 臼 in the character 學 represents the adult hands that guide a child's learning activities – the teachers and adults that foster a student's learning processes and practices in the community – while at the centre of the Manabi practice is the character 子, 'a child.' Manabi, therefore, focuses on the role of community in educational practices, with the child positioned at the centre.

When we think about the educational discourses that could not be reduced to the prevalent concept of 'learning,' we are reminded of the concept of Bildung, which constitutes one of the central terms in German. Bildung refers to a process of personal and cultural maturation, which was originally meant to cultivate godly talents and dispositions that reflect the image of God. In this sense, an educational theory of Bildung differs from learner-centred education and cannot easily be replaced with a single word in other languages. In English, *Bildung* is translated into 'formation,' 'development,' 'culture,' 'self-cultivation,' 'education,' and so on, but it does not have a direct counterpart that can encompass all its meanings. As Bildung indicates cultivation in the image of God, Manebi involves the authentic emulation that is perfectly embodied by the masters. Manebi is also a process of personal and cultural maturation that seeks to harmonise the individual, society, and nature. Instead of assuming a God, classic texts were positioned at the centre in Confucianism, and followers were required to read them aloud (Sodoku) and memorise them. In the Edo period, it was considered that reading Confucian classics, which includes the emulation of truth or authenticity, would lead to self-cultivation.

In Taoism, truth is related to the fundamental principle of the infinite universe that generates everything. Truth or authenticity cannot easily be identified in an explicit way in our ordinary experiences. There is no word other than Nothingness that can represent it. If we assume ego, subject, reason, or consciousness, then confrontation with objects will emerge, and it will cause division from the world instead of uniting with it. Replacing division and separation from the world with unification and harmonisation is thought to be possible through Tao as a way to cast off learning and do nothing. Authenticity does not need any words since the thing itself is thought to reveal the truth. When we are moved by a beautiful landscape, we often lose the words to express it. If we say 'beautiful,' the word is reflectively spoken. When we are completely devoted to something, we often forget our ego-oriented aims and desires and become immersed in doing what we are absorbed in.

It is not the subject–object relationship that constructs Manabi but Nothingness, Emptiness, vacuum, and being incomplete, which are ultimately flexible and are open to encompass everything without coming up against objects. In *Hannya Shingyo* (般若心経, 'the Heart Sutra'), which is a popular sutra in Mahayana Buddhism (大乗仏教), it is explained that 'form is emptiness, emptiness is form' (色即是空, 空即是色), which means that all is vanity, and vanity is all. In other words, the relationship between 'what is' and 'what it not' is not confrontational but 'what is' is 'what is not' and 'what is not' is 'what is.' In doing some important tasks in school activities, such as studying, physical education, painting, singing, or cleaning, students are encouraged to eliminate their externally forced desires and concentrate their consciousness entirely on activity, which means Mushin, or doing nothing.

In the prevalent discourses of learning or Bildung in the West, there is a tendency to highlight the language, reason, logos, and consciousness that would make our recognition and dialogical communication possible by articulating our surrounding objects from the subject. In the original meaning of Bildung, it is aimed at identification with the image of God, and the subject constitutes a vertical relationship that humans need to be subjected to. The constitution of subject is thought to be mediated by language and consciousness, which start from the self and return to the self. Compared with the East Asian theory of learning, Western education is more likely to focus on the language, reason, logos, consciousness, and dialogue and with the strong belief that learning is inseparable from the existence of self-consciousness and dialogical communication.

In Western pedagogies, doing nothing, being empty, being incomplete, eliminating self, and being silent are rarely stressed, and No-mind-ness, not speaking, and not communicating hardly get attention. In Japanese Manabi, more emphasis is placed on eliminating the self, consciousness, words, and language; Manabi is aimed at reaching a sincere and authentic state of learning by casting off learning and doing nothing. It is considered that authenticity does not need dialogical communication and consciousness, since it reveals the essential and fundamental truth without using words. Words and languages are not necessarily reliable things, and people often show suspicious attitudes towards them since they tend to betray us. The Confucian ideas of Ren and Xiao, of 'doing nothing and taking things as they come,' and of 'being ignorant and disinterested' in Taoism all constitute approaches to learning that are different from the Western approach; indeed, including the ideas of Nothingness, Emptiness, vacuum, and being incomplete in educational discourses might give the West an alternative to its current approach to learning.

Conclusion: Manabi and Japanese schooling within globalisation

The Japanese style of learning called Manabi might provide a slightly different and more progressive approach to the prevalent concept of learning that is promulgated by globalised and standardised education. In recent educational practices and with regard to curriculum reform in Japan, there has been a tendency to highlight active learning, competency-based learning, and learner-centred education.

While the Western idea of learning, which more or less overlaps Manabi and Xue in East Asia, has a great effect on educational policies and curricula, and they have contributed to changes in the classroom and in teaching, it is clear that Ren, Xiao, Nothingness, Emptiness, vacuum, being incomplete, and No-mind-ness constitute the foundation of Eastern practices. 'Quit learning' and doing nothing as well as learning by doing are respected in everyday events in schools – as well as moral education that is concerned with benevolent love and filial piety, which prevails in the classroom. Furthermore, studying and club activities in which students innocently practice Nothingness and emulate the model is highly respected. In this sense, the concept of Manabi is mediated not only by language, reason, logos, and consciousness but also by Nothingness, Emptiness, vacuum, and silence. What is lacking in educational discourse is to understand these values as progressive arguments, instead of attempting to restore authoritarian and conservative ideas of education.

In East Asia, education in a global and knowledge-based society has led to the innovative reform of learner-centred education, which is oriented to international academic standards and competencies. School and curricular reforms in East Asia tend to highlight the shift from content-based instruction that focuses on the transfer of deterministic knowledge and its acquisition, to competence-based learning that centres on active, creative, inquisitive, collaborative, and problem-solving learning through which students are encouraged to acquire social and generic skills, logical and critical thinking, and communication skills. There has been a shift to new frameworks of learning such as literacy skills, key competencies, and twenty-first-century skills that comprise skills, abilities, and dispositions that are supposedly required in a twenty-first-century society and workplace.

The current expansion of educational reforms in East Asia has been related to the fact that the highly competitive environment in preparing for the entrance examination of schools and universities is widespread, and the break from a 'cramming' type of education has been named as one of the key issues. Indeed, in international students' assessments and testing such as the OECD's PISA and the IEA's TIMSS, East Asian students including those from Japan, China, Hong Kong SAR, Taiwan, and Korea have attained high ranking scores among the countries and regions surveyed. Tsuneyoshi (2008: 9–18) points out that the results of such high-stakes tests are so influential to the students' future that 'motivation by examination pressure' is extremely high in East Asian countries.

Therefore, based on ordinary experiences, even if problem-solving skills or generic skills that focus more on the practical uses of knowledge are adopted in the test and school curriculum, it will be introduced into the existing examination, and the students will still be required to prepare and train intensively for the exams. Tsuneyoshi (2008: 155) argues that there is an 'effort principle facilitated by Confucian values' and 'the sense of competence equality' in it. In fact, the tradition of the testing system in China and knowledge acquisition by the memorisation of Chinese classics have demonstrable power in bureaucracy jobs. At the same time, it is ironic that East Asian countries such as Japan, China, Korea, among others, where Confucian cultural influences have been strong and Western styles of learning as represented by 'active learning' have not been fully adopted, tend to dominate the top rankings in the international tests that assess problem-solving learning and generic skills (Saito, 2016: 68–69).

In Japan, though there have been widespread reforms that emphasise knowledge, skills, dispositions, and competencies for a globalised, knowledge-based economy in the twenty-first century, the thoughts and traditions in East Asia deriving from Confucianism, Buddhism, Taoism, and so on, which cannot entirely be encompassed in the Western concepts of learning, education, and Bildung, are still maintained. Since the late 1990s, Japanese school and curricular reforms have proceeded to underscore 'zest for living,' 'active learning,' and 'competency-based learning' towards a knowledge-based society in accordance with the dual movements of neo-liberalism, which advocates the liberalisation, marketisation, and deregulation of education, and neo-conservatism, which exalts nationalistic identity. On the other hand, Manabi, which reflects East Asian thoughts and culture in ways that could be interpreted along progressive lines, is still being taught. The ideas of Nothingness, Emptiness, vacuum, being incomplete, No-mind-ness, purposeless, benevolent compassion, kindness, filial piety, and the like remain in everyday practice in education. In schools, students are encouraged to show their attitudes with regard to studying, reading, and concentrating on extracurricular activities with Mushin and to respect teachers and superiors with sincere courtesy.

In addition, school events such as the entrance ceremony (入学式), sports festival (運動会), cultural festival (文化祭), chorus contest, and graduation ceremony (卒業式) are extraordinarily active. School teachers place an importance on lunch instruction, cleaning guidance, school committee activities, and club activities. There are many role committees for students in the classrooms such as the cleaning committee, broadcasting committee, animal-tending committee, recreation committee, and so on. In most of the schools, students take care of animals, birds, fish, and insects – even chickens, pigs, peacocks, and goats. Recent studies have found that Japanese schools are supported by the 'holistic relationship' and 'organisation as a community' (see Tsuneyoshi, 2008) and are guided by the integrated practice of subject learning, student guidance, club activities, and the like, which unites classmates as a whole group as well as individual students (Fujita, 2006).

However, an overemphasis on East Asian culture and traditions may result in a return to a nationalism that facilitates the cultivation of national identity and exclusiveness. Nakajima and Shimazono (2016) criticise the 'ultra-nationalism' and 'religious nationalism' that were promoted by the ideas of *Kokutai* ('the Constitution of the Empire of Japan'), *Koudo* (皇道, 'the Imperial Way'), and the religious trends followed by State Shinto. This nationalism proposes the need to reinterpret 'constitutionalism' and 'democracy' in light of East Asian resources of thought and culture instead of as an import from the West. Since the medieval era, Christianity played a crucial role in Europe, whereas there is no similar centralised and strong common ground in Asia. However, East Asia values the coexistence of various ideas in various ways. Therefore, it is important to consider the religions, minds, and cultures of the East Asian framework and understand about how they relate to the ideas of constitutionalism and democracy.

The question of East Asia has significance in rethinking the thought and practice of Japanese Manabi. Education in East Asia has inherited diverse thoughts and culture, including Confucianism, Buddhism, and Taoism, in a variety of ways. This is happening parallel to the challenge of how to reform education and curricula through the diversity of learning in East Asia amid the formation of the new academic abilities and competencies inherent in globalisation. It has been noted repeatedly that the East Asian school system is inclined to focus excessively on an examination competition and knowledge transmission that originated in Confucian influence and Chinese higher civil service examinations (科擧, 科举). In recent years, there has been a rapid educational shift to focus on students' creativity, logical thinking, problem solving, generic skills, social skills, metacognition, and communication skills, even though East Asian students have acquired high scores in the international student assessments of PISA and TIMSS.

In this situation, Manabi might provide a different perspective in a global and knowledge-based society and open a progressive alternative to the standardised framework of learning. The ideas of Nothingness, Emptiness, vacuum, being incomplete, No-mind-ness, purposelessness, egolessness, and so on are embedded in the various school activities in the everyday learning. Though the ideas of 'casting off learning,' doing nothing, and 'reducing knowledge' are rarely uttered by teachers in the classroom lessons in Japan, an example of 'teaching without teaching' or 'teaching without words' that form part of the educational practices. In Japan, traditional culture has been adopted in such activities as school events, extracurricular activities, cleaning, and lunch instruction. The movement to re-evaluate them from an international perspective is also expanding. However, the philosophy of Manabi is also concerned with the aspect of the education of nationalism, and the risk of the political, economic, social conflicts in East Asia is amplified. The main point is to connect the thoughts and values of East Asian learning, apart from the frenzy of authoritarianism and nationalism, to the school reforms that are rooted in the progressive ideas of democracy and human rights. At the same time, it will become more and more important to re-examine the uniqueness and diversity of the thoughts and culture in East Asia and to realise the reform of school and curriculum by connecting it to democracy and citizenship in East Asian progressivism.

Bibliography

Benesse Corporation (2017) "Kyōikukaikaku no Suishin ni kansuru Chousakenkyu." Benesse Corporation.
Biesta, G. (2017) *The Rediscovery of Teaching*, New York/Milton Park, Abingdon, Oxon: Routledge.
Confucius (1999) *Rongo*, translated by Kanaya, O., Tokyo: Iwanami Shoten.
Cummings, W. K. (1997) "Human Resource Development: The J-Model," Cummings, W. K., & Altbach, P. G. eds. *The Challenge of East Asian Education: Implications for America*, New York: State University of New York Press, pp. 275–291.
Dewey, J. (1897) "My Pedagogic Creed," Dewey, J., & Boydston, J. eds. *The Early Works of John Dewey*, vol. 5, Carbondale: Southern Illinois University Press, pp. 84–95.
Dewey, J. (1916) "Democracy and Education," Dewey, J., & Boydston, J. eds. *The Middle Works of John Dewey*, vol. 9, Carbondale: Southern Illinois University Press, pp. 1–370.
Dewey, J. (1923) "The School as a Means of Developing a Social Consciousness and Social Ideals in Children," Dewey, J., & Boydston, J. eds. *The Middle Works of John Dewey*, vol. 15, Carbondale: Southern Illinois University Press, pp. 150–157.
Dewey, J. (1931) "The Way Out of Educational Confusion," Dewey, J., & Boydston, J. eds. *The Later Works of John Dewey*, vol. 6, Carbondale: Southern Illinois University Press, pp. 75–89.
Dewey, J. (1939) "Creative Democracy: The Task Before Us," Dewey, J., & Boydston, J. eds. *The Later Works of John Dewey*, vol. 14, Carbondale: Southern Illinois University Press, pp. 224–230.
Fromm, E. (2013) *Psychoanalysis and Zen Buddhism*, New York: Open Road Media.
Fujita, H. (2006) "Sekai kara Mita Nihon no Gakko Kaikaku: Nihongata Kyōiku no Cho-sho wo Humaete Seito no Kanousei wo Hiraku," *VIEW* 21, Tokyo: Benesse Educational Research and Development Institute.
Herrigel, E. (2018) *Zen in the Art of Archery*, translated by Hull, R. F. C., Vigeo Press.
Hokusai and Japonisme (2017) Tokyo: The National Museum of Western Art.
Izutsu, T. (1991) *Ishiki to Honshitsu: Seishinteki Toyo wo Motomete*, Tokyo: Iwanami Shoten.
Jung, C. (1964) "Foreword," Suzuki, D. T. ed. *An Introduction to Zen Buddhism*, New York: Grove Press.
Lao Tzu (2001) *Lao-tzu: The Way and Its Virtue*, translated by Izutsu, T., Tokyo: Keio University Press.
Lao Tzu (2016) *Lao Tzu*, translated by Hachiya, K., Tokyo: Iwanami Shoten.
Nakajima, T., & Shimazono, S. (2016) *Aikoku to Shinko no Kouzo: Zentaishugi ha Yomigaeru-noka*, Tokyo: Shueisha.
Natsume, S. (2004) "Roshi no Tetsugaku," *Sōseki Zenshū*, vol. 26, Tokyo: Iwanami Shoten, pp. 71–91.
Nitobe, I. (2007) *Nitobe Inazo Ronshu*, Tokyo: Iwanami Shoten.
Nitobe, I. (2008) *Bushido: The Soul of Japan*, Radford: Wilder Publications.
Okakura, K. (1906) *The Book of Tea*, Start Publishing LLC.
Okubo, T. (2015) *Okakura Tenshin: The Book of Tea*, Tokyo: NHK Shuppan.
Ota, T., & Yamamoto, M. (2016) *Hitonaru: Chigau, Kakawaru, and Kawaru*, Tokyo: Fujiwara Shoten.
Saito, T. (2016) *Atarashii Gakuryoku*, Tokyo: Iwanami Shoten.
Sato, M. (2000) *Manabikara Tousousuru Kodomotachi*, Tokyo: Iwanami Shoten.
Suzuki, D. T. (2005) *Zen and Japanese Culture*, Tokyo: Kodansha.

Tajima, H. (2016) *Shounen to Seinen no Kindai Nihon: Ningenkeisei to Kyōiku no Shakaishi*, Tokyo: Tokyo Daigaku Shuppankai.

Tan, S. (2004) *Confucian Democracy: A Deweyan Reconstruction*, New York: State University of New York Press.

Tsujimoto, M. (2018) "The Corporeality of Learning: Confucian Education in Early Modern Japan," Kwak, D. C., Kato, M., Hung, R. ed. *The Confucian Concept of Learning: Revisited for East Asian Humanistic Pedagogies*, London: Routledge.

Tsuneyoshi, R. (2008) *Kodomotachi no Mittsu no 'Kiki:' Kokusai Hikaku kara Miru Nihon no Mosaku*, Tokyo: Keiso Shobo.

Tsuneyoshi, R., Kusanagi, K., & Takahashi, F. (2016) "Cleaning as Part of TOKKATSU: School Cleaning Japanese Style," Center for Excellence in School Education, Graduate School of Education, The University of Tokyo Working Paper Series in the 21st Century International Educational Models Project, No. 6.

Tucker, J. (2008) "Japanese Confucian Philosophy," Zalta, E. N. ed. *The Stanford Encyclopedia of Philosophy* (Spring 2018 Edition), https://plato.stanford.edu/archives/spr2018/entries/japanese-confucian/.

Ueno, M. (2018) "Higashi Asia no Manabi no Sisou to Gakkou Kaikaku," *Kyōikugaku Kenkyu*, 8(2), 42–50.

Ueno, M., Kashiwagi, Y., Fujii, K., & Murayama, T., (2018) "Manabi as an Alternative Concept of Learning in Educational Discourses," *Philosophy Study*, 8(2), 87–96, February, David Publishing Company.

Chapter 2

The analysis of Manabi
Learning towards Nothingness and Selflessness

Yasunori Kashiwagi

Introduction

Historically, learning in Japan, located at the edge of East Asia, was strongly affected by Mainland China; in particular, its original learning style was established under the influence of China. As mentioned in Chapter 1, in East Asian countries learning has a dimension that cannot be apprehended using the concepts of learning in Western thought. Recently, studies of learning in East Asia have attracted great attention and developed actively all over the world, thereby helping to unveil the learning of East Asian countries.

Studies of learning in East Asia have emphasised the influences of the doctrines of Buddhism, Confucianism, or Taoism as elements that could not be explained with learning concepts based on the theories of Western pedagogy. These elements of East Asia are explained using such words as 'non-subjective,' 'non-active,' and 'non-positive'; we have no choice but to use 'non-' (非－) to convey the essential elements of learning in East Asia to Westerners. When describing the principle of learning and teaching in Japan or in East Asia, we are compelled to state that our learning and teaching are '*not*' learning and teaching as practised in Western countries. In this phrase, as a matter of course, the meaning of 'our traditional learning and teaching' is almost negative, reactionary, and old school at any given moment. Above all, Japanese progressive educational researchers and teachers strongly emphasised those negativities after World War II. In Japan, it is extremely difficult for progressive educational researchers and teachers to accept the traditional authoritarian learning because of its close connections to the past militaristic education that led so many young students to the battlefront. Indeed, we remember such phrases as 'Kamikaze,' 'Banzai Cliff,' and 'the Battle of Iwo Jima.'

In this chapter, I attempt to analyse Japanese traditional learning progressively using the Japanese word *Manabi* to define an alternative perspective on learning. Analysing Japanese learning positively without using the prefix 'non-,' I offer you *the paradigmatic structure of Manabi*, namely the structure of Japanese learning, and I would like to offer a reconstructed learning model and set out the possibility of its application in (post-)global society and education. It has already been more than 130 years since the Western educational system was introduced to East Asian countries. Presently, it seems to us that the pedagogical worth of Western education is recognised in China, South Korea, Japan, Hong Kong, and elsewhere. For example, subjectivity, democracy, (political) freedom, *Areopagitica*, and the freedom of speech, justice, dialogue, and so on – these concepts have been transplanted to many East Asian countries, although some countries do not completely share the view of the worth of Western education, like North Korea or China. Moreover, in Japan many educational researchers have trouble assimilating the value of education from Western countries. No matter how much Japanese learn the necessity of political freedom or democracy, they would like to maintain an authoritarian – or *Chukou* (忠孝) – attitude towards others, towards their community, their school, and their workplace. *Karoshi* (過労死) is one of the typical symbols of the Japanese authoritarian personality.

In any case, there are always two sides, 'two faces,' to everything in the traditional thought of Japan. In Japanese, we refer to *Ura* (裏) and *Omote* (表), or to *Honne* (本音, a person's true/real feelings or thoughts) and *Tatemae* (建前, a person's assumed behaviour or selfless opinions in public). Certainly, Japanese accept the Western principles in Tatemae; they do not, however, recognise those principles in Honne. In the same way, Japanese education has two faces that teachers have in everyday teaching. Therefore, to clarify this structure of Japanese learning, we need to answer the following two questions: 'Why doesn't Western learning become established in East Asian countries?' and 'What is original in the learning practised in East Asia?' The former will reflect the actuality of East Asia, and the latter will reveal the possibilities of alternative learning in the age of globalisation. It is likely that the answer to these questions may come from the analysis and interpretation of Manabi, i.e., Japanese learning, as the learning of one East Asian country.

The question of Manabi underlying learning

The general purposes of pedagogy developed slowly through the course of long historical arguments. No one at the time held the main purposes of learning to be such ideals as democracy, human rights, individuality, or independence, which are now believed to be the most important values for all people in all countries.

After the Meiji Restoration, the Japanese began adopting Western values and educational practices in the late 1860s, which had a huge influence throughout Japan. Of course, they in fact modified their traditional education system on the model of modern Western education systems as a defence against Western colonisation of East Asia. In domestic pedagogy in Japan, the most important issue discussed was how to realise a new educational system in modern Japan based on Western educational models. Yukichi Fukuzawa (福沢諭吉), the founder of

Keio University, wrote a famous book titled *An Encouragement of Learning*, in which he suggests:

> Japan is an island country separated eastward from the Asian continent. From ancient times it has not had relations with foreign countries.... But foreign trade began after the coming of the Americans in the 1850's, creating the situation which has continued up to the present.... Japan and the nations of the west are peoples who live between the same heaven and earth, feel the warmth of the same sun, look up at the same moon, share the same oceans and air, and possess the same human feelings.
>
> (Fukuzawa, 2012: 5–6)

Based on Western thoughts and politics, Japan had not only maintained its independence but had also aimed to develop into a modern nation like contemporary England or France.

Superficially, the aim seems to have succeeded well in the matter of the introduction of Western education. According to OECD's PISA 2015 results, Japan belongs to 'the four highest-performing OECD countries,' namely, 'Singapore outperforms all other participating countries/economies in science. Japan, Estonia, Finland and Canada, in descending order of mean science performance, are the four highest-performing OECD countries' (OECD, 2015). The high Japanese performance in science, reading, and mathematics should be shown objectively (Busemeyer, 2015). Not only that, many East Asian countries have achieved increasingly high average scores on the PISA. The higher school performance of Japanese students has been established in international research. However, few universities in Japan are assessed highly in international research rankings like the World University Ranking. According to *The Japan Times*, it is said that 'the majority of Japanese university students don't read books for pleasure' (*The Japan Times*, 2018). Thus, Japanese students most likely have a superficially higher learning performance, but their learning does not amount to true scholastic learning; that is, it is merely 'counterfeit ability.'

Here are the real intentions of my inquiry. How do Japanese children learn? For what ends do Japanese teachers teach? What kinds of differences are there in learning between the West and Japan? If so, how can the difference be described? Are there even differences between Japan and other countries in East Asia? Furthermore, what should be prized by Japanese teachers and students in the classroom or teaching, or what kind of learning do they hope to achieve? Expressed more formally, what in fact is 'good learning' for them? How should it be defined if an answer is to be given to these questions?

When referring to the learning of Japanese students, their learning styles, plans, attitudes, and behaviour are very different from those of learning in Western countries and moreover even differ from those of learning in other East Asian countries despite their historical geographically strong connections. You would be convinced of these differences everywhere in Japan as soon as you visited a Japanese kindergarten or school. For example, *Souji* (掃除, cleaning activities in school) play a key role in the whole school as part of becoming an educated person. We can describe Souji as the heart of Manabi because it is not only used just as part of the curriculum but is also defined as a traditional key lesson in cultivating the 'good learned person.' Even if outsiders sharply criticise Souji from considerations of safety or health, it would be impossible to remove it from schooling. Not merely teachers and children but almost all Japanese find the meaning of true learning in Souji because Souji as part of Manabi is a fundamental act of the traditional training of Japanese religions, such that Souji and training are related to each other (see Chapter 6).

In the following narrative, I would like to elaborate on the phenomena which are visibly actualised in Japanese schooling, allowing for the differences just described. Silhouetting the main concepts which are concerned with Manabi in different (various) Japanese words or contexts established a long time ago in Japan, I would like to set out and analyse the structure of Manabi to provide a perspective on Manabi as an alternative concept of learning. As a result, we would be able to discuss the educational horizon more deeply in this era of globalisation with concepts that are not used in Western countries. However, this chapter should not be taken as claiming that there is better learning in Japan or that this learning would be a good exemplar of anti-Western learning. In fact, I will never emphasise the superiority of the patriotic education system of Japan. Rather, I would like to elaborate on the implications of Japanese learning, which have been ignored in the learning of Western countries, as this suggests that this emphasis will apply also to the learning of Western children. I want to leave the decision to readers as to whether it is possible that this discussion could apply to learning in Western countries.

A methodological perspective on studying Manabi

In the following discussion, the main concepts of Manabi will be extracted from representative Japanese texts which provide the exact context of Manabi and which have for the most part already been translated into Western languages. Reflecting on these texts from the point of view of traditional philology and educational philosophy, two main concepts, namely Nothingness and Selflessness, are rediscovered in this chapter. But the interpretations of those concepts are very different even between Japan and other East Asian countries. Thus, we must attend to the small differences of each country. Moreover, there are differences between Japanese Buddhism and the Buddhism of other East Asian countries.

It should be noted that it is impossible to present these concepts unambiguously without taking into consideration the historicity, regionality, and differences within East Asia, but we should be able to classify these concepts into several categories and sort them out in terms of educational philosophy.

The following three points are the methodological features of this chapter.

First, this chapter aims to analyse the main concepts related to Japanese learning through reflecting on and deductively, gradually interpreting those concepts. Because of the philosophical nature of the discussion, it must endeavour to devise a general, comprehensive theory; for that, we must distil the abstract concepts which can be included in the learning situation itself, such as *Bildung* in German; also, we cannot present mere learning as practice. The abstract concepts refer to 'the aspect before self-activation (*Selbsttätigkeit*),' namely 'the area (field) of perception before self-activation,' as Imai wrote (Imai, 2015: 314). Hence it is incumbent on us to present this aspect in fact.

Second, this chapter aims to describe the phenomena which are actualised prominently in Japanese learning. However, I do not seek to simply give plaudits to Japanese learning *against* the learning of Western countries because I am strongly conscious of the difference from old Japanese literature and documents written around the beginning of the twentieth century, whose authors constructed their inherent thought in contradistinction to the thought of Western countries, arguing clearly against Western thought. However, today in the twenty-first century, East Asia will need to try not merely to have a dialogue with (or against) Western countries but also to aim at international dialogue, including with all non-Western countries. The latter aim seeks to realise mutual understanding among all countries, not to emphasise the differences from Western countries. For that, we need to find our own language for mutual understanding. Fortunately, our perspective on the world is spreading more and more with the development of our Internet-connected environment and Web-based system. We can receive all types of information from all over the world. For instance, we can not only watch film projecting the whole world onto a screen but also post our own videos using YouTube. Given this, the global infrastructure has already been built for our worldwide mutual understanding. Using a computer, we can always learn about everyday life on the other side of the world and find a new friend online at any time. Also, the border between Western and Eastern is becoming more and more ambiguous.

Third, this analysis seeks to offer *a meta-stage model of learning* based on an analysis of Manabi, which is different from the existing representative theory of development (whether psychological or cognitive) in Western psychology. In this chapter I seek to offer an alternative theory of the stages of the transformation processes of human beings. Existing representative theories of these developmental stages have delineated the processes as aiming towards 'self-actualisation,' 'self-perfection,' or 'identity-establishing.' All these processes are essentially based on self (selfhood). Mayeroff also described this view: 'To care for another person, in the most significant sense, is to help him grow and actualize himself' (Mayeroff, 1972). However, it has been pointed out in recent educational studies that we must confront the ambiguity, the brittleness, and the frailty of 'self' (Nishihira, 2009). Based on the perspective of Manabi focused on learning in Japan, the processes of learning seem to make up a process toward Selflessness, toward Nothingness, namely a process toward the metamorphosis of the self. In the phrase of Takahashi, this process displays the 'dynamism of the metamorphosis that catabolises the merely unambiguous development itself' (Takahashi, 2007: 164). Because of this dynamism, in this process there is neither an end to the process nor the establishment of an ideal human image as imagined by adults. As long as Manabi aims at Nothingness, there is nothing to be restricted and also nothing to be controlled. On this point, we would affirm that there are freedom and emancipation in Manabi. In actual fact, Buddhist practices such as 'meditation,' 'Yoga,' 'Zen,' and 'mindfulness' have come to be highly valued in Western countries in recent years. These practices will be raised as examples of the need for an alternative learning model in the West. It seems to us that Westerners hope to be released from themselves, from their selves that are strongly bound by self-realisation. Western progressive practitioners have also begun to innovate these practices so as to develop their own practice for those who need support, especially in the fields of social work and psychotherapy. Susanne Strobach has already improved upon a variety of 'meditations' for use in caring for the children of divorced parents (Strobach, 2002). In the same way, this new movement of applying meditation and Yoga to educational practice has started in Japan as well, whereas Japanese education aims at identity establishing and values educational programs related to self-perfection.

Based on those methodological perspectives, I would like to analyse the concept of Manabi and describe its structure while indicating practical examples of schooling in which it is involved. Finally, I would like to discuss Manabi comprehensively as alternative learning through this analysis.

The structure of Manabi

First, I would like to present the provisional and paradigmatic structure of Manabi, which will be explained in this chapter. This structure shows the process of Manabi.

Fundamentally, Manabi aims not at self-actualisation but at the *state of Nothingness*, namely at becoming nothing-ness. Therefore, Nothingness becomes the ultimate purpose of Manabi. To actualise this Nothingness, we continue to learn in order to attain the state of 'self-less-ness', i.e., the selfless self. There is not Nothingness without Selflessness. Everything connected with Manabi is related to Selflessness. Therefore, Japanese learning does not exist without Selflessness. In fact, in schooling, there is a variety of practices to learn Selflessness (see Chapter 6).

Selflessness is predicated on a *Silencing* that we must learn. The essence of Zen practice is to sit quietly in silence (Kato, 1940). To sit quietly in silence is not a special thing; children start to learn sitting quietly during teaching, 45 minutes at a time. They stand at the beginning (departure point) of Manabi only after they can Silence (be silent) quietly. In this way, Silencing plays a key role in learning Selflessness. It is *Shugyō* (修行, 'ascetic training,' *sadhana*) to learn this Silencing physically. Shugyō is basically practiced alone, whatever the variety of ascetic training. There is always 'loneliness' (孤独) at the base of Shugyō. This

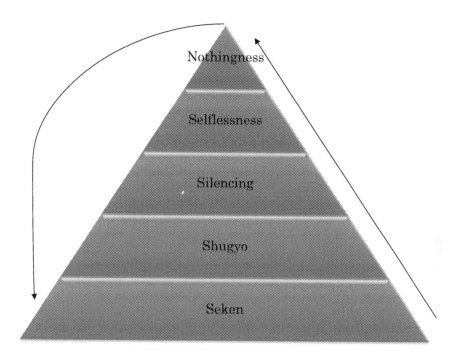

Figure 2.1 Structure of Manabi

training is a lonesome act. Through this lonesome act, learners learn the meaning of Silencing physically, then learn the worth of those who can sit quietly in silence.

Shugyō essentially means separation (disengagement) from the world, namely breaking away from the world. The world here means not only 'world' but also 'worldliness,' 'everyday life,' 'daily individual life,' and 'a society including everyone,' i.e., *Minna*. The practitioners of Shugyō break away consciously from the world for Shugyō. Before that, they have already learned the worldly common sense (knowledge) and the rule for with-living with others (communication skill). At first, they start to apostatise their worldly covenant. Shugyō turns us towards the extraordinary world.

In following discussion, we analyse the conventional and novel learning processes of Manabi.

Nothingness

What have people in East Asian countries fundamentally learned *for*? What have they aimed for in learning? And how have they tried to achieve their aims, and for what in fact have they directed the fruit of their efforts? The ultimate purpose of learning in East Asia is historically to mortify our *klesha* (煩悩) through ascetic training (*sadhana*, Sanskrit *Sādhana*, JP: *Shugyō*), then to reach (1) the state of *Kuu* (空), namely the state of Emptiness which is related with *Tenmei-Kaigo* (転迷開悟) and is suggested by *Buddha* (仏陀, *Siddhārtha Gautama*) (Tagami, 2000: 146), (2) the state of *Mu* (無), namely the state of Nothingness which is illustrated by Lao Tzu (老子). The contents of sadhana are different in individual sectarian persuasions. Whatever the sect, the purpose aimed at is *Nirvana* (涅槃, EN: salvation), attained through the realisation of *śūnyatā* (空, EN: Emptiness) and *Bodhi* (菩提), that is, the state of Enlightenment (正覚). *Sunya* means 'nothing,' 'void,' or 'empty.' In these concepts, we can confirm the importance of Mu, i.e., Nothingness. In the *Heart Sutra* (CN: 摩訶般若波羅蜜多心經, JP: 般若心経), the highest state of Nirvana or Bodhi is called *anuttara-samyak-saṃbodhi* (阿耨多羅三藐三菩提). When reaching the state of this mind, *bhikkhus* (比丘), Buddhists monks or devotees, will obtain the highest truth and an absolute state without any desires. The Buddhists have given this state the most important worth of Nothingness (and/or Emptiness).

Lao Tzu, an ancient Chinese philosopher, also talked about Nothingness. Central to his thought is 'doing nothing and taking things as they come' (無為自然). Therefore, he also said, 'Cast off learning and there will be no worries' (絶学無憂). Additionally, '道常無爲 而無不爲' is also a famous sentence (Chapter 37); namely, 'The Tao, the way, is always to do nothing, but this means not to do nothing.' 無不爲 means 'not doing nothing' (Lao Tzu, 2008). Based on his thought, Nothingness means not merely 'doing not something' but also 'doing something without the intention of Nothingness.' He shows a good example in Chapter 11; 'One cuts out doors and windows to make a house. Precisely in the empty space within is the utility of the house. Thus, if Being profits us, it is due to the working of Non-Being' (Lao Tzu, 2001: 45). And then, according to Chapter 40, 'The ten thousand things under heaven are born out of Being. Being is born out of Non-Being' (Lao Tzu, 2001: 104) Thus, he thought that everything springs from Nothingness. And he has given us an example of Nothingness in Chapter 28: 'If you become the valley of the world, then the eternal virtue, i.e., Tao, would never desert you. And you would go back to being a baby.' Thus, we can interpret the state of Nothingness as the state of a newborn baby with complete No-mind-ness and Selflessness.

In Japan, the idea of Nothingness may also be found in the teaching of Shinran (親鸞), born in 1173, who founded Jodo Shinshu/Shin Buddhism (浄土真宗). '*Even the good person attains birth in the Pure Land, how much more so the evil person*' which was written by him, is one of the most famous sentences in Japan (Tannisho, 1996: 6). He negated the search for *Satori* (悟り, *Siddhi*), which Carter translated as 'absolute nothingness,' through traditional Shugyō and Zen practice (Carter, 1997: 47), and instead of Shugyō and Zen, he aimed at Satori by chanting *Nenbutsu* (念仏), namely Buddhist invocation, so-called *Nianfo*. In Tannisho, in which the teaching of Shinran is told, he said '[W]hen the thought of saying the nembutsu erupts from deep within, having entrusted ourselves to the inconceivable power of Amida's vow which saves us, enabling us to be born in the Pure Land, we receive at that very moment the ultimate benefit of being grasped never to be abandoned' (Tannisho, 1996: 4). The following text seems to show the essence of Shinran's thought:

> The doctrine of attaining Buddhahood in this very body is the essential teaching of Shingon Esoterism, the ultimate attainment of the three esoteric practices. And the purifying of the six sense-organs is the doctrine of the One Vehicle teaching of the *Lotus Sutra*, the attainment of the four blissful practices. These are all difficult practices performed by superior religious adepts and enlightenment realized through perfecting meditative practices. In contrast, the enlightenment that unfolds in the next birth is the essence of the Pure Land way of Other Power, that true entrusting which is settled and final. This is the effortless practices undertaken by inferior religious practices in which the distinction between good and evil is non-existent.
> (Tannisho, 1996: 26)

According to his teaching, if you say simply Nenbutsu, then you are saved by *Amida* (Amitābha). This is expressed more formally as, 'Just say the Nenbutsu, and be saved by Amida.' Daisetsu Suzuki explained his thought as follows (Suzuki, 1972):

> Shinran, the founder of the Shin branch of the Pure Land school, teaches that the way to be absolutely assured of one's rebirth (Ojo) in the Pure Land is to accept wholeheartedly the Original Prayer announced by Amida, and that this acceptance is effected when one has what Shinran designates as a 'side-wise leap' or a 'leaping cross-wise' (Okyo).

In *Tannisho*, Shinran said that 'in the nenbutsu no self-working is true-working; it is beyond description, explanation, and conception' (*Tannisho*, 1996: 56), and he suggested in his *Songou-Sinzou-Meimon* (尊号真像銘文), 'In Other Power (他力) no self-working is true-working; this is the teaching of Honji Shonin.' 'Working' (義, *Gi*) means the mind managing everything by self-working (one's self), i.e., self-centred thinking. Therefore, Gi as everyone's mind managing (or arranging) by one's self means to think something by one's self (to find out by one's self). If you stop working to manage something/everything, then it will be true management – or true thinking. This sentence would be interpreted as '*no-meaning is the true-meaning*.'

Based on this point of view, Shinran also seems to find a positive meaning of Nothingness. In the thought of Shinran, Gi means not only mere meaning but also 'the mind to arrange,' namely *the mind to do something*. Hence, according to Shinran, in the state of Nothingness of Gi, i.e., in the no-meaning, we can learn the true-mind in mindfulness. Nenbutsu has the true-meaning where it is beyond meaning. So he found the true-meaning in the no-meaning.

After the Meiji Restoration, one of the most significant Japanese philosophers, Kitaro Nishida (西田幾多郎), who introduced Japanese thought to Western countries, also described Nothingness from the point of view of 'pure experience' (純粋経験). And, indeed, his explanation of Nothingness is strongly related to the concept of 'pure experience.' Nishida writes:

> The moment of seeing a color or hearing a sound, for example, is prior not only to the thought that the color or sound is the activity of an external object or that one is sensing it, but also to the judgment of what the color or sound might be. In this regard, pure experience is identical with direct experience.
> (Nishida, 1990: 3)

He called this pure experiment the moment 'prior to the judgement of what the color or sound might be.' Based on this thought, he found absolute Nothingness beyond the conflict between being and Nothingness (Hanaoka, 2002). In addition, his 'direct experience' is different from experience in Western philosophy, being, for example, obviously different from experience as discussed by William James. Nishida's experience might be like the learning experience before doing, the so-called experience of doing nothing.

Giving full weight to the moment, namely the moment prior to the judgement of what the colour or sound might be, may be seen in the usual greetings in everyday life. Japanese people greet each other with *Konnichiwa* (Hello). *Konnichiwa* literally means 'Today is. . .'; *Konnichiwa* is not a complete sentence. Therefore, there is no meaning in the sentence, 'Today is. . . .' Etymologically, *Konnichiwa* (今日様) includes 'sun' (天道様). In the same way, 'good evening' is *Konbanwa* (今晩は) in Japanese, which also means merely 'This evening is. . . .' Japanese greetings contain neither 'good' nor 'bad.' To expand on the words of Daisetsu Teitaro Suzuki (鈴木大拙), Japanese greetings show us the way of Mu-Funbetsu-Chi (無分別智) – as Japanese spirituality – which can be interpreted as mind beyond wisdom to ask a question whether good or bad or whether truth or not. In Western countries, people always say, 'How are you?' '*Wie geht's dir?*' '*Comment vas-tu?*' when meeting friends on the street. The Japanese, however, usually say nothing but 'Hi' or 'Hello.' They will not ask whether one's condition is good or bad. The expression of parting (farewell) is *Sayonara* in Japanese, which literally means 'If so . . .' This greeting sentence also says almost nothing regarding something.

We would think that the significant basis of Japanese learning is to stay in the moment prior to the judgement of what something might be or at least attempt to aim at this moment. In other words, the basis of this thought might be that we strive to stay in the moment prior to seeing everything in black and white, namely in an ambiguous world without a judgemental black-and-white point of view. But we should understand that historically it is the ultimate purpose of Japanese learning not to value the moment prior to the judgement of what might be but to learn to aim at this moment.

I will not discuss the philosophy of Nishida further. Suffice it to say here that Nothingness is the most important subject of Nishida's philosophy. As his philosophy is based on the thought of East Asian Buddhism, it is understandable that he finally reached the perspective of Nothingness (Hanaoka, 2002).

However, Nothingness is merely a concept that never became a matter of inquiry or merely a negative concept in the West. I lack the skills to describe it its totality. Yet I cannot ignore discussions of Nothingness in Western history.

The trust in Being and the negation of Nothingness may derive from the thought of Ancient Greece. The thought of Parmenides is a representative example of the absolute trust in being. According to his thought, non-being must be rejected, for there is no temporality or generation or destruction of being. The rejection of non-being seems to be the traditional thought of Western philosophy.

Epicurus (BCE 341–270), one of the Greek philosophers, wrote in the *Principal Doctrines* that 'death is nothing to us: for that which is dissolved is without sensation; and that which lacks sensation is nothing to us' (Epicurus, 1959: 75). He wrote also, 'Take the habit of thinking that death is nothing for us. For all good and evil lie in sensation: but death is deprivation of any sensitivity' (Epicurus, 1959: 67). In this way, Epicurus alleges that death is nothing to us. Therefore, Nothingness is also in opposition to being; this word also means death for him.

In modern times, Nietzsche took into account the meaning of Nothingness. He assumed Nothingness to be a nihilistic state, in which we no longer have any Christian perspectives. When facing the death of god, he called for us to face squarely the demands on us of life without god, namely the time of nihilism concerned deeply with 'the will to nothingness.' Therefore, his understanding of Nothingness seems to be different from that of the philosophers who deal with the problem of Nothingness like Martin Heidegger or Jean-Paul Sartre. Nietzsche writes in *The Genealogy of Morals*:

> [C]onsider its self-hypnotism on the fakir and Brahman principles (it uses Brahman as a glass disc and obsession), and that climax which we can understand only too well of an unusual satiety with its panacea of nothingness (or God: – the demand for a unio mystica with God is the demand of the Buddhist for nothingness, Nirvana – and nothing else!).
> (Nietzsche, 2003: 15–16)

Indeed, Nietzsche understood Nothingness from the point of view of Buddhism. Yet it is for him that Nothingness cannot be presumed as the highest value. At the end of the book, He implies that 'man will wish *Nothingness* rather than not wish *at all*' (Nietzsche, 2003: 118). Moreover, he found his Nothingness in the conception of 'Beyond-man' (overman): '*Übermensch*,' which is one of the most significant concepts in his thought. The Beyond-Man is he who faces the reality of eternal return (*die ewige Wiederkehr*), in which Nothingness appears. Hence, Nietzsche does not deny the meaning of Nothingness. However, the condition of his Nothingness originates in the nihilism in which we should live without a Christian world view, namely in a lost world. As a matter of fact, the concept of nihilism is closely related with such terms as 'lack,' 'denial,' 'anomie,' and the like. In this regard, his Nothingness seems to be different from Nothingness in East Asian thought, which is centred on the highest value of Nothingness.

In 'Being and Nothingness – an Essay on Phenomenological Ontology,' Jean-Paul Sartre also discusses about Nothingness from the point of view of being. He writes:

> [N]othingness which is not, can have only a borrowed existence, and it gets its being from being. Its nothingness of being is encountered only within the limits of being, and the total disappearance of being would not be the advent of the reign of non-being, but on the contrary the concomitant disappearance of nothingness. *Non-being exists only on the surface of being.*
> (Sartre, 1943/2003: 41)

Sartre consider Nothingness as something that exists only on 'the surface of being.' He writes also that 'Nothingness can be nihilated only on the foundation of being,' and then 'Nothingness lies coiled in the heart of being – like a worm' (Sartre, 1943/2003: 45). This 'coiled Nothingness' would be almost a negative thing in Sartre; 'Nothingness must be given at the heart of Being, in order for us to be able to apprehend that particular type of realities which we have called *négatités*' (Sartre, 1943/2003: 46). For him, Nothingness is strongly related with the heart of being.

Moreover, in the thought of Erich Fromm, 'being' is contrasted not with Nothingness but with 'having;' for him, the opposite of Being is not Nothingness but Having. He determines the meaning of human being from 'being' (Fromm, 1976).

> By being I refer to the mode of existence in which one neither *has* anything nor craves *to have* something, but is joyous, employs one's faculties productively, is *oned* to the world.

This thought of Fromm seems to imply basically an absolute trust in being. However, he could not notice the deeper difference between Being and Nothingness. He actually cited the poem of Basho Matsuo (松尾芭蕉) about a flower: 'When I look carefully/I see the nazuna blooming/By the hedge!' He noted about this poem, 'What Basho wants is to see, and not only to look at the flower, but to be at one, to "one" himself with it.' Fromm compared Basho's poem with the poems of Tennyson and Goethe. Then he wrote, 'Basho's and Goethe's relationship to the flower each sees is in the mode of being.' Even Fromm could not find the state of Nothingness. He interpreted the thought of

Buddha from the standpoint of either Having or Being. 'The Buddha teaches that in order to arrive at the highest stage of human development, we must not crave possessions' (Fromm, 1976). At the centre of his thought, there is no difference between Being and Nothingness, only the difference between having and being.

In this way, the word 'being' has a meaning of basic importance in Western languages. Also, Carter explains that 'indeed, it is generally assumed in the West that *being* is the primary category of understanding and that 'nothingness' is simply a term which refers to the negating, denial, or removal of being' (Carter, 1997: 81).

However recently, Nothingness has become a subject of discussion, and this argument seems to deepen little by little in small steps. For instance, Carter asked, '[W]hat does nothingness add to human understanding?' (Carter, 1997), and he attempts to clarify the whole image (picture) of Nothingness. Mohsin (2017) asked also, 'How did creation happen?' and answered, 'Nothingness theory describes it with a new approach considering "Nothing" as a new kind of thing which we have been ignoring in our logical conception' (Mohsin, 2017). In this way, Nothingness theory is becoming a new progressive approach to reconsidering our logical conceptions which is related with learning.

What effect, then, does Nothingness have for today's human beings? Why do Japanese frequently use the word 'Nothingness,' and why do they tend to learn something aiming towards Nothingness? To live in Nothingness, in the most significant sense, is to practice Shugyō and actualise a life lived in *Satori* (悟り, *Siddhi*), which is the final purpose of the ascetic training of Shugyō. In East Asia, Nothingness is closely related with the Shugyō of Buddhists who wish to attain the world of supreme enlightenment called Satori. Now we should ask the question, 'What is Satori?' Wakimoto explained Satori:

> Buddhism teaches us to attain enlightenment (*satoru*) of the truth of '*anitya*' (無常, 'impermanence') and '*anatta*' (無我) as the fundamental order of universe, and to attain '*moksha*' (解脱) from the suffering of life by attaining enlightenment.
>
> (Wakimoto, 1997: 94)

In countries influenced by Buddhist thought, it is exactly the ultimate purpose to attain enlightenment for truth, and all the difficulties of Shugyō are practised in order to achieve this purpose. As a result, the truth is undoubtedly Nothingness, which is shown in impermanence and Selflessness (無我, *Muga*), which will be described in the next section.

Nothingness, which was just discussed, is not shown explicitly in Japanese school curricula. No schools aim at Nothingness as the main purpose in schooling. However, many teachers require that the students concentrate on the teaching of class through an approach to Nothingness, namely through strong concentration without self-working, and many teachers make a special effort not to let the children understand the meanings of their textbook but rather to let them concentrate on reading it aloud without self-thinking. Additionally, for example, lunch in silence (無言給食) and the cleaning activity in silence (無言清掃) are practices cultivating Nothingness (see Chapter 6). Whereas Nothingness is clearly shown in school curricula, this is strongly hoped for by teachers who emphasise students' attitudes in learning more than their understanding the textbook in teaching. Therefore, we can say that Nothingness always has and already should have been noted as existing implicitly as the ultimate purpose of the 'hidden curriculum.'

In addition, Nothingness would apply not only in East Asian countries but also in Ancient Greece. Socrates said, 'I know that I know nothing.' This means, on the one hand, 'The only good is knowledge and the only evil is ignorance.' But on the other hand, we can reinterpret this sentence as meaning that 'I know that *I am nothing-ness*,' for at least, based on East Asian thought, it is more important for us to know that I *am* Nothingness than to know that I know nothing.

Finally, in 1907, Inazo Nitobe (新渡戸稲造), a professor at Tokyo University, a philosopher, and the author of *Bushido*, suggested the superiority of 'something of everything' as the purpose of education in comparison with 'everything of something.' He used this word to emphasise the importance of cultivation and the liberal arts (Nitobe, 1907). However, both words are false from the point of view of Nothingness. We should emphasise that the purpose of education must be to learn the 'nothing-ness of everything;' this is the suggestion of the theory of Nothingness. There is something more ultimate and important in East Asian countries than cultivation or liberal arts.

Selflessness

Similar to the concept of Nothingness, there is another concept that is representative of the essence of Manabi learning, namely *Selflessness* (無私, *Mushi*; 無我, *Muga*). This concept is strongly related to Nothingness. Strictly speaking, Selflessness is the last step of the process toward Nothingness. There is no Nothingness without Selflessness. Fundamentally, Selflessness is deeply related with Buddhism (Nakamura, 1963: 3). In the context of Buddhism, its origin is 'anattan' or 'anattā,' which means 'not a soul' or 'without a soul' (Nakamura, 1963: 3).

At the roots of this thought may be found 'the three marks of existence' (三法印) of the *Tattvasiddhi-Śāstra* (成実論) in Buddhism. The three marks are:

1 All forms are impermanent (諸行無常, *anicca*).
2 All things are Selflessness – or 'non-Self' (諸法無我, *anatta*).
3 Nirvana is Silencing (涅槃寂静, *nirvāṇa*).

And it is possible to say 'the four marks of existence' by adding a fourth mark: (4) 'Everything is suffering (一切皆苦, *dukkha*).' This teaching is the inherent thought that would be affirmed in all Buddhist cultures. In anatta, or anatman, we can find the conception of Selflessness. By now, it should be clear that Selflessness is impressed by these cultures. *Mushin* (無心) of Zeami Motokiyo (世阿弥) is also closely associated with this Buddhist thought.

Zeami, a Japanese aesthetician, actor, and playwright, also makes an exhortation for the *feeling of Mushin* (無心の感), namely the *feeling of no-mind*. Nishihira, an educational theorist interested in the feeling of no-mind of Zeami, wrote: 'Zeami stated that Mushin isn't "achievement of learning way" (習道). But he said also that "It is impossible to learn Mushin without learning the way." In this confused talk, the depth of Mushin in Zeami appears' (Nishihira, 2009). Thus, basically it is impossible to attain Mushin without exercise, but we cannot also attain this as an achievement of exercise. Nishihira defines it as follows: 'We don't wait merely for Mushin by doing nothing; nonetheless, we do not create this directly. That is to say, Mushin comes as a consequence, without our realising it.'

Selflessness is one of the most important principles that Japanese children learn. We can say that Manabi is the process by which children become selfless people. Although they leave themselves by being selfless, they learn to control themselves. Nitobe also wrote, in Chapter 11 on self-control, 'Imagine boys – and girls, too – brought up not to resort to the shedding of a tear or the uttering of a groan for the relief of their feelings' (Nitobe, 1905/2008: 171). Despite the fact that this sentence was written in 1900, it explains how the Japanese learning style came to be possible. In fact, Selflessness has ethical and moral worth in Western countries, too. For example, there is the expression 'selfless love.' What does selfless love mean? Generally, selfless love means *agape* love in Western thought. It is possible to say that Selflessness is a comprehensive word that has universal worth. Japanese words like Muga or Mushi truly name the phenomenon of Selflessness. Therefore, it will be worthwhile interpreting the meaning of this universal word as an academic concept.

Because of Mushi and Mushin, Japanese people do not explicitly have a view of their clear self. For this reason, they do not assert themselves against each other (they are not assertive of their rights) and do not make strong personal statements to each other, because they have a weaker subjectivity than Western people. They have no split in the relationship between I and you (others). In this way, they have lived selfless lives by having ambiguous selves.

Even after the Meiji Restoration in 1867–1868, whereas Japanese people have taken to themselves the Western concept of independent 'self,' they have consciously or subconsciously continued to maintain this selfless lifestyle. Selflessness is, on the one hand, one of the traditional ethical concepts. On the other hand, however, there is the negative aspect of Selflessness. The most symbolic existence of the ultimate Selflessness in this negative meaning is so-called *Kamikaze*, namely the special suicide attack corps. About 6,000 kamikaze pilots participated in World War II, aged 17–30. They committed suicide, which is to say they threw themselves away by giving their lives for the nation. This seems be the essence of Selflessness in its most negative meaning. Therefore, we should point out this negative element first when discussing Selflessness. We may be able to term this Nothingness as '*authoritarian Selflessness.*' If this Selflessness relates to Authoritarianism, then these terrible consequences may possibly arise again. Selflessness always includes this ambiguity.

Today, many people in Japan still criticise this Selflessness as a negative element of being human and value a strong (tough) self from the point of view of the Western context. Therefore, I must note that a great conflict between those who value a tough self and those who value a selfless tender person, and we can find this conflict in a single person.

Carl Löwith pointed out this conflict in the Japanese as 'ambivalent' already in 1948. After he said '[T]he whole relationship of the Japanese to the West is necessarily discordant and *ambivalent*,' he wrote:

> They live as if on two levels: a lower, more fundamental one, on which they feel and think in a Japanese way; and a higher one, on the European sciences from Plato to Heidegger are lined up. And the European teacher asks himself: where is the step on which they pass from the one level to the other? In principle they love themselves as they are; they have not yet eaten from the (Christian!) tree of knowledge and lost their innocence, a loss which *places* human beings *beyond themselves* and makes them critical of themselves.
>
> (Löwith, 1995: 232)

As shown in this critique, Japanese people live as if in a two-level house. Löwith also wrote: '[T]hey learn what is foreign in itself, but they do not do so for themselves;' 'they do not come from others back to themselves; they are not free, or – to put it as Hegel does – they are not with themselves in Being-other.' This suggestion seems to prove the existence of Selflessness as typical of the Japanese.

In any case, self-realisation as a Western concept is clearly related to the educational issue of establishing identity, not only in Western countries but also in all developed countries. This issue has been recognised by many educators and psychologists, whence the establishment of identity is valued especially in pedagogical contexts. Nevertheless, as a purpose of Manabi, Selflessness before (or after) establishing identity should have been the aim of many Japanese educational researchers and teachers. If you express yourself to others in Japan, then the Japanese would recognise immediately that you are a selfish, egotistical person. In the Japanese context, expressing something to others is rejected as well as disliked. Why is the self rejected? What kind of causation is there in this rejection? Fundamentally, what is Selflessness that absolutely rejects the existence of self?

Daisetsu Teitaro Suzuki rediscovered Selflessness as a significant spirit of human beings after the Meiji Restoration. By describing Harmony (和) in the chapter on *Sado* (茶道), the Japanese art of the tea ceremony, Suzuki wrote in *Zen and Japanese Culture* (Suzuki, 1938/2005: 198):

> [F]rom the spiritual point of view, Christians and Buddhists alike know how to follow Dōgen to appreciate the significance of Selflessness or 'sort-heartedness.'

Based on his perspective, Christians have recognised the significance of Selflessness also. Historically, this Selflessness is closely related with *Mushin no Shin* (無心之心, 'mind of no-mind'), namely Mindlessness, which generally has a very negative meaning in English. But this mind of no-mind is the ultimate value in East Asian countries. In the thought of Suzuki, the fundamental figure (*Gestalt*) is that of the ideal human being in the condition of a mindless self; he also wrote, 'When there is no self, the heart is soft and offers no resistance to outside influences' (Suzuki, 1938/2005).

These thoughts are confirmed in *The Book of Five Rings* (五輪書), by Musashi Miyamoto (宮本武蔵), the famous Japanese swordsman and philosopher before the Meiji Restoration. He advances the idea of the Strike of *Munen-Musou* (無念無想); *Mu* means 'Nothingness' (literally, 'without'); *Nen* means 'intention' or 'thought'; *Sou* means 'concept' or 'imagination.' Generally, *Munen-Musou* means 'throwing away all remembrances which are risen in our mind'; namely, if you throw away all kinds of wishes and hopes, then you can arrive at a state of Selflessness. Miyamoto wrote:

> When you think that both you and your opponent are ready to strike, your body becomes a striking body, your mind becomes a striking mind and your hand instantaneously strikes with strength emerging from nothingness and leaving no wake. This is the most important strike, that of No Thought–No Concept. This is often an effective strike, and you should practice and master it thoroughly.
>
> (Miyamoto, 2012)

This No Thought–No Concept should be the kind of being (*Seinsart*) of the ideal human being that is imagined by Japanese people. They strike with the samurai Japanese sword in the state of no-mind, namely in Munen-Musou.

From this analysis, it is clear that Selflessness as an ultimate purpose of human beings is the aim of those who live in all East Asian countries. Indeed, Selflessness is closely related with the tough, hostile natural environment of Japan. In this island, there are many natural phenomena such as typhoons, tsunamis, earthquakes, and volcanic eruptions. All our lives may come to naught through those natural phenomena. Japanese live in this hostile environment. Therefore, all Japanese people must always confront the possibility that everything will melt down and be destroyed someday. The Japanese have already learned empirically what impermanence is. In this way, they learned the impermanence of everything as the landscape of the original state of Selflessness.

As well as Nothingness, Selflessness is also a concept that is never discussed in learning in Western countries. Whereas there are different discussions of the theory of self-definition and self-formation, I have never heard discussions in learning theory on Selflessness in pedagogical discussions. Hence it seems worthwhile to discuss learning with respect to Selflessness; for example, Zen is now one practice worldwide that Westerners have heartily taken up. The alternative method to Zen is the 'mindfulness' which has already been introduced into the schools. It might be said that the time has come in which we are to attempt to learn to throw ourselves away and forget ourselves. Instead of establishing the self, we ought to think about learning towards Selflessness.

However, Self-less-ness does not mean that the self is becoming perfectly nothing, namely nobody. The austere training for the vanishing self, so-called Shugyō, postulates that there is a self that attempts to make my self vanish. Based on the phrase, 'Throughout heaven and earth, I alone am the honored one' (天上天下唯我独尊), assuredly 'I alone' subsist in the world. Therefore, Selflessness and solipsism (唯我) would be two sides of the same coin. In either case, 'the others' that form one of the bases of Western thought are not assumed in East Asian philosophical thought. Just the selfless self is assumed as well as selfless others, in *Silence*.

Silencing

We must absolutely take Silencing into account if we wish to reach for the state of Selflessness. We cannot understand Selflessness without thinking about Silencing. In the same way, Nothingness is also related to Silencing, namely to practise silence in stillness, to be quiet, to avoid saying something, and to contemplate without speaking. Silencing is a prior condition of Nothingness and Selflessness. The typical practice of Silencing is *meditation* (瞑想), which is already widely practised in Western countries. In schooling, Silencing is emphasised every so often, intentionally or unintentionally.

Silencing is based on the Japanese aesthetic sense. Basho Matsuo (松尾芭蕉), the most famous Japanese poet of the Edo period, wrote:

> Furuike ya kawazu tobikomu misu no oto;
> An old silent pond, a frog jumps into the pond, splash! Silence again.
> (Translated by Harry Behn)

In profound silence, the deep silence was broken by the sound of a frog jumping into the pond (Matsuo, 1979). This poem expresses the East Asian idea of the evanescence (はかなさ) of this broken moment and shows the beauty of deep Silencing. As shown in this haiku, Japanese children are always told that they must be silent in school as a process of Manabi. Not only in teaching but almost everywhere else, they should be silent. They also have to line up in order and stand at attention. There is an aphorism also in the West: 'He who knows most, speaks least.' In the process of Manabi, it is of ultimate significance to become a Silencing person. Japanese people find the true learning of children in this silence. If you observe the children in a Japanese or East Asian school, then you can immediately find that all teaching orients the children toward Silencing.

For example, Japanese children 'button it up' (take to silence) in class. No matter how much they learn to speak in their schooling, they tend to keep silent in many cases. Students do not speak in class throughout their lessons as if they were in a church, even though they talk loudly with their classmates during recess. In elementary schools, students are encouraged to raise their hands firstly and then to answer loudly after the teacher asks questions.

In the process of Manabi, especially in junior high school, they begin to lose expression and remain silent during class. They merely listen in silence to the teacher's talk, look at the blackboard, and take notes of what the teacher writes. In addition, they do not express their ideas by saying 'I think that...' or, 'In my opinion....' It is believed to be wrong for Japanese students to insist on their opinions in the classroom. Therefore, active dialogue seldom occurs in class. Dialogue rarely arises even if so-called active learning, which has become popular, is introduced because nobody wants to talk in class.

Silence is one of the highest virtues for the Japanese. In the same way, Self-Silencing is the aesthetic behaviour in which we would realise our highest ideal condition. When the Japanese hear a call for *Mokutou* (黙祷), a moment of silent tribute, then they would visualise a scene of sober ceremony, mainly to commemorate a death.

In this respect, Silencing has been discussed in the history of Western thought as well. 'Many people have searched for silence,' wrote Alain Corbin (2018: 41):

> [I]t is an ancient and a universal quest. It provides the whole of human history: Hindus, Buddhists, Taoists, Pythagoricians and, of course, Christians, Catholics and perhaps even more Orthodox, have felt the need for and the benefits of silence; and this desire has been felt beyond the spheres of the sacred and the religious.

As pointed out here, silence is a universal quest. However, there is a major difference between Western *Silence* and Eastern *Silencing*.

In classical times, Epicurus wrote: 'The just person enjoys the greatest peace of mind, while the unjust is full of the utmost disquietude.' And he found the greatest peace of mind in tranquillity (*ataraxia*), whereas he thought the unjust found themselves in disquietude. *Ataraxia* can be interpreted as 'stillness of the soul' (Fromm, 1989). He put up the slogan of '*lathe biosas*' (live covertly). We can probably find an element of Silence in this living covertly as a main aspect of Epicurean thought. He wrote also: 'We must free ourselves from the prison of public education and politics.' It sounds as if he knew everything about Zen or Shugyō, including Silencing. However, Epicurus found a significant meaning in philosophy with friends, namely in 'dialogue.' In the heart of Western thought, there is always this insistence on dialogue as the unshakable basis of learning after Socrates. Additionally, dialogue is closely related with discussion and debate using varied words. He wrote: 'In a philosophical dispute, he gains most who is defeated, since he learns the most' (Epicurus, 1980: 95). Thereby, how we should lead dialogues in learning will be questioned in pedagogy (philosophy of education).

However, if East Asian people do not recognise the essential worth of this dialog in the Western tradition as an initial premise, then how should we think about it? Is it possible for those who recognise the worth of dialogue and communication to have a dialogue with those who never recognise the essential worth of dialogue? I would like to show a good example: When Japanese or other East Asian people see Westerners who speak so much, then they think truly that Western people speak very much – too much. Nevertheless, East Asian people try never to speak so much in public spaces as Western people do and probably only listen carefully to Western people who want to speak much.

The worth of listening carefully to someone without speaking is noted in a work of Michael Ende, a German author. He suggests in *Momo*, one of his masterpieces, the importance of listening (*Zuhören*) to someone without saying anything. On this point, we may be able to argue that Japanese people can listen better to others than Western people; it seems to be very difficult for Westerners to listen carefully to someone without saying anything. Because the Japanese have already found the absolute worth of Silencing without saying anything in silence, they have already built their own relationships with others in Silencing. But this is also proof that there is no dialogue in Japan: Japanese thought is based essentially *not on dialogue but on Silencing*. In addition, Silencing is also sometimes required in Western countries. For example, at Western classical music concerts, the audience must be absolutely quiet in Silencing except for the sound of music; they need to let others listen to the music undisturbed. Thus, Silencing as a moral concept applies not only to the Japanese but also to Westerners attending classical music concerts to listen to the music (Corbin, 2018).

Zen and meditation are also fundamentally based on Silencing. Suzuki described it thus: 'Hence Zen's motto, no reliance on words' (不立文字, *Furyu Monji*) (Suzuki, 2005). Historically, Japanese have no reliance on words. The concept of this phrase in Zen declares, 'Do not believe words.' The suspicion of words is shown in the thought of Ekken Kaibara (貝原益軒), who wrote *Yojokun* in the Edo period (Kaibara, 1961).

> Guard your words, save your deadwood (needless) words, decrease your words. If you talk too much, then you will be mentally exhausted or lose your temper. You will lose all your basic energy. To guard words is also the way (道) to learn goodness (virtue) and cultivation.

Hence Silencing would mean to guard one's words as the way of the Tao. Silencing is a moral, ethical, and didactic concept based on the traditions of Japanese thought.

Now I would like to introduce the example of Teaism (茶). *The Book of Tea*, written by Kakuzo Okakura (岡倉覚三), is the most famous book of thought of Teaism. At the centre of the thought of Teaism is the thought of Silencing while drinking and enjoying tea. According to Okakura, the old Teamen (茶人) were ex-learners of Zen; hence they aimed to introduce the mind of Zen into the real world. The tea room, *Sukiya*, has an average size of 4.5 tatami mats, about 7.3 square meters. Before they enjoyed drinking tea, they had to meditate in Silencing.

Silencing is closely related with ephemerality. In Chapter 6, Okakura described the life and death of flowers:

> Said Laotse [Lao tzu]: 'Heaven and earth are pitiless.' Said Kobodaishi: 'Flow, flow, flow, flow, the current of life is ever onward. Die, die, die, die, death comes to all.' Destruction faces us wherever we turn. Destruction below and above, destruction behind and before. Change is the only Eternal, – Why not as welcome Death as Life? They are but counterparts one of the other, – the Night and Day of Brahma.
>
> (Okakura, 1997: 54)

In the change from life to death, he found the eternity of everything. Hence, he asked, 'Why not as welcome death as life.' At the base of Silencing, there is the concept just presented, impermanence, namely *Mujo* (無常), or, expressed in another word, *Hakanasa* (はかなさ), which can be interpreted as ephemerality. Okakura wrote also, 'Why were the flowers born so beautiful and yet so hapless?' Haplessness means impermanence, in which the Japanese find beauty. There is the aesthetic thought called *Mono no aware* (もののあはれ) based on Heian medieval literature of Japan, which may be translated as 'the pathos of things,' 'the sorrow of human existence,' 'a sensitivity to things,' or the 'meaningfulness of Mono,' and the like. In any case, *Mono no aware* means 'the profoundly deeper affections appearing when you encounter the various things around you like natures and persons' (Kitahara, 1987). This thought is related to impermanence or ephemerality because the Japanese values how you felt about what you saw, not what you did. So we might interpret the sense of impermanence and ephemerality as causing this Japanese aesthetic idea of *Mono no aware*. This is also the essential issue of Silencing.

Hence also in Manabi, it is not enough for Japanese people to simply silence. Silencing should be related with ephemerality; it has always been a matter of Mujo as well. The matter of Silencing is always also a matter of Mujo; i.e., Silencing exists only in a moment. If so, then what is Mujo fundamentally? How is it related to Silencing in the Japanese mind?

For example, the Japanese love the sakura, Japanese cherry blossoms; in particular, they love the *Somei Yoshino* (*Prunus yedoensis Matsumura*), which is cloned from a single tree. The sakura blooms in profusion at one moment; however, the sakura leaves will fall from the trees right at the same time as the blossoms bloom. As shown by this example, the Japanese are not only fascinated by the beauty of the sakura but are also strongly affected by the ephemerality of the transitory life of the sakura. The *Somei Yoshino* blooms all at once because it is a clone; then the blossoms fall immediately and all at once a few days after. The ephemerality of aesthetical things has taken deep root in the aesthetic consciousness of the Japanese. In Western countries, the word originated historically in *ephemeros*, meaning 'lasting only one day' in Greek; i.e., it refers to 'Things that exist or are used or enjoyed for only a short time' (*Oxford Dictionary of Foreign Words and Phrases*). We cannot, however, read a positive meaning in this word. The Japanese word for ephemerality, *Hakanasa*, includes an especially strongly positive meaning.

Hōjōki (方丈記), written in 1212 by Kamo no Chōmei (鴨長明), provides us a good example in understanding the positive meaning of ephemerality. The opening sentence of this book is the most famous phrase to explain ephemerality. I now present two translations as varying interpretations:

> Incessant is the change of water where the steam glides on calmly: the spray appears over a cataract, yet vanishes without a moment's delay. Such is the fate of men in the world and of the houses in which they live.
>
> (Natsume, 1891)

> The river flows unendingly. Its waters pass and shall never return. Where the water eddies and pools, bubbles from only to vanish the next moment, while others are born in their stead. So it is with man and his dwelling in this world.
>
> (Kobayashi et al., 2018)

Utakata is translated here as 'spray' or 'bubbles.' Both words are good examples to explain the meaning of Japanese ephemerality. The Japanese love bubbles that will only vanish the next moment. Perhaps spray or bubbles have no worth in Western countries; it may be nonsense to experience the beauty in bubbles for them only to vanish the next moment. But the Japanese find ultimate worth in such ephemerality. We may say also that the Japanese learn Silencing in order to feel the ephemerality of things like sakura and bubbles on the water. Additionally, not only the Japanese but all the peoples of East Asian countries have a more or less unconscious aesthetic sense that values impermanence and ephemerality based on Buddhistic thought without one true god.

Shugyō

The practice of reaching for the state of Silencing just presented, finally arriving at the state of Selflessness, or Emptiness, is *Shugyō* (修行). Shugyō is a lifelong learning process based on the thought of the Ancient Brahmanism and Buddhism of absolute Nothingness beyond god (Kashiwagi, 2015). The ultimate purpose of Shugyō is Satori: supreme enlightenment. In Satori, all desires, all kleshas, and all anxieties vanish from the minds of the practitioners. From this they attain Silencing at the same time.

Incidentally, indulging in luxury or addiction should be prohibited and inhibited in any cultural sphere of the world. In Christian nations, *asceticism* (禁欲) is an important ethos, virtue, or norm. Temperance (節制) as self-control is one of the virtues or norms in Western thought too. In *Galatians* (22–23) in the New Testament:

> But the fruit of the Spirit is love, joy, peace, longsuffering, kindness, goodness, faithfulness. Gentleness, self-control. Against such there is no law.

Self-control in Galatians 5–23 is often interpreted using the word 'temperance.' Temperance is a significant purpose of Shugyō as well; note, however, that the semantic context is ultimately different in Western and Eastern thought. Furthermore, even the hedonists in Ancient Greece who accepted their desire strove against excessive luxury and addiction themselves. Indeed, even in the United States of America, the birthplace of pragmatism and consumerism, excessive luxury seems to be viewed as a bad thing contrary to an ethos based on Christian thought.

Although the Japanese and other East Asians also seek such an ethos, they seek not an ascetic life to temper the several desires forbidden in the Bible but rather the ultimate ascetic life to temper unconditionally all desires, including eating, drinking, and sleeping. This temperance far transcends mere self-control. The best example of this ultimate temperance is Shugyō, that is, traditional ascetic training or ascetic practice. More than that, *Shugen-do* (修験道) includes stricter training than Shugyō. Both Shugyō and Shugen-do are methods that evolved in Japan, whereas the idea of Shugyō came fundamentally from ancient India: *sadhana* (or *Sādhanā*).

Historically speaking, almost all of Buddhist theory and practice in Japan was imported from Ancient China, originating in India. From this source the Japanese, especially Buddhists with authority, urged the imposition of Shugyō on the people so that they can learn to vanquish all *Bonno* (EN: Kleshas – earthly desires, blind foul passion; JP: 煩悩; CH: 煩惱) in order to reach the state of Satori (Yuda, 2000).

What, then, is Bonno in actual fact? How do we understand this word; how can we interpret it for Westerners? According to Taitetsu Unno (海野大徹), Bonno means 'deep rooted and ineradicable self-centeredness contained in the unconscious which is one with the body, causing mental, emotional, and physical afflictions, which no amount of self-powered practice can overcome' (Unno, 1996). In short, Bonno is the self-centredness as described. Shugyō aims to overcome Bonno at any time and in any place. Bonno is, for example, the

Three Poisons, *Moha* (癡), *Raga* (貪), and *Dvesha* (瞋), or the Five Hindrances. And Tachikawa wrote, '[T]he essence of Shugyō in Buddhism is to deaden or to reject the *Karma* (業) and Bonno as the profane.' Then he suggests, 'by rejecting the profaned, Satori as the sacred appears' (Tachikawa, 2003: 122); Shugyō aims to deaden the profane and make way for Satori, which belongs to the sacred. Several traces of this practice may be confirmed as still active in today's Japan. The activities toward Selflessness are traces of Shugyō. For the purpose of vanquishing the profane, the Japanese tend to practice the strict training of Shugyō.

The most easily imagined practice in Shugyō would be *Zen* or *Zazen*. Similar to Zen, *Yoga* is famous already in Western countries. Additionally, for example, there are *Suigyo* (水行), *Takigyo* (滝行), *Kito* (祈祷), fasting (断食), the thousand-day chanting walk through the mountains (千日回峰行), *Kagyo* (加行) from Buddhist Tantrism, and the like. As a matter of fact, the contents of Shugyō differ greatly depending on the branch of Buddhism.

In Shugyō, the relationship between master and disciple is of the most profound importance; this relationship is called *Shi-tei*; *Shi* (師) means 'teacher,' and *Tei* (弟) means 'disciple' or 'younger brother.' In Japan, the relationship between teacher and student is always understood in the image of the traditional relationship just presented: the *Shi-tei relationship*. Using Western philosophical concepts, this relationship is based on 'no explanation' and 'mimicry.' In this relationship, there are no word, no dialogue, and no discussion. The teacher need not explain; he only sets the best example for his students. By setting a good example, the students can experiment to discover what it is. Then, through continuous trial and error, again and again they strive until they can recreate what their teacher set before them. Shizuka Sasaki calls such an education 'back shot education' (後ろ姿の教育) (Sasaki, 2012: 38). Additionally, all traditions are brought to fruition in Silencing through living together beyond word and dialogue (see Chapter 3).

Basically, the learning of children in school is also strongly influenced by aspects of this model, such as the Shi-tei relationship and the strict training in Shugyō. Here is why I attempt to explain Manabi from the point of view of Silencing.

Based on the perspective of Western countries, namely that of globalisation, MEXT (Ministry of Education, Culture, Sports, Science, and Technology) insists nowadays on the importance of '*proactive, interactive, and deep learning*,' so-called *active learning*. However, in fact, such proactive learning or interactive learning is not fully expected by teachers and students or even by parents, except for some progressive educational researchers, due to the Japanese reason that learning is closely related with Shugyō, namely with long strict training in Silencing, as a result of which the Japanese have no idea that they can enjoy learning in school. Therefore, learning works not so actively, although we can see signs of active learning in recent years. In any case, the majority of Japanese still find the deep meaning of learning in Shugyō, for example, in suffering, in asceticism, in patience, and in dilemmas.

In the same way, the Japanese display a feeling of disgust against expressing their own emotions because they greatly value the selfless attitude of seeking Nothingness. Therefore, *Expressionlessness* and *Emotionlessness* are the most honoured compliments for the Japanese. These compliments seem to be the result of sympathy for the practitioners of Shugyō. The tendency to value expressionlessness and emotionlessness would be shown not only in Japan but throughout East Asia; we hold that expressionlessness belongs to a specific kind of being (*Seinsart*) of East Asian people.

Seken: the selfless self and Japanese micro-society

The selfless self in Japanese thought consists essentially in the relationship with the world (social world), namely *Seken* (JP: 世間; CN: 人世). The selfless self exists not solely by itself. Similarly, the selfless self consists not just in the relationship with others because there is fundamentally no concept of 'others' in Japan. In the same way, the selfless self subsists not in dialogue with others because they have no conception of dialogue in their tradition. As previously presented, there is no basis for Western dialogue anywhere in East Asia, including Japan. *The opposite of the selfless self is not others but Seken.* Seken means simply the sum of selfless persons; Seken is explained conceptually with the word *Minna* in Chapter 4 of this volume. If described more formally, *there is a fundamental relationship between the selfless self and Seken* in Japan, whereas there is a fundamental relationship between *I and Thou* (*Ich und Du*) in Western thought (Abe, 1989). The principle of this relationship is the basis of Manabi, which is different from learning in Western countries.

In Western anthropology, the concept of 'experience' and 'understanding' has always been valued if we want to know and discuss other minds, namely the alter ego. Above all, understanding (*Verstehen*) is recognised worldwide as a main anthropological approach, including a different dimension from explanation in the context of descriptive psychology. In this approach, the following question appears: How should we understand the other as a person who exists in a different form from ourselves (myself)? '*Intersubjektivität*' of Husserl (1973) and the *Du* in *Ich und Du* by Buber (1923) are widely known as the main Western concepts of one's relations to others. Because Western philosophy values the traditional problem of other minds, Japanese philosophers or East Asian philosophers have also desired to reason out the same problem in the same way in East Asian countries.

However, the problem of other minds, or simply the 'other,' is an everyday concern in Japan as well as in East Asia, even if this problem serves as the theme of modern academic argumentation because, as just presented, the Japanese, or East Asian peoples more generally, value Nothingness, Selflessness, Harmony, Emptiness, or Silencing as having the highest ethical worth. In Japan, flowers are beautiful because the Japanese find Nothingness, Selflessness, or Emptiness in flowers themselves. They even find those elements in the others. For example, if you live somewhere in Japan, then you are a foreigner, a *Gaijin* (外人). The Japanese, especially Japanese children, will shout, 'There is a Gaijin!' They are interested in foreign people on the surface level, but for them it is not a matter of your *otherness* (*Andersheit*) or *foreignness* (*Fremdheit*). Therefore, they will not attempt to understand who you are. It would not be an issue for them to understand others. Even though the otherness and foreignness of others are an academic concern of Western countries, the Japanese or East Asians do not take into account who you are, namely your otherness. You need only be a selfless self in Silencing, then you can live well in East Asian countries.

Instead of the other, the Japanese strongly value Seken, i.e., the World. They ask, 'What is Seken?' This question has endured for a long time in Japan (Sato, 2001). Just as Western people ask what the other is, the Japanese ask what Seken is. The question about Seken exists prior to the question about the others in Japan.

Though Western people attend to the eyes of others, the Japanese worry not about the eyes of the others but rather about the 'eyes of Seken' (世間の目), the so-called neighbourhood eyes. Their concern is not the eyes of the other but the eyes of Seken, namely the eyes of the Japanese social world based on the sum of selfless persons. The concept of Seken is not an abstract academic word but one of the common words in everyday life (Abe, 2014).

The most important task for the Japanese is to correctly understand what Seken thinks and how it expects. For example, (1) Japanese tend to have very high expectations that you won't bother them; this expectation does not mean bothering a certain individual but bothering the sum of persons (or children, students, etc.). It is said in Japanese, '*Hito ni Meiwaku wo Kakenai*' (人に迷惑をかけない). Also, (2) they absolutely value reading the mind of Seken, getting the message of Seken, empathising with Seken, assuming the atmosphere of Seken. It is said in Japanese, '*Hito no Kimoti wo Sassuru*' (人の気持ちを察する). In both examples, the word *Hito* (人) is used. *Hito* means 'people,' 'person,' 'man,' 'individuals,' or ' human being.' Thus, Seken refers to human beings.

In the real situation of having a talk with someone, Japanese pay special attention to the individual in order not to cause him discomfort. As a result, they become people of few words: Self-Silencing. They do not enjoy conversing freely. When conversing with someone in Japan, it is more important for Japanese not to bother each other (i.e., Seken) than it is to talk freely or to enjoy conversing. Therefore, as a result, they are intolerant of those who do not read the mind of Seken and who bother them. They are necessarily intolerant of everyone who causes inconvenience because they always want to avoid inconveniencing others. However, now it is not a matter of others in the Western context but of Seken; This Seken consists of the will of individuals. Abe suggests that Seken is seen as a datum, i.e., *given* (Abe, 2004).

In Japan, where it is expected that no one will bother anyone, those who create a scandal face public outrage because of the act of treachery to Seken, not to individuals. There is the custom of *Shazai-Kaiken* (謝罪会見) in today's Japan, meaning 'a press conference to apologise to the public.' When a famous actor or actress, politician, or sports player causes a scandal, then he or she absolutely must hold this type of press conference for the public. Otherwise, those who caused the scandal will suffer consequences to such an extent that they can no longer retain their position in the world. Those causing scandal must absolutely apologise immediately. But to whom do they actually apologise? The answer is very simple; *nobody*. Seken, which is the sum of each person, is fundamentally nobody.

It may be possible to interpret Seken as similar to '*the they*' (*Das Man*) which Heidegger analysed in his *Sein und Zeit*, namely 'the who is not this one and not that one, not oneself and not some and not the sum of them all' (Heidegger, 1993: 126). He stated, 'The "who" is the neuter, *the they*.' In fact, many Japanese philosophers have attempted to explain Seken from this statement. So who is *Das Man*, 'the they'?

Heidegger provides the following interpretation:

> We enjoy ourselves and have fun the way *they* enjoy themselves. We read see, and judge literature and art the way *they* see and judge. But we also withdraw from the 'great mass' the way *they* withdraw, we find 'shocking' what *they* find shocking. *The they, which is nothing definite and which all are, though not as a sum, prescribes the kind of being of everydayness.*
>
> (Heidegger, 1996: 127, emphasis in original)

What Japanese value is not individuals but just '*nobody like everybody*.' Thus, Seken seems to be like 'the they,' although Heidegger's concept has a negative connotation which is a mode of inauthenticity.

> The they has its own ways to be. The tendency of being-with which we called distantiality is based on the fact that being-with-one-another as such creates *averageness*.
>
> (Heidegger, 1996: 127)

Seken also has its own ways of being: The 'average *nous*.' However, the *nous* of Seken would not to be caused by averageness, as Heidegger suggests. In contrast to averageness, it can be said that Seken is made by *Kuuki* (空気), not by a concrete someone. Kuuki means 'air' or 'atmosphere.' This Kuuki wears several hats. We can physically feel this Kuuki directly because Kuuki is air itself. Therefore, the Japanese really feel Seken through Kuuki. In Japanese, there are aphorisms like 'The wind of Seken is cold (i.e., cruel)' or 'The wind of Seken blows hard badly.' These aphorisms do not mean that individuals are cold/cruel but rather that they feel the coldness of unspecified human beings – an unnamed human circle – with respect to themselves. Moreover, Seken in Japanese is not a fixed-average *nous*; it fluctuates greatly depending on the place or generation (period). Additionally, it is always changing fluidly at all times. Therefore, it would be also possible for one-time *nous* (old common sense) to be upset all at once overnight. Also, there is a famous cliché in Japanese: '*Wataru Seken ni Oni wa nashi*' (渡る世間に鬼はなし), literally, 'In the living world, there is not only the ogre' (鬼, Oni), namely, 'There is kindness to be found everywhere.'

In any case, Japanese regulate their own behaviour patterns based not on principles or doctrines but on each varied situation or the liquid *nous* of Seken (Holloway, 2000). Nevertheless, this *nous* itself is fickle like the wind and thus cannot be controlled by particular people. Therefore, Japanese behaviour and expressions are always characterised by ambiguity (fuzziness).

At the basis of the Japanese Haiku, as a teaching of Basho, there is the thought of *Fueki Ryuukou* (不易流行), which means 'Immutability and Fluidity' or 'Permanence and Change' (Renato de Guzman, 2010); 'If you don't learn immutability, then you can't know the basis of Haiku. And if you don't learn fluidity, then you can't bring a new movement.' We can interpret this in two ways: First, we find immutability in the fluidity, and second, we find fluidity in the immutability. At any rate, Fueki-Ryuukou teaches us how we should learn; although we learn truth within our tradition, we must find our new style through fluidity (Imoto, 1968). As a matter of fact, Seken is closely related to fluidity. But the blowing wind winnows everything into Nothingness. According to this thought, everything is fluid and liquid like a river to Nothingness.

Seken will become an important research question because Seken typically appears in the classroom. In each classroom, each Seken constructs itself naturally, whereas the classroom consists of all classmates. The Seken in each classroom seems to be constructed not by each classmate, still less by the teachers. For the students, the Seken as Minna, the air of the classroom, is more important than the existence of teachers because they value a selfless harmony (和, 調和) as the greatest worth. This perspective will be explained more deeply in Chapter 4 through the concept of Minna.

Not only students but also teachers value selfless harmony as Seken in the classroom. Therefore, the understanding of others is almost out of the question except for the interests of several academics because the interest of teachers and students is concentrated only on Seken in the classroom. In the everyday life of students, the question, 'How do we understand Seken?' is more important than the philosophical question of, 'How should we understand others?' Described more formally, only those who learned philosophy mainly in Western countries will ask, 'Who are the others?'; for almost all Japanese who do not seek the understanding of the other, only the understanding of Seken is aimed at and valued or plays a crucial role in Japanese society (Abe, 2004). The ambiguous relationship between 'Selfless self and Seken' is focused on anytime and anywhere in Japan, although the dialogic relationship between 'I and thou' is based on Western thought. Additionally, this ambiguous relationship should be observable in Western countries, too.

In Japan, possibly also throughout East Asia, it is highly valued to care about and think how someone (or Seken) feels, to read or enter into someone's feelings. At the same time, Japanese and perhaps other East Asians do not care about you, that is, they care not about each individual person but rather about the nameless faceless Seken. Thus, they care for Seken; they think and read about how Seken feels; they enter into Seken's feeling.

In conclusion, as previously noted, the selfless self of Japanese consists essentially in the close relationship with the Seken which is the sum of selfless persons. However, this ambiguous relationship between the selfless self and Seken is not a destination but a starting point from which we aim to reach the world of Nothingness. Therefore, it will be the first step for us to leave this selfless relationship and to be *absolutely alone without bonds* (ひとり). Also, we can say that it is the departure point of the long Shugyō way toward Nothingness and Selflessness to leave this world that consists of the selfless self and Seken.

The alternative dimension of learning toward Nothingness and Selflessness

Based on the preceding discussion, I conclude that Japanese learning, Manabi, consists of (1) learning the world of Seken and leaving it, (2) imposing gruelling Shugyō on themselves, (3) learning to sit quietly in Silencing or to chant words, (4) aiming at the condition of Selflessness, and finally (5) reaching the ultimate state of Nothingness. Manabi will be actualised through all this. This is the fundamental mechanism of Manabi whereby the Japanese learn that *they are nothing*.

In Manabi, there is no 'dialogue,' 'others,' 'comprehension,' or 'discussion' in the context of traditional Western thought. In the process of Manabi, we seek for Silencing instead of dialogue, for Seken instead of the others, for taking care of one another instead of comprehension, and Nothingness instead of being. Therefore, you can understand that Manabi has a completely different principle from the learning of Western modern education. However, this suggestion need not imply a confrontation between East and West, but it does constitute a *Higan* (彼岸), the far shore of the so-called Sanzu River, like the River Styx, that separates the living world (この世) from the afterlife (あの世): The difference between the West and East Asia does not reflect a confrontation in same dimension but rather reflects different directions in different dimensions (Sato, 2018).

In that sense, we should evaluate the analogy of a 'two-level house' described by Löwith as correct. Superficially, Western thought and methods have been introduced in Japanese schooling, indeed probably in all schooling in East Asia, but the stronger educational power is still exercised as a hidden curriculum within the curriculum. Accordingly, *East Asian education orients itself towards an education directed towards Nothingness and Selflessness*. If we use the analogy of Löwith again, we live in a two-level house. He asked, 'Where are the steps to pass from one level to the other?' We can now answer his question: 'There are no such steps in this house.' Nevertheless, we can live in this two-level house without steps because the differences between the West and East Asia lie along different directions in different dimensions. Thus, both thoughts can coexist in one house.

Recently, the Westerner, who has always lived in a one-level house, seems to want to add a second level to his one-level house: Many Euro-American Buddhists, or so-called '*night-stand Buddhists*,' 'might place a how-to book on Buddhist meditation on the nightstand' (Tweed, 1998: 74–75). They also seem to wish to live as if on two levels: a lower, more fundamental one on which they feel and think in a Western way, and a higher one on which East Asian thought is lined up from Confucius to Banana Yoshimoto. Additionally, they eat hamburgers, spaghetti, cheese fondue, and fish and chips on one level, then eat sushi, ramen, mapo doufu, kimchi, pho, and Peking duck on the other level (Kashiwagi, 2015). In the same way, they dialogue about the meaning of being with others on one level, then practice Zen, Yoga, meditation, and mindfulness on the other level. Additionally, they don't need to add steps to their new two-level house. *Both levels can coexist without steps because they have an absolute difference in different dimensions.*

Conclusion

It would probably be unacceptable for Japanese progressive educational researchers to discuss East Asian education based on Nothingness and Selflessness. For them, the discussion in this chapter would have a negative meaning only because the old traditional words like Nothingness or Selflessness are reminiscent of past militaristic education. Additionally, these concepts are not suited to the idea of democratic education in post–World War II Japan. However, the old traditional learning of Japan is highly valued by recent conservative educational researchers, whereas this old learning would be rejected strongly by many progressive educational researchers.

Nevertheless, *not all of the elements of Japanese Manabi described in this chapter can be explained by the concept of 'control.'* Indeed, '*liberation from the self,*' as well as '*rebirth to a selfless new self,*' is included in these elements. On this point, it may overlap '*Liberating Education*' in Western pedagogy. At the least, learning towards Nothingness and Selflessness would contribute a great deal to our liberation from the deep desires inside each of us and from biased views, and perhaps those who would really know the value of this liberation are Westerners.

In the end, I would like to distil the fundamental essence of Manabi. Manabi requests that learners abstain from self-assertiveness, maintain silence in public spaces to avoid conflict, take a hint from the group, and live selflessly. By synthesising all these requests, Manabi will finally help learners to experience both the Nothingness and Selflessness that have been the main concepts of East Asian Buddhism. Accordingly, those who have learned Manabi would subjectively live a passive life for the sake of good learning. In Manabi, this *active* passivity will be the fundamental basis for learning anything.

The next chapter will mainly discuss the issue of body and soul in Manabi, and the relationship between master and pupil will be clarified in the historical context of Japan, whence the deeper dimension of Manabi will be uncovered.

Bibliography

Abe, K. (2004) *Nihonjin no Rekishi Ishiki*, Tokyo: Iwanami Shoten.
Abe, K. (2014) *Kinndaika to Sekenn*, Tokyo: Asahibunnko.
Abe, M. (1989) *Zen and Western Thought*, Honolulu: University of Hawaii Press.
Buber, M. (1923) *Ich und Du*, Leipzig: Insel verlag.
Busemeyer, M. R. (2015) *Bildungspolitik im internationalen Vergleich*, Konstanz: UTB GmbH.
Carter, R. E. (1997) *The Nothingness Beyond God: An Introduction to the Philosophy of Nishida Kitaro*, Minnesota: Paragon House.
Chomei, K. (1891) *Natsume Soseki's English Translation of Hojoki*, Seattle: Amazon Services International, Inc.
Corbin, A. (2018) *A History of Silence: From the Renaissance to the Present Day*, Cambridge: Polity Press.
Ende, M. (2005) *Momo*, translated by Kaori Oshima, Tokyo: Iwanami Shoten.
Epicurus (1959) *Epicurus*, Tokyo: Iwanami Shoten.
Epicurus (1980) *Briefe Sprüche Werkfragmente*, Stuttgart: Reclam.
Fromm, E. (1976) *Haben oder Sein*, München: dtv Deutscher Taschenbuch.
Fromm, E. (1989) *Vom Haben zum Sein*, München: Wilhelm Heyne Verlag.
Fukuzawa, Y. (2012) *An Encouragement of Learning*, Tokyo: Keio University Press.
Hanaoka, E. (2002) *Zettai Mu no Tetsugaku-Nishida Tetsugaku Nyuumon*, Kyoto: Sekai Shisou Sha.
Heidegger, M. (1993) *Sein und Zeit*, Tübingen: Max Niemeyer Verlag.
Heidegger, M. (1996) *Being and Time-A Translation of Sein und Zeit*, translated by Stambaugh, J., New York: State University of New York Press.
Holloway, S. D. (2000) *Contested Childhood: Diversity and Change in Japanese Preschools*, New York: Routledge.
Husserl, E. (1973) *Zur Phänomenologie der Intersubjektivität*, Heidelberg: Springer.
Imai, Y. (2015) *Bi, Media, Kyouiku*, Tokyo: University of Tokyo Press.
Imoto, N. (1968) *Basho-his Life and art-*, Tokyo: Kodansha.
Japan Bible Society (1988) *The New Testament*, Tokyo: Japan Bible Society.
The Japan Times (2018) "Majority of Japanese University Students Don't Read Books for Pleasure, Poll Shows," *The Japan Times*. Retrieved from www.japantimes.co.jp/news/2018/02/28/national/majority-japanese-university-students-dont-read-books-pleasure-poll-shows/#.W_wItzj7TIV.
Kaibara, E. (1961) *Yojokun*. Tokyo: Iwanami Shoten.
Kashiwagi, Y. (2015) *Manabi no Jissengaku*, Tokyo: Ikkei Shobou.
Kato, T. (1940) *Zen ni Ikiru Michi*, Tokyo: Daito Shuppansha.
Kitahara, Y. (ed.) (1987) *Zenyaku Kogo Reikai Jiten*, Tokyo: Shougaku Kan.
Kobayashi, M. et al. (2018) *HOJOKI – The Account of My Hut*, Tokyo: Babel Press.
Lao Tzu (2001) *Lao Tzu-the Way and Its Virtue*, Tokyo: Keio University Press.
Lao Tzu (2008) *Lao Tzu*, translated by Hachiya, K., Tokyo: Iwanami Shoten.
Löwith, K. (1995) *Martin Heidegger and European Nihilism*, New York: Columbia University Press.

Matsuo, B. (1979) *Oku no Hosomichi*, Tokyo: Iwanami Shoten.
Mayeroff, M. (1972/1990) *On Caring*, New York: HarperPerennial.
Miyamoto, M. (2012) *The Book of Five Rings*, Boston: Shambhala.
Mohsin, S. M. (2017) *Nothingness-Thus Creation Happened*, Seattle: Amazon Services International.
Nakamura, G. (1963) *Jiga to Muga*, Kyoto: Heirakuji shoten.
Nietzsche, F. (2003) *The Genealogy of Morals*, New York: Dover Publication, Inc.
Nishida, K. (1990) *An Inquiry Into the Good*, New Haven and London: Yale University Press.
Nishihira, T. (2009) *Zeami no Keikotetsugaku*, Tokyo: University of Tokyo Press.
Nitobe, I. (1905) *Bushido*, New York: G. P. Putman's Sons.
Nitobe, I. (1907) *Kyouiku no Mokuteki*, IN, Zusouroku, Seattle: Amazon Services International.
OECD (2015) "PISA 2015 Results in Focus," Retrieved from www.oecd.org/pisa/pisa-2015-results-in-focus.pdf.
Okakura, K. (1997) *The Book of Tea*, Seattle: Amazon Services International.
Renato de Guzman, R. (2010) *World Literature: Asian, African, Islamic and South America*, Manila: Katha Publishing Co., Inc.
Sartre, J. P. (1943/2003) *Being and Nothingness*, London: Routledge.
Sasaki, S. (2012) *Buddha -Shinri no Kotoba*, Tokyo: NHK Shuppan.
Sato, H. (2018) *"Shinkoku" Nihon*, Tokyo: Kodansha.
Sato, N. (2001) *SEKENN no Gennsyougaku*, Tokyo: Seikyusha.
Strobach, S. (2002) *Scheidungskindern Helfen*, Weinheim: Beltz Verlag.
Suzuki, D. T. (1938/2005) *Zen and Japanese Culture*, translated by Momo'o Kikugawa, Tokyo: Kodansha.
Suzuki, D. T. (1972) *Japanese Spirituality*, Tokyo: Japan Society of the Promotion of Science.
Tachikawa, M. (2003) *Kuu no Shisoushi*, Tokyo: Kodansha.
Tagami, T. (2000) *Buddha no Iitakatta koto*, Tokyo: Kodansha.
Takahashi, M. (2007) *Keiken No Metamorphosis*, Tokyo: Keisou Shobou.
Tweed, T. A. (1998) "Night-Stand Buddhists and Other Creatures: Sympathizers, Adherents, and the Study of Religion," Williams, D. R., & Queen, C. S. eds. *American Buddhism: Methods and Findings in Recent Scholarship*, London: Routledge.
Unknown Author (1996) *Tannisho*, translated by Taitetsu Unno, Honolulu: Buddhist Study Center Press.
Wakimoto, H. (1997) *Shukyogaku Nyumon*, Tokyo: Kodansha.
Yuda, Y. (2000) *Upanishad-Honyaku oyobi Kaisetsu*, Tokyo: Daito Publishing Co., Inc.

Chapter 3

Body and mind in Manabi
Focusing on Kata and Shūyō

Tomoya Saito

Introduction

This chapter discusses traditional methods of Manabi in Japan, paying particular attention to the relationship between body and mind.

The Eastern tradition and the Western tradition differ in their ideas about the relationship between body and mind. Generally, this relationship has been explained in the traditional Western view since Descartes as mind–body dualism (心身二元論), but in the traditional Eastern view, it is explained as mind–body monism (心身一元論). However, Japan's acceptance of Western study and culture in the process of its modernisation has resulted in the spread of mind–body dualism among Japanese. Moreover, once the mental disease that the author Sōseki Natsume (夏目漱石) described as the 'modern disease' (nervous breakdown due to instability of identity) spread mainly among the youth from the end of the nineteenth century to the early twentieth century, folk remedies based on mind–body monism and physical exercise became more popular, leading to an increase in the number of people who used these remedies to restore balance between their minds and bodies.

Thus, a mixture of mind–body dualism and mind–body monism continues to date. This situation arose from the termination of body and mind balance through the acceptance of modern Western knowledge. It is paradoxical, but we can reconsider the mind-body relationship by looking at the state of knowledge.

Until the end of the Edo period (1603–1867), mind and body were regarded as one in Japan. The basis of this was the aspect of 'discipline' (しつけ, *Shitsuke*) in education (Tsujimoto, 2012). It is not clear when discipline originated, but at least in popular education until the close of the Edo period, children learned various actions and techniques necessary for life firstly by *observing* what their parents and other adults were doing and secondly by actually carrying out these actions and techniques independently. In other words, they did not acquire knowledge from parents and other adults per se, and only when they made mistakes would they be cautioned by their parents and other adults, allowing them to repeatedly correct their actions. Thus, using one's body and learning by actually performing the observed actions was the ordinary way of learning in Japan. The way the character for 'discipline' (躾) is written implies 'make the body (身) beautiful (美).' Manabi ensures that the body is being used suitably because the very usage of the body contains the knowledge necessary for living. This stems from the contemporary thinking known as *Yōjō* (養生).

On the other hand, the focus often turns to the effects of Zen and bushido when discussing Japanese education. Let us briefly summarize the reasons why these are thought to have had an impact.

Education in reading, writing, and arithmetic (the 3 Rs), which support the high literacy rate among Japanese, began in civilian educational institutions called *Terakoya* (寺子屋) in the Muromachi period (1338–1573). Terakoya were primarily located in Buddhist temples, demonstrating the effect of Buddhism, primarily Zen Buddhism, on education.

Similarly, *Bushido* (武士道) inspires the image of a spirit that is quintessentially Japanese and therefore must have affected education for many years. However, bushido did not have a serious effect on education until the late 1890s. There are two reasons for this disconnect between the image and the reality. The first reason is the proportion of the warrior class to the total population at the time. The Edo period divided society into four classes under the *Shinōkōshō* (士農工商) system. *Shi* (士, 'warrior') was the ruling class, and *nō* (農, 'farmer'), *kō* (工, 'artisan'), and *shō* (商, merchant) were the ruled classes. The entire population when the Edo shogunate fell was about 30 million people, but only about 3.5% of these were in the warrior class. Given this population ratio and the relationship between the rulers and ruled, it is somewhat difficult to conceive of the members of the farmer, artisan, and merchant classes, which account for almost the entire population, adopting bushido as their own mentality.

The second reason is the time during which the term 'bushido' came into general use. The use of 'bushido' in writing began from the second half of the sixteenth century, albeit sparingly, and its use exploded from the end of the nineteenth century (Saeki, 2004). Considering this information, we must conclude that the trigger for the popularisation of 'bushido' was the publication of Inazō Nitobe's (新渡戸稲造) world-famous *Bushido: The Soul of Japan* (1899).

This conclusion shows that at the centre of traditional Manabi in Japan was mind–body monism in the sense of 'changes in the body changing the state of the mind.' Keeping this conclusion in mind will assist the reader in understanding the characteristic method of Manabi in Japan, involving *Kata* (型), *Keiko* (稽古), *Shugyō* (修行), and *Shūyō* (修養).

Kata in Manabi

The traditional approach of Manabi in Japan is Kata. Until the late twentieth century, Japanese people referred to learning outside of school as Keiko, which frequently entailed calligraphy, abacus, piano, kendo, and the like. However, the choices have increased in the twenty-first century, adding options such as swimming and soccer, so Keiko are now called lessons (習い事).

The use of the word *Keiko* rather than 'learning' to express the acquisition of knowledge outside of school is quite interesting in light of Manabi. This is because Manabi, in addition to being school-based learning, is centred on the acquisition of skills and involves the learning of 'Kata' in Keiko. This, then, is what was considered to be Manabi.

In the first place, Kata was a central concept in Manabi tea ceremony, traditional performing arts (such as noh and kabuki), and martial arts (kendo, judo, and kyudo, among others) in Japan. However, Kata is an extremely complex concept, which makes translating it into English difficult. Possible candidates for a translation include 'pattern,' 'archetype,' 'type,' 'form,' and 'style.' Of these, 'style' is closest to the Japanese *Kata* (型).

Saito (2003: 115) defines style as a 'coherent deformation of mode.' This definition by Saito originates from the ideas of Maurice Merleau-Ponty. Let us look at Merleau-Ponty's (1973: 61) definition of 'style' for reference.

> For each painter, style is the system of equivalences he builds for himself for this work of manifestation. It is the general and concrete index of the "coherent deformation" through which he focuses the signification still scattered in his perception and gives it an express existence.

According to Merleau-Ponty, style appears as a 'coherent deformation' to 'give it an express existence' to 'signification still scattered' because 'signification occurs where we subject the given elements of the world to a "coherent deformation".' However, Saito's definition is not identical to Merleau-Ponty's. This hints at the concept of Kata. Saito's style concept adds what is meant by 'mode' (様式) to Merleau-Ponty's style concept. Saito tries to capture the essence of variability by treating the consistency of the way of deformation as 'mode.'

This rearrangement by Saito is based on his own experience of karate (空手). Karate, which Saito practised and which is generally popular, involves competing to perform the best Kata rather than directly striking an opponent. For this reason, Saito's ideas can be regarded as an explanation of Kata in the physical sense. The author, who has also practised *kendo* (剣道) for 35 years from a young age and who currently holds sixth Dan (qualification of kendo) and the title of *renshi* (錬士, instructor), finds Saito's concept of style convincing. To summarise, Kata can appropriately be considered to include the meanings of style and mode.

In that case, let us consider Manabi in Kata. Minamoto (1989: 68) explains Kata:

> The Kata of physical acts include Kata narrowly defined as the forms that physical movements depict in space. In other words, the basic forms of Kata, in addition to Kata that one internalizes over time through 'Keiko'. The latter Kata of internalization is the '"Kata" of self-discipline' within a

single culture and the Kata of the process of maturation as a person, and in this context, is it not a question of 'Kata of culture'?

Minamoto shows that the process of Keiko and internalizing Kata leads to an expectation of 'maturation as a person.' This shows that the Manabi of Kata has something in common with Bildung and also explains the philosophy of Manabi in Japan.

In that case, how is Kata internalized? Next, the process of internalizing Kata is explained using the concept of *Shuhari* (守破離). Shuhari was presented by Fuhaku Kawakami (2019: 138), an eighteenth-century tea master who wrote:

> *Shu* (守) means to 'obey,' *Ha* (破) means to 'break,' and *Ri* (離) means to 'leave.' To disciples, teach only *Shu*. Once the disciples can master *Shu*, they will naturally break away from it of their own accord. This is an advanced stage, where obeying is one wheel, and breaking is the other wheel. Detaching from these two is to become a master: connecting these two and detaching from them while still obeying them.

This meaning is expressed by the single word *Shuhari*. Following this, once Zeami's (世阿弥) 風姿花伝 (*Fūshikaden*, a treatise and manual on noh) was released to the public and read at the start of the twentieth century, *Shuhari* was frequently used when explaining the training process for martial and performing arts. Next, Shuhari is broken down into its three constituent parts – Shu, Ha, and Ri – and each of them is explained.

The first stage is Shu. At this stage, learning a martial or performing art begins with faithfully *imitating* the Kata. Disciples faithfully imitate every one of the fixed ways of behaving and moving their bodies and repeat them over and over again for their bodies to internalize them until they can do them without thinking. At this stage, disciples cannot accurately understand the meaning of the Kata – or rather, they can hardly understand them. They also have not developed a sense of unity between body and mind at the Shu stage.

The next stage is Ha. Once disciples have become somewhat familiar with Shu, they begin to develop a sense of unity between body and mind. At this stage, they can at least perform Kata formally and without hesitation. They have also experienced many challenges, and by conquering them, they have learned how to converse with their own bodies. Then they attempt to reconstitute Kata in their own styles, according to the characteristics and habits of the way they move their own bodies. When disciples reach this stage, others observing them can perceive the disciples' *particular traits* in the performance. This is the Ha stage.

The last stage is Ri. When disciples ultimately master this process, they gain a deep understanding of the meaning of the Kata and establish their own unique style that no one else can imitate. It is paradoxical, but the lack of freedom in Kata produces freedom. This may be easier to understand if we think of a batter in baseball, for example. Each batter has his or her own batting style, but if we break the style down into a series of actions, they all use their bodies in the same way at each point, beginning from the way they use their hands at the moment when the bat hits the ball. This is not limited to baseball: Whether in soccer or golf, once players reach the professional level, everyone performs the same basic actions, even if they appear different. This is the Ri stage. When the three stages are thus explained separately, they are easier to understand.

However, ultimately reaching the Ri stage does not necessarily mean that the Kata disappears because arriving at the Ri stage allows disciples to understand the meaning and importance of Kata. Although they are leaving Kata, they return to Kata. Reaching the Ri stage allows students to become aware of the 'coherent deformation of mode.' Herein lies the difficulty in understanding Kata.

The difficulty in understanding Kata comes from its relationship with form (形). Nishihira (2009: 108–109) focused on the ambiguity of Kata and summarised the relationship between Kata and form:

> Kata is distinct from form. Form is concrete. However, Kata is not a form. The perfected form is not Kata. Kata and form exist in different phases. Kata is extracted from the accumulation of forms with a wide variety of appearances, as a principle that precedes them. We could also say that we intuitively see one Kata behind a range of forms. However, in reality, Kata manifests only as forms. Kata does not directly manifest in the same capacity as forms. Thus, a cycle is born. Kata is drawn out of forms, and forms arise from Kata. In the former, Kata is extracted from various concrete

This is the translation of the Japanese text in Figure 3.1: *Left pair of arrows:* Concrete form

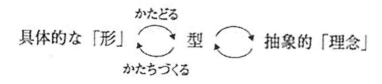

Above the arrows: Model
Below the arrows: Shape
Between the arrows: Kata
Right pair of arrows: Abstract concept

Figure 3.1 The relationship between Kata and form
Source: Nishihira, 2009

forms (かたどる, *katadoru*, 'imitate, model'). In the latter, a variety of forms are created from Kata (かたちづくる, *katachizukuru*, 'form, shape'). However, in this debate, it is important to note that forms are concrete and individual whereas Kata has a higher level of abstraction.

Nishihira explains that Kata is a *principle* that precedes the accumulation of variously manifested forms. However, Nishihira says that 'Kata' is not an abstract concept but is 'immanent in the movements of the body' and 'exists as occurrences that are achieved as a necessity.' He ultimately concludes that '*Kata* [is] an intermediate item between the two [concrete forms and abstract concepts], and a means of going between the two.'

Summarising what has been just discussed, the act of going back and forth between the concrete and the abstract via the medium of Kata is called Keiko, and the entire process is called Manabi.

What is Shugyō?

In Japan, when someone seeks to thoroughly acquire some sort of skill, people use the word *Shugyō* (修行). Even today, terms like *Hanayome Shugyō* (花嫁修行, 'domestic training,' or 'bride training') and *Musha Shugyō* (武者修行, 'knight errantry,' or 'warrior training') are used. In this way, the word *Shugyō* is at the root of the image that modern Japanese people have of Manabi.

However, *Shugyō* is a word that came into use in *Shugendō* (修験道), an old religion that has been practiced in Japan since ancient times. Shugendō was systematised in the Heian period (794–1192), as a form of belief combining Shinto and esoteric Buddhism and adding Taoist and other philosophies (Suzuki, 2015). *Yamabushi* (山伏), people who perform Shugyō in Shugendō, went into the mountains for long periods, refrained from contact with people, and conducted activities individually or in Yamabushi groups. These activities included, for example, walking the ridge line of mountains or peaks to travel around Shugyō locations and learning to manipulate fire. In this way, Yamabushi used their whole bodies and holistically acquired spiritual power. In Shugendō, this activity is called Shugyō.

That may be the origin, but considering the modern age, would it not be comical for a bride preparing to marry to hide away in the mountains and practice housekeeping duties all alone? Of course, modern Japanese people do not perform Shugyō as in Shugendō in everyday life. In that case, why do Japanese people still use the word *Shugyō* today?

The first reason is that Shugyō is thought to contribute to Bildung (Kadowaki, 1978). The second reason is related to loneliness (孤独, *Kodoku*), which is a characteristic of Shugyō because the traditional Japanese view of Manabi includes loneliness, and Manabi is perceived as something that one does solitarily. Japanese people subconsciously share the perception that working on Shugyō in loneliness allows the practitioner to reach a state of Nothingness (忘我, *Bōga*; 無, *Mu*). Nothingness in Manabi is analysed in detail in Chapters 1 and 2.

Originally in Shugendō, Shugyō would sometimes be performed in groups, but perhaps due to the suffering that the word suggests, Shugyō is generally considered to be an individual activity. Further, behind the use of the term *Musha Shugyō* (武者修行, 'knight errantry') lies the effect of Bushido as previously discussed. This is because '武者' (*Musha*, warrior) means '武士' (*Bushi*, 'samurai'), and samurai are considered to distinguish themselves from others. Naturally, distinguishing oneself has something fundamental in common with loneliness. Whether it is performed in a group or solitarily, Shugyō has an unbreakable bond with loneliness.

This understanding of Shugyō is thought to have been transmitted to the fact that career or social success through effort to help oneself (刻苦勉励, *Kokku Benrei*, 'diligent self-application') has been accorded significance in Bildung in modern times. In Japan, during the Meiji period, it became possible to select a job and to escape one's class by gaining admission to a good university, unlike during the Edo period, and this has enabled people to gain social prestige as well as to earn higher incomes. For this reason, competition to join the best universities (受験戦争, *juken sensō*) became fierce and remains so to date.

Success is closely related to Bildung in the history of education in modern Japan, and this has been described through the concept of Shūyō, not Shugyō. However, closely resembling Shūyō is the concept of Yōjō, so let us discuss the concept of Yōjō.

What is Yōjō?

Neo-Confucianism uses the term *Yōjō*, which is similar to *Shūyō*. Until the middle of the nineteenth century, Yōjō was broadly known by the public and used every day. Ekiken Kaibara's (貝原益軒) *Yōjō-kun* (養生訓, 1731) is the most famous work related to Yōjō. The book is written from the point of view of the *Ki* (気) phenomenon and *Ri* (理) (a position in harmony with Neo-Confucian's logical nature), and it is still read and passed down now as an exemplar for developing individual health. The reason for its ongoing popularity is understandable, given also that Saigusa (1958) curtly describes Yōjō as 'building one's body and thereby building one's humanity.'

Takizawa (2003) conducted historical research on the concept of Yōjō and gave many suggestions, but the three important matters pointed out in relation to this chapter are as follows. First, Yōjō in the East has long been 'a culture of health-related skill and philosophy' and 'a free and autonomous act in accordance with the laws of nature to seek physical and mental stability.' Second, the concept of Yōjō expanded to a form that included development from the second half of the eighteenth century to the first half of the nineteenth century. Third, Takizawa clearly shows the fact that nineteenth-century Japanese Yōjō increased the possibility of human development as a philosophical proposition. Foucault's 'care of the self,' Heidegger's '*Fursorge* and *Sorge*,' and Mayeroff's 'care for others and oneself' suggest a philosophical universality that is similar to Yōjō.

From Takizawa's points, Yōjō, which was a Neo-Confucian term, underwent its own evolution in the living environment in Japan, and it might have developed as a method of Bildung in a form that harmonises Eastern philosophy and Western philosophy. In other words, development, being an Eastern view of Bildung and a Western view of education, could have fused harmoniously. However, the appearance of Shūyō meant that this ended up being nothing more than a possibility.

The concept of Shūyō in modern Japan

Shūyō was a term known only to Neo-Confucian scholars until the end of the nineteenth century. *Shūyō* is a term from Neo-Confucianism that was coined by taking one character each from *mi wo osame* (身を修め, 'improve oneself') and *kokoro wo yashinau* (心を養う, 'cultivate the spirit'). Considering the origins of the word, *Shūyō* means 'enriching the spirit by correcting the body.'

However, the use of Shūyō by Masanao Nakamura (中村正直, 1871), when translating *Self-Help*, spread knowledge of this word broadly. Incidentally, he was motivated to translate the book when he studied in Great Britain from 1866 to 1868. He received *Self-Help* as a parting gift from a British friend and read it on-board the ship on his return journey to Japan, where he got the impression that the book contained things that were necessary for the children and youth of Japan to live out in the coming age. For this reason, he translated and published it upon his return to Japan.

Nakamura translated cultivation and culture as *Shūyō* and education as *Kyōyō*. In some cases, he reversed the relationship between them in his translation. He also translated cultivation as *Kyōiku* (教育, 'education') at times. Distinguishing these during translation evidently gave Nakamura a lot of trouble in his translation effort. Before travelling for study, Nakamura was a teacher who taught Neo-Confucianism at a school in the Edo shogunate. This caused him to worry about how to translate *Self-Help* based on his experiences in Great Britain. Thanks to his abundant knowledge and understanding of Neo-Confucianism, he chose the Neo-Confucianist term *Shūyō*.

Nakamura's uncertainty about the term hints at the meaning he imbued *Shūyō* with. Working from what he had seen and heard in Great Britain, Nakamura thought carefully about how to advance modern education in Japan, a country in transition from a feudal society to a modern one. The result was choosing *Shūyō*, which potentially could speak to the people's subconscious mentality with regard to Manabi, as the central translation for cultivation and culture.

However, the use of *Shūyō* as a translation for education proves the uncertainty in Nakamura's thinking. In any case, *Shūyō*, as well as *Kyōyō* and *Kyōiku*, were used as translations for cultivation according to the context (Saito, 2019).

What is important in Nakamura's translation is that *Shūyō*, *Kyōyō*, and *Kyōiku* are all interchangeable. Moreover, culture, which Nakamura translated as *Shūyō*, is now translated as *Kyōyō*, which Nakamura used as a translation for education – a concept that is interesting considering modern education in Japan. When explaining the modernisation of education, Nakamura used words that were easy for Japanese people to understand in his translation, depending on context.

Unfortunately, the manner in which the concept of Shūyōhas spread since then shows that Nakamura's inventiveness went completely unnoticed. This has resulted in the characters for *Shūyō* (修養) bringing to mind *Shugyō* (修行), the traditional method of learning, which is contrary to the purpose of advancing the modernisation of education. From this situation, the reason for the lack of understanding of the inventiveness of Nakamura's translation and failure to make the most of the possibility of Yōjōwill become clear.

Nakamura's use of the word *Shūyō* with the aim of spreading modern education throughout Japan severed the link between the body and knowledge. For the Japanese, the body and knowledge were originally one because knowledge was identified through the experiences and sensations of the body. In Japan, knowledge was thought to be immanent in the body, not thought in the head, whether it was something directly needed for life or something like the martial or performing arts. For this reason, knowledge was to be obtained by conversing with one's own body.

In the process of modernisation, however, Japan sought to receive Western knowledge that was new and had no connection to physical sensation through the medium of the term *Shūyō*, which gave rise to the situation where the meaning Nakamura had given to *Shūyō* was not understood. Conversely, Yōjō grew and incorporated elements of modern Western development in line with the experience of the Japanese people until the first half of the nineteenth century, but at the end of the Edo period, it was replaced with the term *Shūyō*.

Upon confirming the changes to the word *Shūyō*, we understand that Sato's (1999: 6) explanation of Shūyō (the tradition of learning by which one seeks to restore one's holistic nature and to approach perfection through culture and education) is accurate. However, *Shūyō*, *Kyōyō*, and *Bunka* (文化) are all translations of culture, making it difficult to define in Japanese.

Shūyō and the principle of cultivation

The term *Shūyō* was revived in the form of the principle of cultivation (修養主義) to play a role in promoting nationalism under the pro-Japan sentiment that came to the fore after the Sino-Japanese War (1894–1895). Shūyō was revived as 'the Invention of tradition,' as indicated by Hobsbawm and Ranger (2012). By linking Shūyō with a principle, the meaning and function of education that Nakamura had given Shūyō was lost. As is apparent from the link with nationalism, the body was used through the term *Shūyō* to resurrect the term in the form of being the principle of cultivation, in order to change it into a particular ideology.

Segawa (2005) organises the state of Shūyō into (a) '*Shūyō* as a traditional Japanese concept of Bildung' and (b) '*Shūyō* as a device for the permeation of the ideology of the Emperor system in Japan.' This organisation is very clear and easily understandable. The two kinds of Shūyō that Segawa defined spread suddenly and rapidly from the mid-1890s through the 1900s.

There are three reasons for this. The first is that Shūyō was used as a device to ensure that the ideology of the Imperial Rescript on Education, which was enforced in 1890, permeated the Japanese populace. The Imperial Rescript on Education defined the concepts of subject education. The second reason is the effect of the nationalism that spread throughout the country in response to the tripartite interference Russia brought upon Japan after the Sino-Japanese War. The fact that Inazō Nitobe's publications *Bushido* (1899) and *Shūyō* (1911) were widely read at just this time also furthered this second effect. The third reason is the instability of the identity of the youth. The rapid Westernization of all aspects of life was too quick for the younger generation's bodies and minds to keep up. For example, the suicide of Misao Fujimura (藤村操), a student at First Higher School under the old system, by throwing himself over Kegon Falls in Nikko in 1903 was a symbolic event. 'At the Top of the Falls' (巖頭之感), the suicide note he left at the scene, caused a significant stir in society, and it later became an important reference which young people who worried in the same way he did read committedly. The note offers insight into the anguish of the youth at the time; therefore I have quoted it here (Delphi no Kai, 2018: 41):

> At the Top of the Falls
> How spacious Heaven and Earth are!
> How eternally Time flies!
> I have been trying hard to measure the greatness with my little five-foot figure!
> What authority does Horatio's philosophy have?
> The truth of the whole universe can be expressed in a single word 'inscrutable.'
> I have suffered many mental agonies, and I have finally decided to die.
> Now I stand at the top of the falls.
> I have no fear whatsoever.
> For the first time in my life,
> I have realized that great pessimism is equal to great optimism.

In Japanese:

巖頭之感
悠々たる哉天壤、

遼々たる哉古今、
五尺の小躯を以て　此大をはからむとす、
ホレーショの哲學竟に
何等のオーソリティを價するものぞ、
萬有の眞相は唯だ一言にして悉す、
曰く、「不可解」。
我この恨を懐いて煩悶、終に死を決するに至る。
既に巖頭に立つに及んで、
胸中何らの不安あるなし。
始めて知る、
大いなる悲觀は　大なる樂觀に一致するを。

Thus, the increase in the number of young people suffering from nervous breakdowns is also a result of the permeation of Shūyō. It is an attempt to adjust one's mental state by coming face to face with one's own body.

Let us now explain forms (a) and (b) of Shūyō in detail. (a) '*Shūyō* as a traditional Japanese concept of Bildung' played a major role mainly in youth self-formation as extracurricular education. For example, Shūyō-dan was a representative organisation that strove for youth Shūyō in extracurricular education. Shūyō-dan was formed in 1908 by Monzō Hasunuma (蓮沼門三). At the time, Hasunuma was a student at the Tokyo Prefecture Normal School. However, despite being in a position where he ought to have aimed to be a teacher, he was dissatisfied with the state of school education at the time. His dissatisfaction stemmed from the way the educational style of imparting knowledge reduced the character of the students and caused physical and mental damage. For this reason, he called to fellow boarders who also aimed to become teachers and began Shūyō-dan activities by cleaning the dirty boarding house. (However, after graduating, Hasunuma did not become a teacher but pressed on with activities for Shūyō-dan.)

The purpose of the organisation was 'cultivation of character.' The specific methods used to achieve this purpose were 'meditation,' 'sweating,' and 'worship of the great,' and these were known as 'the three philosophies of cultivation.' The most distinctive of these is 'sweating.' Hasunuma (1969) explains that 'sweating washes away the worldly passions in one's heart, cultivates a character of sympathy and purity, trains the muscles and spirit, and builds a personality that will not be frustrated at difficulty.' Upon its establishment, this organisation raised issues about school education, and support from politicians and businesspeople allowed it to expand the scope of its activities, and it ultimately emphasised social education movements and collaboration with local young men's associations.

Shūyō-dan had two particular features. The first was its aim of rejecting doubt and cultivating the mind by training the body. This is a traditional method of Bildung founded on the ideas of mind–body monism. The second was the way it formed a community for Shūyō consistently from its establishment. This is a major difference from Shugyō, which is based upon loneliness, and it shows that Shūyō succeeds through mutual aid and support.

On the other hand, (b) 'Shūyō as a device for the permeation of the ideology of the Emperor system in Japan' penetrated from the mid-1890s, mainly through links with the old-system teachings on morals in school education. This originated in the Imperial Rescript on Education that was issued in 1890. The Rescript was announced by Emperor Meiji, and it listed important virtues as the purpose of education and discussed the modern Emperor system. The concept of *Chūkun Aikoku* (忠君愛国), meaning loving one's country and being loyal to the Emperor, gives a straightforward explanation of the contents of the Imperial Rescript on Education. Students learned this philosophy as part of the subject of morals. However, the loyalty and patriotism that was taught in morals was formalist, and the ideology of the Imperial Rescript on Education did not spread much. Just as that problem arose, the Sino-Japanese War broke out, nationalism came to the fore, and attention returned to the need to cultivate the spirit through Shūyō. As a result, Shūyō was listed as an item to learn in textbooks on morals from the second half of the 1890s.

Further, Masatarō Sawayanagi (澤柳政太郎), who was also a bureaucrat in the Ministry of Education, published *The Spirit of the Educator* (教育者の精神) in 1895 and argued that Shūyō was important for teachers. Sawayanagi served successively as the principal of high schools and junior high schools under the old system, acted as the chancellor of Kyoto Imperial University, and furthermore founded Seijō Gakuen, a symbol of the Taisho Liberal Education Movement (大正自由教育運動). These are merely a few examples demonstrating the large impact that Sawayanagi had on modern Japanese education. Sawayanagi was also well informed about Buddhism and had been influenced by Manshi Kiyosawa (清沢満之), a friend and Buddhist priest. The two of them resonated on a philosophical level and advocated 'spiritualism' in relation to Shūyō. (b), unlike (a), emphasized the spirit.

What changes did Shūyō, classified as a philosophy, undergo after this? Karaki (2013) indicated the characteristics of the Japanese society in the 1910s from the point of view of Shūyō and Kyōyō, saying that Japanese society lost its Kata and moved from Shūyō to the era of Kyōyō at the turning point in 1917 and 1918, against the background of the effects of the Russian Revolution.

Karaki defines Kata as something that 'controls our thinking and living systems.' Specifically, he refers to thinking systems that assume grounding in Chinese classical literature. He points out that owing to rapid progress in modernisation, Western knowledge has the upper hand in Bildung too.

The Japanese term *Kyōyō* was a term coined by Nakamura that he used in translation in regard to Kyōiku (education) (Saito, 2019). However, while Kyōiku is widely recognised as education, Kyōyō became known in the context of Bildung. Specifically, after receiving the teaching of Dr. Koeber in the First Higher School in the old system, the principle of culture (教養主義) spread, centred on the young people who gathered around Sōseki Natsume. *Santarō no Nikki* (三太郎の日記, Santarō's diary), written by one of these young people,

Jiro Abe, was widely read across a range of ages as a bible-like book relating to self-formation for young men. The young men from the 1920s onward then held that self-formation by reading Western classics, focusing on Western philosophy such as Descartes, Kant, and Schopenhauer, was the principle of culture, creating a boom.

Practice of Shūyō and mindfulness in school education

To summarise the discussion so far, the spread of the principle of cultivation in the mid-1890s led to a realignment of identity, and the relationship between spirit and body was modernised. The appearance of the principle of culture about 20 years later in the mid-1910s then pushed the modernisation of knowledge forward all at once. This lag contains the unique qualities of Kyōyō in modern Japan. Ironically, *Kyōyō*, which used to mean education, completely lost the meaning it had in the early Meiji period when it changed to the principle of culture.

However, drawing a distinction from such social trends, Shūyō demonstrated further power under the Taisho Liberal Education Movement in school education from the 1920s. I will present three items selected for their notability.

The first is the method of *Gyōnen* (凝念法) of Seikei Elementary School. This school was founded by Haruji Nakamura and is known for 'self-assisted education,' 'Eastern training principles,' and 'education in small numbers.' The method of Gyōnen involves doing abdominal breathing at the beginning of lessons. Abdominal breathing calms the consciousness and creates a physical and mental state of readiness for learning.

The second is the practice of posture instruction by Takeji Kinoshita (木下竹次) of the Elementary School attached to Nara Women's Higher Normal School. In his instructing position at the school, Kinoshita aimed to create a state of concentration by having the children perform abdominal breathing to straighten bent backs and breathe deeply. This is like Nakamura's approach and the practice aimed at 'independent learning.'

The third is the practice of Shūyō by Enosuke Ashida (芦田恵之助). After retiring as a teacher, Ashida travelled to schools throughout Japan to give visiting lessons. This on its own would be Shūyō for the purpose of Ashida's own growth, but he performed a practice known as the Okada sitting method that resembles Zen meditation. He started the Okada sitting method because he suffered a nervous breakdown. The strenuous duties of teaching pushed his mental and physical capacities past their limit, but he restored his balance of body and mind by following the 'tanden' breathing method while sitting. This experience caused him to realise that Shūyō is important for teachers too, and he engaged in activities that sought to spread Shūyō throughout Japan.

These practices prepared a foundation for totalitarian education in Japanese education from the 1930s. However, what is important is that, although knowledge is closely related to physical sensations, Manabi will paralyse the intellect through the body if a particular ideology is assumed. In other words, it reduces the body to a void. Ideology steals the body's intelligence. For precisely this reason, control using intellect becomes necessary as well. However, the hidden potential of the body should not be denied. The body's balance with intellect, or with the spirit, is important.

Breathing to control the body should be done to enrich our lives. The preceding three educational practices were initially intended for seeking out rich, engaged Manabi and an enriched life by creating the mental and physical state for Manabi. However, due to its contribution to totalitarianism in the 1930s and later, education that pays attention to the body tended to be avoided in Japanese education after World War II. The reason was that in Japan, thought had been given to the relationship between the body and the spirit, but no thought had been given to the relationship between the body and Western knowledge.

In Europe and North America, mindfulness based on Buddhism has drawn attention in recent years. Mindfulness is discussed in education as well, in the form of the 'mindful teacher.' The key method is meditation through abdominal breathing. This is similar to the practice performed in Taisho Liberal Education.

What is mindfulness in the first place? Let us check the definition of mindfulness by Thich Nhat Hanh and Jon Kabat-Zinn, who were instrumental in spreading mindfulness. Thich Nhat Hanh is a Vietnamese-born Zen monk and was the first person to propose mindfulness in the United States. Thich Nhat Hanh (2013) explains mindfulness:

> Mindfulness is the energy of being aware and awake to the present. It is the continuous practice of touching life deeply in every moment. Practicing mindfulness does not require that we go anywhere different. We can practice mindfulness in our room or on our way from one place to another. We can do very much the same thing we always do – walking, sitting, working, eating, talking – except we learn to do them with an awareness of what we are doing. . . . Awareness of the breath is the essence of mindfulness.

The important aspect of Hanh's definition is 'being aware of and awake to the present' and 'awareness of the breath.' Being aware of the state of our breath allows us to re-examine the state of our clothing, food, and housing. By being aware of what our own bodies are seeking, we improve our lives.

Next, let us review the definition of mindfulness given by Kabat-Zinn, a professor at the University of Massachusetts Medical School. He is known for conducting activities to introduce mindfulness meditation into medical and social locations in the United States and for proposing 'mindfulness-based stress reduction.' Further, he is a founding member of the Cambridge Zen Center.

> Mindfulness is an ancient Buddhist practice which has profound relevance for our present-day lives. This relevance has nothing to do with Buddhism per se or with becoming a Buddhist, but it has everything to do with

waking up and living in harmony with oneself and with the world. It has to do with examining who we are, with questioning our view of the world and our place in it, and with cultivating some appreciation for the fullness of each moment we are alive. Most of all, it has to do with being in touch.

(Jon Kabat-Zinn, 2005)

It is important for Kabat-Zinn to show that mindfulness originated from Buddhism, but he says it has nothing to do with being a Buddhist. In other words, mindfulness is not a training method for a particular religion but a technique for enriching our lives. Further, he does not define 'ancient Buddhist practice,' but concretely it means activities centred on breathing methods. By practising deep breathing, you can encounter yourself again.

Looking at both definitions of mindfulness, you will notice that they have elements that are strikingly similar to those of Yōjō in Japan while also having similarities with Shūyō. Shūyō, as a principle developed in modern Japan, also emphasised breathing. Regulating one's breathing allows them to adjust their physical state and ensure an optimal mental condition. Doing this improves the physical and mental states making it possible to re-examine life and ensure optimal performance.

Many people may find the concept of meditating by controlling breathing odd, but while breathing is essential for human life, it is too ordinary in everyday life and is unconscious. For this reason, consciously concentrating on breathing allows us to bring forth our own subconscious powers. By controlling breathing, we can actively engage in learning. This could be considered the greatest characteristic of Manabi.

Conclusion: Manabi and Shi-tei kankei

The relationship between the teacher and the learner in Manabi is called the *Shi-tei kankei* (師弟関係). The teacher is the *Shishō* (師匠, 'master'), and the student is the *Deshi* (弟子, 'disciple').

Shi-tei kankei (master–disciple relationship) exists even today in martial and performing arts. Deshi who live in their Shishō's house and learn from them are called *Uchi-deshi* (内弟子), whereas those who come to their Shishō's house to learn are called *Soto-deshi* (外弟子) to distinguish the two types. However, the expressions *Shishō* and *Deshi* are also used generally outside the martial and performing arts contexts. For example, phrases like 'my Shishō is so-and-so' and 'I am Deshi to such-and-such' are common. The usages of the words *Shishō* and *Deshi* strongly retain the true nature of the Shi-tei kankei. The Shi-tei kankei is basically a one-on-one relationship between Shishō and Deshi.

The Shi-tei kankei is like an apprenticeship but different because the Deshi's learning is individual and therefore cannot easily be conceptualised as 'legitimate peripheral participation' (Lave & Wenger, 1991).

The Shishō hardly ever uses direct words to tell Deshi what and how they should learn and internalize. How then, do Deshi learn?

Deshi's methods of learning can be divided in two types. The first type of learning is to *watch* and then to *imitate* the Shishō's every movement and action. Deshi learn holistically, including the Shishō's way of life and manner of talking, and even the way they should behave and live as people. Japan has an idiom '*senaka wo mite manabu*' (背中を見て学ぶ, 'to learn by watching someone's back'), which is precisely what this is. The *Deshi's* second type of learning involves receiving concrete instructions from the Shishō about what to do, without being told in advance what these actions mean. They must perform the actions as instructed by the Shishō and find their meaning independently. Accordingly, in the second method of learning, a Deshi may find instructions unreasonable if they cannot detect the Shishō's intentions, and Deshi sometimes leave Shishō of their own volition.

Uchida (2014: 245–247) describes the Shi-tei kankei:

> When a 'Deshi' studies under a 'Shishō,' the 'Deshi' does not know what they are going to learn when they begin training. The 'Shi-tei kankei' does not necessarily succeed merely because the teacher is a great person. No matter how great the 'Shishō' is, if the 'Deshi' is not prepared to learn, the 'Shi-tei kankei' will not succeed or continue. Conversely, if the 'Deshi' studies under that 'Shishō' and performs 'Keiko' as he or she is told, despite being unsure of the Shisho and the benefit of their role, they may develop rapidly and become a worthwhile person. I think that is the most dynamic part in the Shi-tei kankei. The 'Shi-tei kankei' is not bidirectional, and it cannot succeed if the 'Deshi' does not embrace the 'Shishō's' wisdom and skill. From the point of view of the 'Deshi' who believes that the 'Shishō's' every movement, action, word or utterance is overflowing with wisdom, no matter what the teacher does – even just sneezing or yawning – the 'Deshi' will pay attention thinking 'what could the teacher be trying to tell me by doing that?' and look on with eager intent as they begin an infinite interpretation. Once the 'Deshi' believes that 'the "Shishō's" every movement, action, and word or utterance is overflowing with wisdom' the 'Manabi' exercise is never-ending.

This citation was somewhat long, but it accurately captures the key points of Manabi in a Shi-tei kankei. The important thing in a Shi-tei kankei is that the Deshi trusts the Shishō. Otherwise, the Deshi will not succeed in Manabi because the Shishō will not teach what needs to be learned with close and careful attention – watching and learning. Repeatedly practising what the Shishō instructs, even when the Deshi does not properly understand the meaning, is the process of Shugyō and of Manabi under Shuhari.

In the case of a Shi-tei kankei, the community of Deshi under the same Shishō is referred to as *Ichimon* (一門). The Deshi share their worries and help one another, while deepening their Manabi and improving their skills. However, important insights and learning require them to face themselves and independently overcome loneliness.

Shi-tei kankei consist of relationships among individuals, so they are not bound by systems or affiliations. Thus, they still play a role today as Manabi relationships in various fields. Shi-tei kankei are made up of various elements of Manabi.

Bibliography

Delphi no Kai (2018) *The Appeal of Tochigi*, Tochigi: Zuisōsha.
Hasunuma, M. (1969) *Shūyō-dan no Risō*, Tokyo: Shūyō-dan.
Hobsbawm, E., & Ranger, T. (2012) *The Invention of Tradition*, Cambridge: Cambridge University Press.
Jon Kabat-Zinn (2005) *Wherever You Go, There You Are: Mindfulness Meditation in Everyday Life*, London: Piatkus.
Kadowaki, K. (1978) *Shugyō to Ningen Keisei: Gyō no Kyōikuteki igi*, Osaka: Sōgensha.
Karaki, J. (2013) *Gendaishi he no Kokoromi & Soushitu no Zidai*, Tokyo: Chukouron-shinsha.
Kawakami, F. (2019) *Fuhaku Hikki*, Tokyo: Chuokoron-shinsha.
Lave, J., & Wenger, E. (1991) *Situated Learning: Legitimate Peripheral Participation*, Cambridge: Cambridge University Press.
Maurice Merleau-Ponty (1973) *The Prose of the World*, Evanston: Northwestern University Press.
Minamoto, R. (1989) *Kata*, Tokyo: Sobunsha.
Nishihira, T. (2009) *Zeami no Keiko Tetsugaku*, Tokyo: University of Tokyo Press.
Saeki, S. (2004) *Bushido no Seishinshi: Bushido to iu gen'ei*, Tokyo: Japan Broadcast Publishing.
Segawa, D. (2005) '"Shūyō" Kenkyū no Genzai' (English subtitle: 'A Research on the Studies of "Shuyo" (Cultivation)'), Bulletin of the Education History and Philosophy Division, Faculty of Education, the University of Tokyo (31), Tokyo.
Saigusa, H. (1958) *Seiōka Nihon no Kenkyū*, Tokyo: Chuokoron-sha.
Saito, Takashi (2003) *Iki no Ningengaku*, Yokohama: Seori Shobō.
Saito, Tomoya (2019) "Seinen no Jiritsu ni okeru 'Kyōyō' to 'Kyōyō Shugi' 'Seinen no Jiritsu to Kyōiku Bunka'," 61st Bulletin of the Noma Education Laboratory, Tokyo.
Sato, M. (1999) *Manabi no Kairaku*, Yokohama: Seori Shobō.
Suzuki, M. (2015) *Sangaku Shinkō: Nihon Bunka no Kontei wo Saguru*, Tokyo: Chuokouron-shinsha.
Takizawa, T. (2003) *Yōjōron no Shisō*, Yokohama: Seori Shobō.
Thich Nhat Hanh (2013) *Happiness: Essential Mindfulness Practice*, Berkeley: Parallax Press.
Tsujimoto, M. (2012) *'Manabi' no Fukken: Mohō to Shūjuku*, Tokyo: Iwanami Shoten.
Uchida, T. (2014) *Machiba no Kyōdōtairon*, Tokyo: Ushio Publishing.

Part II

Practices of Manabi

Chapter 4

The resonance of Minna's voice in Japanese schooling

Kayo Fujii

Introduction

How does the concept of Manabi in Part I appear in Japanese schooling? What is the feature of Manabi in Japanese school education? How do children experience Manabi at school? We will discuss these questions in Part II, 'Practices of Manabi.'

This chapter philosophically examines the characteristics of Japanese schooling by focusing on the word *Minna* and the Japanese conception of the self. *Minna* (みんな) usually represents 'everybody' and is a term used by teachers, students, and parents throughout all levels of primary school, junior high school, and high school in Japan. Minna corresponds to the Chinese characters '皆、未那、未奈、衆' (みな, *Mina*). Some Chinese characters are used because the word *Mina/Minna* was originally in Japanese. *Mina* means 'all people who live together,' 'all people,' and 'all things.' The first recorded citation of 未那 can be found in correspondences from the *Nihon Shoki* in CE 720 (Nihon kokugo dai jiten second edition editing committee, 2001: 774). In Japanese schools, Minna is frequently used in educational activities and creates a unique learning environment. In this chapter, I propose that Manabi is a living art in our unpredictable and unprecedented world facing an era of globalization, and I discuss unique learning styles in Japan.

Considering Japanese education in a VUCA world

Volatility, Uncertainty, Complexity, and Ambiguity (VUCA) represents the state of the future (Fadel et al., 2015: 13). VUCA indicates that our world is difficult to predict and uncontrollable. How can people pursue learning in a society in which the future cannot be predicted? According to Charles Fadel et al., learning that responds to future societies comprises not only knowledge and skills but also meta learning and character qualities. Character qualities related to learning refers to attitudes such as mindfulness, curiosity, courage, resilience, ethics, and leadership (Fadel et al., 2015: 130). In other words, in a complex and ambiguous society, learning can be promoted through a positive character.

Is leadership always constituted by positive character? According to the Japanese philosopher Kiyokazu Washida, Japan needs a leader like *Shingari* (しんがり, 殿) because of the nation's population decline. A Shingari is someone who moves at the end of a team of mountain climbers while checking on the safety of Mina (everyone) (Washida, 2015: 140). The leader image of Shingari does not represent a person who leads strongly at the forefront but someone who is located behind the group and ensures the safety and livelihoods of the people concerned. A leader does not necessarily have to be at the forefront of the group; leadership methods can vary according to cultural background. This is also true for Japanese education.

In Japan, traditional sports such as Kendo (剣道), Judo (柔道), Japanese archery (弓道), and Aikido (合気道) are practiced to master Tao (道) (see Chapter 3). One can learn to master Tao through the relationship between the master and pupil, *Shiteikannkei* (師弟関係). From his experience learning *Budo* (武道), the Japanese philosopher Taturu Uchida compares learning Tao to acquiring one's mother tongue. He states that people do not think about the effect or usefulness of learning their mother tongue before learning it. They only learn of its usefulness 'after learning' (Uchida, 2009: 137). In the same way, those who learn Tao do not understand the usefulness of Tao before learning it. In other words, the significance of learning Tao is acquired ex post facto.

When a pupil learns Tao, the master teaches his pupil a 'learning way' or 'way of learning' (Uchida, 2009: 143–144). The most important aspect of learning Tao is to assume a posture of learning, so the material that one learns in the process is secondary (Uchida, 2009: 144). The syllabi of university courses are in direct contrast to Tao learning. Syllabi state the material that learners will learn; they are an 'explanation written so that beginners can understand the meaning and usefulness of learning before beginning learning' (Uchida, 2009: 138).

In addition, the relationship between masters and pupils in Tao is not clearly separated in the conventional master/teacher–pupil/learner dichotomy. Both the master and the pupil are trying to understand Tao. Learning Tao is ambiguous, so the master and pupil do not know when and where the end point of learning will come. Considering the unpredictability of future society, we must seek a way of learning together even while the final point cannot be seen by the pupil or the master.

Self-formation and Manabi

In contrast to mind and body dualism, the idea of body called *Mi* (身) works as a body not in physical space but 'in social space,' according to the Japanese philosopher Hiroshi Ichikawa (Ichikawa, 1993: 139). In Japanese, *Mi* is used for expressions related to emotions and hearts. For example, it is used in the phrases 'sink deep into one's mind' (その言葉は身にしみる, *Sono Kotoba ha Mi ni shimiru*) and 'thing experienced for oneself' (それは身をもって経験したことである, *Sore ha Mi o motte keiken shita koto de aru*). This usage concerns the personal and social body and expresses the 'subjective–objective' quality of the body (Ichikawa, 1993: 139–140). In other words, the body (身体, *Shinntai*) is not a physical thing that can be counted. It is instead the foundation that creates one's sense and perspective of place by being here in the moment. We can perceive the atmosphere and comfort of the place throughout the body. Therefore, it is tied to society and personality.

Through Mi, persons know things, understand the meaning of their experiences, and learn. Learning through Mi is an ambiguous and co-occurring event in which 'the world is segmented by Mi and, at the same time, Mi is segmented by the world' (Ichikawa, 1993: 188). Learning through this process of dual articulation causes people to feel the self's body and to reflect on the self. Manabi is also a self-formation art through which a learner can seek a better way to learn. Manabi occurs in the interaction between the body and the self.

The education scholar Manabu Sato has actively used the words of Manabi rather than of 'learning' since the mid-1990s in Japan; he suggests education that combines Western learning linked to Dewey's thought and Vygotsky's social constructivism and Manabi. According to Sato, 'Manabi is a trinity of interactive mediation between world-making (cognitive and cultural practice), searching for oneself (ethical and existential practice), and fellowship-making (social and political practice)' (Sato, 1995: 75). Based on this idea of Manabi, he has redefined the school as a place of reorganisation of identity and community and suggests that small school communities should be created with about 200 students and 10 teachers (Sato, 1997: 170). He states what the teacher should do in such a school: 'The teacher must design the environment of the classroom as an active and collaborative place, design experiences with meaning and appeal as educational content, and create an active, autonomous, and cooperative interactive practice' (Sato, 1995: 86). In other words, school education should promote cognitive world-making, self-formation, and friend-making based on each individual's experience rather than merely promoting the acquisition of knowledge. In addition, he asserts that conflicts between individual freedom and the greater community good should respect the goodness of the community, so that, when individual rights and community ties conflict, the community's bonds are considered superior (Sato, 1995: 69).

This theory is the learning theory that mixes several elements. It shows us that Manabi is not accomplished by one person and envisions the body, language, and space from a combined viewpoint. From the viewpoint of Manabi, school education emphasizes experiences and activities through the Mi, and the children position themselves in nature and the universe based on some feeling arising from them. The self's position comes from a relationship that brings together activities and experiences. Children perceive their position in the universe, and they are aware of their selves again.

Even in the following indicators, created in response to global learning, we can read the essence of Manabi. The educational committee of Yokohama city in Japan outlines career stages, which enables a teacher to see the qualities and abilities necessary from the time they are newcomers to the mature stage of their career. In these human resource development indicators, the necessary qualities and abilities for teachers are divided into 'the characteristics of the teacher' (including 'humanity and sociality, communication, passion, and educational affection') and 'professional expertise.' 'Humanity and sociality' is defined by 'building a relationship of trust with children, faculty staff, guardians, and communities with a wide, human-rights-based perspective,' while 'communication' refers to 'drawing out the circumstances and the minds of one's partner, communicating one's ideas appropriately, and actively supporting others.'[1] In short, teachers are required to create a space that children can experience through Mi with confidence through helping others and building relationships of trust. Even using such indicators, what is at the core of Manabi is that children's experiences of Manabi occur through relationships (among teachers, students, faculty members, people, and things), awaking to the self, and knowing it through Mi.

The practice of knowing: structure of the Japanese language

The idea that education is fostered by relationships is influenced by various characteristics that are particularly Japanese. According to Tetsuro Watsuji, a Japanese philosopher who studied in Germany, Chinese language was developed with academic terms, while native Japanese words were used as part of a daily language. Due to this daily usage of the language, experiential expressions in Japanese are very rich and expressions of emotions are highly developed (Watsuji, 2016: 11). For this reason, academic terms expressing concepts and logic and everyday terms expressing experiences are distant from one another in Japanese (Watsuji, 2016: 13). Japanese lacks distinctions between singular or plural, one or general, and masculine, feminine, or neutral nouns. This ambiguity of the Japanese language deeply conforms to situations and forms of human existence (Watsuji, 2016: 16). For example, the phrase 'young people' (若い衆, *Wakai Shuu*) means both one young person and a group of young people; this implies that human beings are personal and social (Watsuji, 2016: 16–17). In addition, verbs do not change with personal pronouns. This means that 'human actions are not fixed to any person's position as personal or social,' and when describing the act of seeing, the verb 'to see' does not need to change its form to identify the viewer (Watsuji, 2016: 17).

The Japanese word for 'know' not only refers to the function of knowing content, it also means a knowing person and a knowing people. According to Watsuji, it is focused only on the subject who knows. When elder Japanese people express cognition, they state that they learn and know Tao (Watsuji, 2016: 23). Here, the goal and the content to be known are Tao, not knowledge. Tao means the way people walk, what leads to a certain goal that will never disappear, and the trend itself (Watsuji, 2016: 23). Tao is also a 'trend towards a spiritual goal,' and the expression 'walking with Tao in question' refers to asking for spiritual guidance (Watsuji, 2016: 23). Therefore, Tao also means 'the way of humanity,' 'the way of function,' and a 'method,' not the target or object itself (Watsuji, 2016: 24). To know Tao, Manabi begins without setting goals. In addition, those who begin Tao do not always end by reaching the ultimate, although they are constantly orienting themselves toward the ultimate. Knowing Tao is not merely an intellectual problem; it is closely tied to the practice of imitating a way (Watsuji, 2016: 24).

After all, to know is to learn Tao. Knowing is a practice that includes experience and awareness through learners' Mi. In other words, knowing something is a practice that does not clearly distinguish among actors to know, acts of knowing, and objects to be known.

The Japanese self: both social and personal

According to the criminal law scholar Sato Naoki, in Japan, people conceive 'shame' (恥, *Haji*) or 'ignominy' (穢れ), *Kegare* in the *Seken* (世間, 'world'), rather than the individual-based idea of equality under the law (Sato, 2001). Of course, words such as 'society' (社会, *Shakai*) and 'individual' (個人, *Kojinn*) exist in Japanese, but they are translated words. 'Society' was translated as 社会 in 1877, and 'the individual' was translated as 個人 in 1844 (Abe, 1995: 86). Both society and the individual appear in Meiji era language, when many Western books were translated, and these terms are now widely used.

According to Sato, the Seken has the following four main characteristics. The first is the relationship of giving and receiving (Sato, 2015: 17). For example, this relationship occurs when one receives letters or comments from someone else. The widespread development of social networking services (SNSs), such as LINE, that are used by young people in Japan has given rise to a new communication problem that might be called 'not replying to the received message' (Sato, 2015: 19). Those who receive mail are expected to answer it. If there is no reply, senders may feel that the receiver is ignoring them or may doubt the personal qualities of those who do not reply. The second characteristic of the Seken is the 'class system.' In the Seken, there are 'upper and lower rankings' such as 'upgrade/downgrade,' 'superior/inferior,' 'older/younger,' 'senior/junior,' and 'male/female' (Sato, 2015: 21). Since the Seken is not based on individual relationships, people are positioned in groups according to their attributes. The third characteristic of the Seken is 'common time consciousness.' In the Seken, 'everyone is living at the same time' (Sato, 2015: 26). Therefore, a person who mentions different acts or different ideas by an individual may be perceived as not being able to read between the lines or, as the Japanese phrase states, read the *Kuuki* (空気, 'air'). In Japan, it is 'necessary to read the air of the Seken' (Sato, 2015: 30). The fourth characteristic is that Seken cannot be reasoned or rationally grounded but is instead operated through the world of polytheism.

The influence of the Seken in Japan means that neither society nor individuals are as rooted as they are in the West. Rather, Japanese conceptions of society and individuals are both personal and social. As discussed earlier, this dual personality is also embedded in the structure of the Japanese language.

Modern Japanese schools first developed in the Meiji era. At first, schools using desks and chairs did not suit Japanese culture. Gradually, however, the school system was established, and more children were able to attend classes. While they incorporated Western culture, Japanese schools also utilized Japanese traditions and culture. Children as the learners, along with adults as the teachers, are accustomed to Western methods while living in the Seken. Community learning in schools comprises this cultural gap. How do children in Japan experience Manabi in schools that are influenced by different cultures?

Making a place to learn: Minna

When I visit Japanese schools (elementary schools, junior high schools, or high schools) and observe classes, I frequently hear the word *Minna*. *Minna* is used when a teacher asks a question of all the children in the class, such as, 'What did Minna (everyone) do?' or 'What do you all (Minna) think?' In addition, the titles of several textbooks for moral classes in Japan include Minna, for example, 'A school student who thinks and discusses with Minna (everyone)' and 'Minna's (everyone's) moral.' Also, in relation to contents, there are stories of living comfortably with Minna, cherishing Minna's pleasant feeling, and Minna and society. Thus, the expression *Minna* is used very often in Japanese education.

When a teacher asks children 'What do you all (Minna) think?', students understand that they are being asked a question, and each person starts thinking. In this way, even children who do not understand the flow of the lesson can feel that they are participating. The teacher may ask children who are feeling sleepy, 'Are you thinking?' In response to this question, some children will begin talking to their friends, while other children will raise their hands and give their opinions. When a teacher addresses a Japanese class with Minna, each child in the class is set into action. The question 'How did Minna think?' is magical.

Children in school experience thinking with Minna in class. Through thinking with Minna, children can learn about other children's thoughts, modify their own ideas, and clarify them. Minna refers to all classmates, but Minna's idea ultimately represents one idea. Teachers may identify Minna's idea by considering what lies between opposing viewpoints within a group. Through class, children learn about the uniqueness of their ideas in comparison with Minna's thoughts, as well as the kinds of ideas that are the closest to their own. Through Manabi in the classroom, students learn more about their own thoughts in light of the ambiguous and fluid criteria set out by Minna's idea. This means that, in Japanese education, one's own ideas are not formed by confrontation with others. They are formed through recognition from the ambiguous Minna criteria.

When a teacher asks, 'Is Minna ready?', most children will look what the other children nearby do. They will then check whether the nearby children are preparing in the same way. If a difference is confirmed, the child will observe the other children and correct their difference. In short, children imitate the appearances of others nearby. As a result, the class is in a state of readiness. In this way, the use of the term *Minna* in Japanese schools encourages children to imitate others and promotes Manabi.

Through imitating another person's action, Manabi involves learning through the body. Words cannot fully explain the actions of classmates who are to be imitated. According to Masasi Tsujimoto, an educational history researcher, this form of Manabi was also a feature of education in the Edo period (Tsujimoto, 2012). When students learn by imitation, the teacher becomes the model for the learner. Imitation is more focused on imitating a model than on expressing one's own ideas and words. The learner gradually learns by imitating the teacher and other children. Teachers provide discipline when children divert from the norm supported by the model. This type of Manabi teaches children to socially recognise things that are not linguistic.

The practices of considering Minna in the classroom and imitating others are maintained by Japan's current education system. According to the educational researcher Ryoko Tsuneyoshi, Japanese schools are shaped by a mechanism that involves intrinsic entrainment. In Japanese schools, cooperative goals such as 'Minna gets along' are proposed, and small groups conduct activities such as morning meetings, lunch, and cleaning. These small group activities are a system in which students closely interact with one another and 'accumulate knowledge about each other through a common experience' (Tsuneyoshi, 1992: 48). It creates a situation that makes it possible for students to understand one another without having to mediate with words, a foundation that functions as communication through empathy (Tsuneyoshi, 1992: 48). Schools in Japan share the work of school life with children, and each group has specific responsibilities. For example, in each class, each child is charged with a role, such as lunch helper, music staff, blackboard staff, health care staff, or bulletin board staff.

The ideas and opinions of which Japanese children speak during class are different from those of children in the West. Japanese voices are a kind of amalgam of many different voices. These are the voices of 'everyone,' not of 'individuals.' According to the educational philosopher Hiroyuki Numata, 'I' in European culture differs from 'I' in Japanese culture. He compares Rousseau's 'The Reveries of the Solitary Walker' with Touson Shimazaki's 'Chikuma River Summertime' and describes the differences in the perception of the individual in each culture.

Although Rousseau seems to leave himself naturally by listening to the sound of the waves, the sound confronts him and makes him focus his consciousness so that 'he does not feel the need to forget himself' (Numata, 2009: 281). Through this experience, Rousseau is not becoming integrated with nature. He feels in his consciousness clearly that it reacts with the rhythm of the universe while reacting to and moving with that rhythm. In this case, the self is made up of 'the power to force oneself, life force, energy' (Numata, 2009: 282). On the other hand, the Japanese 'I' is like the 'atmosphere' that spreads around rather than a core like the nucleus that supports the self (Numata, 2009: 282). 'I' as 'the place' is not focused on the inside of self but on the self with ambiguous and blurred boundaries between the outside world and the self. This means that the self changes according to changes in the world, making the boundary of the self more clarified or blurred.

The Japanese-self consists of a self that goes through Nothingness (無, *Mu*). According to Shizuteru Ueda, an academic and Buddhist, Selflessness is not becoming nothing or forgetting everything. Selflessness means that 'there is no one,' which means that 'everything is in relation' and 'existence appears in relationships' (Ueda, 2000: 155). The idea that relationships cause existence implies 'that related things are established from relationships' (Ueda, 2000: 155).

However, this does not mean that everything is reduced to a relationship (Ueda, 2000: 153). As we have seen, Nothingness implies the perception of an absence, not that there is only a relationship. 'I' exists at the intersection of relationships and at the point of connection. The uniqueness of the node contains the expression of 'I' (Ueda, 2000: 156). Here, 'I' is creation from the Nothingness. In other words, Nothingness is a state that is satisfied with the relationship. The self is connected to the eternal Nothingness of opening without limit that passed through the relationship, occurring in the relationship that passes through Nothingness (Ueda, 2000: 157).

'I' can accept other people as 'others who are not him/herself' and 'touch nature in their own way' in a state other than oneself (Ueda, 2000: 158). 'I' is enriched through contact with others who pass through Nothingness. In this way, it is necessary to establish a relationship with the absence while referring to a real person or thing to establish oneself. For this reason, self-formation via Nothingness becomes education that emphasises educational relations in school education. That is, 'place/atmosphere'–oriented Japanese education places a great emphasis on human relations.

Efforts of a Japanese elementary school: 'Minna's classroom'

As part of inclusive education in Fujisawa city in Japan, open classrooms are named Minna's (everyone's) Classroom, and children who have difficulty learning in the classroom are supported. In Minna's Classroom, the teacher is a children's support expert who understands the embarrassment of children who have trouble and supports them through learning. Any child in such a classroom can learn regardless of their abilities or disabilities. The principal of a public elementary school that has Minna's Classroom has said:

> This classroom is not just a comfortable place (居場所, *Ibasho*), it is made to function as a place of learning. We are preparing the contents of support so that children can gain confidence through education. Considering a

child's living and home environment, I can understand when children do not feel like learning. However, the central role of a school is to guarantee learning, and we want to support children's learning while caring for their minds. Minna's classroom is also a place where children can be confident and where they will want to return to class.[2]

Learning is central in Minna's Classroom, unlike in nurse's offices that are set up to respond to non-attending children. In this situation, when such children go to school, they cannot go to the classroom and are instead sent to the nurse's office, where the school nurse supports the child's growth by focusing on caring for the child's mind. However, no learning function is attached to this relationship. Even today, listening to the voices of children who cannot adapt to the classroom or to children who come to the nurse's office complaining of a stomach ache, the nursing teacher cares for children who wish to tell their stories.

Empathy from Minna and unity of Minna

Annual targets for school education have appeared in recent years, such as accept, learn, help, and enhance one another. Accepting and learning are specifically recommended. These efforts indicate that it is necessary for students to respect one another before they learn. In other words, we cannot learn unless we recognise each other. In Japanese education, recognition and learning are deeply related.

In Japanese classrooms, in order to listen to one's own voice, it is necessary to be recognised from the standard of Minna (everyone). If each person's idea or opinion is proposed without such recognition, Minna is not formed, opinions remain unacknowledged, and children cannot learn in the class. By making all students members of the class, the Minna, and by recognizing that each person has something to say, a classroom becomes a space for learning. This expression of mutual recognition means that two things get close to each other and not only do not conflict but are united (Takeuchi, 2012: 27). This promotes Manabi.

Therefore, the voice born by recognition in a coherent class will be different from the individual voice in the West. It is a symbiotic voice, a voice of a group of friends rather than an individual voice.

Japanese classrooms are very sensitive to differences of opinions, and such differences are emphasised. These differences are not those between individuals; they are different from the perspective of Minna. The voice of Minna is an ambiguous, fluid voice that cannot be easily defined. Minna is something more than a group of individuals. The use of Minna in education in Japan has promoted the inclusion of ambiguous ideas rather than the totalizing of diverse individuals' ideas.

Children who are learning to position their thoughts in light of the fluid standard of Minna are likely to be influenced by the opinions of other children. Therefore, they are not skilled in thinking by themselves. On the other hand, such children seem to be proficient in sympathizing with others and thinking about others' feelings.

The spirit of respecting one another and keeping harmony without excessive self-assertion is developed through educational activities to foster children's minds. In sports, festivals, and chorus competitions in Japanese schools, for example, classes compete, but it is considered most important to get involved in the competition as a team rather than to win the competition. Therefore, when a class wins the tournament, the certificate is posted on the blackboard visible to 'everyone.' The victory that the class wins is praise not for an individual but for Minna.

In addition, some educational activities in Japanese schools involve taking care of plants and animals such as rabbits, turtles, and parrots. Children take turns caring for and cooperating with these animals and plants. In addition, children participate in special activities such as classroom cleaning activities, club activities, and student council activities. The educational objectives of special activities are as follows:

1 Understand the significance of various collective activities that require cooperation with diverse people and how to engage in such activities.
2 Identify problems in the group, students' lives, and human relations, then discuss them to solve problems, form a consensus, and make decisions.
3 Make use of what we learn through voluntary and practical collective activities, form better human relationships in groups and society, and cultivate attitudes to deepen our thoughts about our way of life and to realise self-actualisation.[3]

These activities allow children to form their selfhood through group activities with other children.

In addition, Minna may refer to some of one's classmates involved in an activity, depending on the context. For example, when children state that 'Minna knows,' they mean that many of their classmates know, rather than all of their classmates know. In this case, a small number of children do not know and do not say 'I do not know well.' Rather, the children who do not know are silent and act as if they are included in Minna. Educational scholar Sato explains, although only the individual and its relationship exist in the classroom, it is conscious of a group called Minna that exists with a collective will. There is 'no other person in the schools' and classrooms of the Japanese education system from the beginning (Sato, 2012: 61).

There is no self in a classroom in which there is no other. This means that each child gives priority to the 'I' or role in the group, and the child's own outline becomes obscure. In Japanese schools, teachers refer to themselves as 'teacher' – even teachers make themselves ambiguous. In addition, if a child is recognised as a leader of a class, the criterion for recognition in the community of classes is not clear. For example, the criterion of approval will not only be identifiable by the class, in order to limit dissatisfaction, but will also help to differentiate criteria for recognition according to the class.

Conclusion: does Minna include people who are not present?

Finally, I would like to critically consider the Japanese education that I have observed. If the standard of recognition of Minna contributes to nurturing cooperativeness, will it nurture a public nature in students? The educational scholar Akio Miyadera says that mutuality, which refers to scenes in which students support all their own activities, does not have the same meaning as 'publicness' (Miyadera, 2014: 95). In terms of the condensability and cooperativeness created by activities involving Minna, he separates the openness of everyone and the public nature characterised by universality. From that point of view, actions for the class community to which the children belong are private acts, while critically reviewing the class's conduct from a third-person viewpoint is a public act. The viewpoint of a third person not only refers to 'judgment levelled by a neutral professional like a judge,' but an 'opinion or criticism that may be brought from others outside the community' (Miyadera, 2014: 95). That is, the public nature of 'pursuing objective and universal correctness rather than protecting what the parties think is good' (Miyadera, 2014: 95) is a different feature from cooperativeness.

If activities and thought by Minna do not include a 'normative occasion to invite the judgment of a third person' (Miyadera, 2014: 95), that activity cannot be regarded as a public activity. Actions in Minna and thinking with Minna, in order to become public activities, must consider objective correctness beyond the correctness of Minna and Minna from the viewpoint of those who are not there. In other words, too much emphasis on Minna in class may cause students to lose sight of publicness. The publicness of Minna's action has to be considered for everyone based on diversity, including those who have never met or those of different generations. The publicness of the Minna's actions has to be considered 'for anyone.'

Educational activities in which people work together do not contradict this community and public nature. Even if there is an emphasis on nurturing mutuality, including everyone who is not there when a person thinks about something, it changes to public activity 'for Minna.' In this way, the activity of Minna has an ambiguous nature that shifts between cooperativeness and publicness, making the quality of activities, such as how children work, important.

The results of the Programme for International Student Assessment (PISA) indicate that Japanese schools have focused on language activities since 2000. However, as previously discussed, it is very difficult for students to state their own ideas in Japanese classrooms. Communication mediated by Minna is different from communication in the present global society based on the opinions of individuals. Therefore, in Japanese classrooms, there are cases where rules for discussion are set. In the classroom, although teachers encourage students to reveal their thoughts, children do not positively speak about their own ideas. Children in the classroom face a dilemma because they are in the classroom as ambiguous selves even though they must express their thoughts in class. Even explaining the environment of each child is difficult when considering others in the class.

On a daily basis, children at Japanese schools practice communication based on empathy. For that reason, words are not the means of expressing desires and intentions and are instead the means of connecting one's thoughts with others' thoughts and expressing ideas in this connection. A student who says 'my idea' does not mean 'my perfect idea.' In the classroom, children are not highly conscious of themselves; they exchange opinions, including empathy for other people while reading the *Kuuki* (空気, 'air') in the classroom and promoting communication that closely connects language and sensibility.

Takashi Saito, a Japanese educational researcher, stated that Kuuki is composed of 'the context of the talk' and 'each Mi (body),' and the state of the body of each individual participating in communication creates air in the place (Saito, 2004: 126–127). For example, since a sour person emits a mood from the whole body, the air on the spot is worse, so a speaker changes the content of discussion while talking with the other person. In this way, 'the Kuuki of the place has a great influence on communication' (Saito, 2004: 128). Saito talks about communication reading Kuuki:

> First breathe in and out and relax. Calm down and look around firmly. Be careful of your eyes and take care. Those who are bored should not show emotions of outrage, those who are loners, who talk too much, and who are cold should consider how each person faces the place they are involved. Each person cultivate[s] the atmosphere of a place. By observing each person carefully, the sensibility of the atmosphere of the place also increases.
>
> (Saito, 2004: 129)

This communication style can accelerate today's child recognition problem if it is advanced without consideration for the human body's conditions. The sociologist Takayoshi Doi regards the characteristics of communication between children and young people in Japan as 'characterisation' and 'friendly relationships.' Children hone delicate and sophisticated communication skills in order to acquire recognition and places in groups, rather than to express their own claims clearly and build relationships with others (Doi, 2009). In post-modern society, the certainty and commonality of values and norms are relieved, and children in the growth process seek recognition by familiar people and establish themselves as significant beings through it. Therefore, children believe things because Minna believes them. Rather than believing in group values, they dare to trust and achieve recognition, even though they do not truly believe in the value of the group (Yamatake, 2011: 35).

The delicate communication skills found in Japanese children have developed in response to the fluidization of recognition order and are necessary for continuing to consider Minna in small groups. The objects imitated in the group are familiar people, fellow groups, and Minna. In other words, one's recognition in fellow groups is desired not because the value of the group is important but because by mimicking the action and beliefs of the group, one becomes a fellow and may achieve recognition from the group. The fluidization of the criteria for such recognition will accelerate the vague self. Collective learning through Minna always includes ambiguous self-formation.

Can we think not only about those who are present in Minna but also about persons who are not there? This form of imagination is the key to 'publicness.' In other words, in order for collective learning through Minna to maintain a public nature, it is important to use imagination to think about the absentee. As SNS technologies have evolved, people now may have no difficulty in thinking of Minna as including absent people.

Furthermore, self-formation via Nothingness also promotes an ambiguous self. The absence of the end point of self-formation is a feature of education that digs out the unfinished self as Nothingness. This type of learning promotes education that grows with consideration for others and relations through Nothingness.

Children are part of a group of peers and a learning group, and they encounter recognition in the process of growth. The self is formed through both intimate and public relationships. Japan's concept of Manabi and care for ambiguous groups and Minna is not a growth model in which individuals and society collide with one another to form a self; it is a growth style learned in the Seken.

Today, Japanese teachers attempt to help children develop the skills and abilities required in a global society. At the same time, they also try to build good relationships with local people in the Seken by participating in regional events. Thus, Japanese teachers live in a dualistic world as adults living in the Seken and as professional teachers.

Notes

1 See the following resource: www.edu.city.yokohama.jp/tr/ky/k-center/shihyou-1.pdf [referred to December 29, 2018]
2 The author interviewed the principal on February 2, 2018.
3 See the following resource: www.mext.go.jp/component/a_menu/education/micro_detail/__icsFiles/afieldfile/2018/05/07/1387017_15_1.pdf [referred to December 29, 2018]

Bibliography

Abe, K. (1995) *Seken to ha Nanika*, Tokyo: Kodansha Gakujutu Bunko.
Doi, T. (2009) *Kyaraka suru/sareru Kodomotachi*, Tokyo: Iwanami Shoten.
Fadel, C., Bialik, M., & Trilling, B. (2015) *Four-Dimensional Education: The Competencies Learners Need to Succeed*, Boston: Center for Curriculum Redesign.

Ichikawa, H. (1993) *Mi no Kouzou*, Tokyo: Kodansha Gakujutsu Bunko.
Miyadera, A. (2014) *Kyouiku no Seigironn*, Tokyo: Keiso Shobo.
Nihon kokugo dai jiten second edition editing committee (2001) *Nihon kokugo dai jiten*, Tokyo: Shogakukan.
Numata, H. (2009) "Nihon no Roussou Kenkyuusya kara mita saikinn no nitihutu kyouiku kaikaku," Sonoyama, D., & Sabouret, J-F. eds. *Nitihutu hikaku hennyou suru syakai to kyouiku*, Tokyo: Akashi Shoten.
Saito, T. (2004) *Komyunikeishonryoku*, Tokyo: Iwanami Shinsho.
Sato, M. (1995) "Manabi no Taiwateki Jiisen he," Saeki, Y., Fujita, H., & Sato, M. eds. *Manabi he no Izanai*, Tokyo: Tokyo Daigaku Shuppan-kai.
Sato, M. (1997) *Manabino Shinntaigihou*, Tokyo: Tarojirosya.
Sato, M. (2012) *Gattkoukaikaku no Tetugaku*, Tokyo: Tokyo Daigaku Shuppan-kai.
Sato, N. (2001) *'Seken' no Gensyogaku*, Tokyo: Seikyusha.
Sato, N. (2015) *Hanzai no Sekengaku*, Tokyo: Seikyusha.
Takeuchi, S. (2012) *Yamatokotoba de tetugaku suru*, Tokyo: Shunjusha.
Tsujimoto, M. (2012) *Manabi no huuken*, Tokyo: Iwanami Shoten.
Tsuneyoshi, R. (1992) *Ninngennkeisei no Nichibeihikaku*, Tokyo: Chuko Shinsho.
Uchida, T. (2009) *Nihon Henkyoronn*, Tokyo: Shincho Shinsho.
Ueda, S. (2000) *Watashi toha nanika*, Tokyo: Iwanami Shinsho.
Washida, K. (2015) *Shingari no Sisou*, Tokyo: Kadokawa Shinsho.
Watsuji, T. (2016) *Nihongo to Tetugaku no Mondai*, Aichi: Keibunkan Shoten.
Yamatake, S. (2011) *Mitomeraretai no Syoutai*, Tokyo: Kodansha Shinsho.

Chapter 5

Inclusiveness in/of Manabi

Taku Murayama

Introduction

This chapter provides a description of Manabi in a special and inclusive practice. While it is worth noting the exclusive trends in education, it is inclusive education that is promoted in Japanese schools as well as in other countries, and the concept of Manabi refers to inclusive learning. Japanese schoolteachers and students value Manabi in a collaborative and reciprocal way. These days, the individualized educational plan and the learning of special education in Manabi have aspects of the change and the development both of the individual learner and of the static learner. Japanese culture does things according to Minna, a concept that suggests not a rigid group of members but the gradual and flexible connection of members' reciprocity. Japanese historian, Shirakawabe (2019) suggests that Japanese society is rooted in the culture of *Tanomu*. The Japanese verb *Tanomu* may be translated into English as 'leave,' 'call on,' 'ask for,' and so on, but Shirakawabe is attentive to the notion that the act of Tanomu includes the actor's responsibility for the person or neighbour (*Tanomareta* in Japanese) in the principle of reciprocity. Japanese schools also have an unconscious basis in this culture.

Inclusive education in Japanese schooling is constructed in a culture and comorbid system of inclusive schooling and partially segregated schooling. Though MEXT (Ministry of Education, Culture, Sports, Science and Technology, Japan) has been proposing a model project forming an inclusive education system, students with disabilities, illness, and other exceptional needs are not fully included but are only partially included. This is not the abandonment of full inclusion but the practical application of Manabi to the symbiotic culture of Minna (*Minna no Manabi*) and has a historical background.

Special needs education in Japan

Over the past decades in Japan, policy and opinion regarding how special education for children with disabilities should be conducted in regular classes have been expanded and promoted, as influenced by the United States and the United

Kingdom. But on the practical side, we can find the original context for disabled learners and workers. For example, in the early modern period, the disabled, especially the blind, have had a unique position in society, having been endowed with the exclusive right to get specific jobs and utilize specific tools. Small schools, *Terakoya* (寺子屋), have many students, with and without disabilities, who learn in the same schoolhouse *Manabiya* (学び舎, literally, 'the house of Manabi').

When discussing Japanese special needs education for the primary and secondary levels, it is necessary to separate the case for lower secondary education from the case for upper secondary education. This is due to fact that education at the primary and secondary levels is compulsory and the educational and social expectation that all students should attend the compulsory education system (*Minna ga Gakko ni iku*). The primary and secondary level educational system for meeting special educational needs is categorized into three main types according to the type of school. The first type consists of the special education school. Special schools exist in both the lower and the upper secondary levels and are prepared for students with five types of disabilities and illness: blindness and low vision, deafness and hearing disability, intellectual disabilities (including students who are diagnosed with autistic spectrum disorders with intellectual disabilities), physical impairment, and illness. Schools for children with intellectual disabilities have the greatest number of students, schools, and teachers. Target students of the special schools constitute about 1% of all students at the secondary level. Many regulations have been prepared for special education schools. For example, the School Education Act regulates the role of special education schools, the targets for the types of disabilities of the students, and the obligation of each prefecture (local government) to establish special schools for meeting student needs. The Ordinance for Enforcement of the School Education Act regulates the subjects and the contents for special education schools. All special schools are required to practice the contents of the 'self-care activities' for improving and diminishing the difficulties resulting from the disabilities and illnesses of individual students. In principle, the schools, except the schools for children with intellectual disabilities, are to prepare a program and curriculum based on regular schooling. The schools for children with intellectual disabilities are required to create a program that differs from those of the other types of schools, the main differences relating to the goals and content of the subjects taught in the schools. In the case of students with multiple and severe disabilities, the curriculum for children with intellectual disabilities is distinct even if they learn in the special schools. The roles of the special education schools parallel those of the regional centre for special needs education. The teachers and coordinators are required to collaborate with secondary schools, counselling centres, medical centres, and hospitals near the schools.

The second aspect concerns special education classes. These classes are supported by the regulations regarding public schooling and the aim of schooling all students in the area at the same schools (*Minna Onaji Gakko de Manabu*). These classes are established in the regular primary and junior high schools, but there is no systematically compulsory system for this type of class at the upper secondary level. In some limited examples, senior high schools have a section for students with disabilities, but most of these students are in a separate section in special schools. The special classes are divided into seven types in accordance with the target disability and illness: low vision, hearing difficulties, intellectual disabilities (including autistic spectrum disorder with intellectual disabilities), physical impairment, illness, emotional disturbance, and speech disorders. The number of students in the special classes are 1–2% of all students, but the number of students has been increasing despite a decrease in the total number of students of school age (Ministry of Education, Culture, Sports, Science and Technology, 2018). Almost half of the lower secondary schools have special classes, and the students partly commute to the regular classes with students of the same age. The maximum number of students in one class is eight, and the feature of the special classes is the smaller size of the learning community. As a general rule, since they are established in the secondary schools, the curriculum and programs are based on the regular secondary schools, but the Ordinance for Enforcement of the School Education Act authorizes exceptions if it is necessary to plan and practice a program based on the national curriculum of special education schools. The difference in the curriculum for the special classes is linked to evaluations and report cards. The differentiation of the report cards is said to be a risk factor when students in special classes apply for the entrance examination for high schools, since it is necessary to submit the achievement record of each student when applying for the high school entrance examination.

The third aspect is regular educational classes with attendance in special classes for specialized and effective learning and training in accordance with the special educational needs of the students. This system, utilizing the resource room, is common at the lower secondary level but in 2018 began at the upper level, where there are few practical examples as yet. There are nine categories designated as targets of student disabilities and illness: low vision, hearing disability, physical impairment, illness, emotional disturbance, speech disorders, learning disabilities, attention-deficit hyperactivity disorders, and high-functioning autistic spectrum disorders. At most, guaranteed attendance is eight hours per week, and the students are in regular classes for most schooldays. The number of students in this type of class are 4–6% of the total number of students, but the number has been rapidly increasing since around 2004. The number of students with emotional disturbances, maladjustment, and psychosomatic diseases especially has risen sharply. While half of the secondary schools have these types of classes, there are discussions about the gap in opportunities for attending these classes (Ministry of Education, Culture, Sports, Science and Technology, 2018). This system is based on the assumption that it is desirable for students to learn in regular classes with typical students and with longer school time, and it has been reflected in the policy and thought for inclusive education.

The selection and allocation of students at the lower secondary level are based on discussions and requests by the council for special needs education in each municipality (cities, towns, villages, and the districts in the largest cities). Discussions in the council are based on a medical diagnosis, psychological assessment (WISC, K-ABC, DN-CAS, and others), observation records of the student's behaviour in classrooms and so on. In the revision of the national course of study in 2017, there is an obligation to teach self-care activities in the special classes based on the special schools program. As a general rule, education in inclusive settings is the principle, but special education schools and classes are utilised if the special needs for each student can be realised only in separated environments. Even in this the case, students are to be placed in regular classes as soon as possible. After graduation, following the course for the upper secondary level is recommended, and many graduates proceed to the upper secondary section in the special schools. However, in some cases, entrance examinations have been established, especially in schools where value is placed on vocational education.

In recent years, policies for 'schools as teams' have been put forward for special needs education, and some professionals have committed themselves to this kind of schooling, typically school counsellors, assistants for learning support, school social workers, and so on. In the special schools, caregiving staff for severely disabled children, occupational therapists, physical therapists, and speech therapists are partly engaged in special needs education. Teachers and other school personnel carefully support diverse learners with special educational needs in a contingent place of learning. In Japanese schooling, special educational needs include not only disabilities and the illness but the teachers' sense of the students' worrying or troublemaking. Only doctors diagnose and confirm children's disabilities and illness, but teachers may sense the exceptional needs of children when they are learning individually or in the group settings in Minna. Classroom teachers may suggest that the parents consult a doctor or psychological counsellor regarding the exceptionality of their children. The students' ratio of the special educational needs is 6.5% according to the national survey, but many teachers have a sense that the ratio is more like 20%. The rise in the number of students going to the resource room and in the number of personnel aside from teachers is reflected in the school climate as the number of exceptional students increases. Given this rise in the numbers, the need to guarantee Manabi in the schools and the importance of the roles of staff have led to a growing awareness that meeting students' needs must be performed as a team. These efforts are related to the thought of educating and caring for all students (Minna) not only by classroom teachers but by all staff within and outside the schools.

Social change for inclusion in the Japanese context

After World War II, as a general rule, special education for physically and mentally disabled children effectively segregated them from students in the regular/ordinary education system. This pervasive segregation in the education system reflected the development of the principle of ability education in the 1960s. In other words, thorough classifications were made according to the principle of ability and depending on the kind and degree of a students' disability. In the Japanese context, especially on the systemic side of special education, the organization of the school system remained subdivided and fixed in the latter half of the twentieth century. The traditional thought in special education placed much value on the disabled child's ability to focus when dealing with the value and culture of non-disabled persons. For example, educational opportunities were decided based on the capacity for work and the potential for becoming a member of the taxpaying public.

Educational policymakers and researchers have not rigidly protected the segregated or dual system, but recently the movement and policies for inclusive education have rapidly been promoted. The practice of Manabi in inclusive settings has been explored in many ways in educational practice, including the places where Manabi takes place.

Researchers, practitioners, and policymakers have been sensitive to the movements and shifts in educational policy, and after the 1990s, the shift toward integration and inclusion has increased under the influence of the 1994 Salamanca Declaration. Integration or inclusion may seem to be an expression of a dominant humanistic ideology in special education (Oliver, 1996; Swain & Cook, 2005). Oliver has indicated that the educational literature on integration sees the whole issue as non-problematic. But, strictly investigated, inclusion involves selection for inclusion and thus becomes an exclusive process (Swain & Cook, 2005). This is especially true of the gap between the spoken language and sign language in the public schools in Japan.

Given the compulsory education requirement, entrance to special schools such as schools for the blind or disabled versus general education schools has caused conflict. Parents and guardians of disabled children insist that their children or charges receive normal, integrated, and inclusive instruction, while the Board of Education wants parents and protectors to cease any negative behaviour toward non-disabled students.

Opposition between two conventional ways of thinking continues to exist regarding concrete solutions for the education of disabled children with special educational needs. The first way of thinking respects the idea that children with disabilities have their needs most effectively met in schools for disabled children (a segregated education approach). On the other hand, others have a normalized way of thinking about disabled children's education and believe they should generally learn with other children in mainstream schools; this viewpoint is represented by the term 'normalization' (integrated or inclusive education theory).

Besides these opposing opinions, there is another difference in the way of thinking about the rights of a disabled child to receive education. One argument claims that only segregation can efficiently correspond to the specialized educational needs of disabled children, making it best to educate those with disabilities in segregated environments. In contrast, those who insist on integration or inclusion argue that 'a right to receive an integrated or inclusive education' is a leading factor in disabled children's right to education and can be considered essential to 'the personal dignity' that the Constitution of Japan is based on, and it is therefore essential to 'normalization' (Shibasaki, 2000). In other words, integration or inclusion is given top priority over the correspondence to special needs promoted by the segregation perspective, and from the integration and inclusion theory perspective, it will ultimately benefit a disabled child to learn with normal children, even if, to some extent, this means sacrificing the correspondence of education to needs. Multiple meanings can be derived from the Constitution of Japan and from other laws and ordinances concerning whether the segregated education theory or the integrated and inclusive theory is fair. Moreover, regarding the perspective expressed by the Convention on the Rights of the Child, a child has the right to express his or her own opinion, and, depending on the child's developmental stage, this viewpoint, which leaves a lot of room for self-decision on the part of the disabled child, should be adopted. Backed by integration trials in advanced countries, the United Nations demanded that each country promote integration during the International Year of Disabled Persons. However, it was assumed that Japan was already 'concerned with the basis of the educational system' and did not need to comply with this request.

The duality of the education system did not arise to any great extent from the general idea of integration but was rather socially and historically formed in response to the development of the modern educational system. Additionally, 'integration' had been introduced as a theoretical device to overcome this dual system, considering both its merits and its drawbacks, the general idea being that such a theoretical device would be sufficient. On the other hand, lumping all education together ineffectively and continuing to forgive the dumping and various other tropes such as 'segregation' should not be allowed. In other words, it seems that one of the reasons why integration as a general idea is criticised is that integration as a theoretical device to overcome dualism is related to the phenomenon that recognizes dualism as the reality of the situation. Thus, integration is confused with integration as a theoretical device and a phenomenon. Traditionally, education for disabled children has occurred in spaces different from those used for other children. In Europe and the United States, the nineteenth century is considered to have been the beginning of the creation of educational opportunities for physically and mentally disabled children as part of the modern education system, and educational institutions for the disabled were formed that differed from those for normal children. The conventionally segregated education paradigms are declared an impropriety and are disputed by supporters of the integrated and inclusive paradigm. The situation that we face can be described as a maelstrom of this paradigm shift. The integrated and inclusive paradigm is not always theorized clearly in Japan. Thus, in the present condition, I cannot identify a clear point of agreement.

Some introductions and commentaries also address the distinction between integration and inclusion. There is, however, no unified education policy, due to a lack of clarity about the meaning of the switchover from integration to inclusion for the practicality of education in Japan, where these issues have not yet been definitively debated. Compared with Europe and the United States, Japan has an extremely peculiar structure. The chance of an 'isolated' child taking a step is low, even in a developed nation with strong unification of society and research and clear definitions for education policy. Additionally, other children themselves can guess that education paradigms are not unified when the support system for disabled children in general education classes is completely insufficient.

The aim to change the social whole into something more inclusive by realising more inclusive schools can be seen in the Salamanca Declaration. This was expected to act as an antithesis to the existing Japanese 'segregated education' approach because the maintenance and availability (total number) of schools that educate students with disabilities may not always be adequate. The Japanese education system has also been influenced and stimulated by international trends.

The argument over places of attendance for children with disabilities has tended to drift between 'segregation or unification' and 'development security or symbiosis education' or an argument for an alternative vocational education. In contrast, in the mid-1980s, suggestions for the reform of education for physically and mentally disabled children began to appear from countries overseas that encourage special needs education and integration because all students have the right to education. The Education Ministry persisted in its 'education for the disabled' system, bringing it to a head at the beginning of the 1990s. Meanwhile, however, the number of disabled children per class in each school remained below 1%; this was a situation in which reform of the existing system could not be avoided. Consequently, the 1994 Salamanca Declaration was introduced into Japan, and systemic reform was to be based on the idea of special needs education as something inclusive, which would become a point of debate. Until recently, it has certainly been rare for 'regular' educators to show real consideration for disabled children during both curricular and extracurricular activities in the classroom, although these educators claim to embrace 'integration.' For this reason, disabled children attending regular schools stand alone, educationally and socially. In the discussion of integration, procedural paradoxes seem to emerge regarding the terms 'integration' and 'inclusion.' Because the latter term's intended use was to improve the former conceptually, there has been much discussion of the integration of certain categories of disabilities. However, discussions of integration differ according to the category of a disability. Particularly, according to the theoretical base of disability studies, hearing disabilities, including deafness, are addressed comprehensively in the discourse (Sakata, 2002). Attention is focused on deaf people and their group, and it is argued that deaf children develop positive identities as deaf adults if they have constant contact with other deaf children, which eases inner conflict. It is thought that the only way to overcome disabilities and to succeed in socially competitive communities dominated by hearing people is to obtain an education in a school for the deaf and to learn sign language. In contrast, a child with a hearing impairment attending a general school must use a hi-tech hearing aid, and, as a result, may feel isolated from the community and culture of people with hearing disabilities. In Japan, especially following the 'deaf culture' declaration in 2000 (Kimura & Ichida, 1995), the distinctiveness and foreignness of the language of the deaf from the Japanese language have been recognized, and discussion has addressed how Japanese sign language and the culture of the deaf differs from Japanese spoken language. From this point on, the aim of this chapter is to discuss the literacy of hearing-disabled children through a review of preceding studies, and to further address the themes of the special nature of deaf culture and its position in the context of cultural studies. Cultural studies has moved from its earlier emphasis on adult literacy, class analysis, and youth cultures to its late concern with feminism, racial popular culture, and identity politics (Giroux, 1996). Literacy and identity politics are treated in the following sections.

A short review of deaf education in Japan

Oda (2002) organized and conducted a historical review of issues related to the literacy of children with hearing impairments. He established that the reason the use of the word 'literacy' had become common in the area of education for the deaf stemmed from the widely held opinion that the connection between the mastery of language and different types of abilities, especially the ability to write, should be discussed. First, Oda introduced Tashiro Furukawa and his book *Mou A Kyojyu Sankosho* (*A Reference Book for the Instruction of the Blind and the Dumb*), written at the time (1878) of the opening of *Kyoto Mou A In* (Kyoto House for the Blind and the Dumb), a school that coincided with the beginning of literacy discussions in deaf education. Furukawa thought that traditional sign language was not enough for deaf students and that their practice of Manabi should visually teach them the form of the Japanese language through letters and lip reading, as well as sign language.

Around this time, an oral teaching method was completed, the education of the deaf became professionally established, and deaf education switched to a teaching method mainly based on sign language due to the faultiness of pronunciation guidance and hearing training. This was a theoretical and practical forerunner of the oral method. Unosuke Kawamoto called Furukawa's method 'multilingualism,' as his method included the language of sound, fingers, writing, four kinds of sign language, and a wide variety of lip-reading methods. Kawamoto's concept of multiculturalism does not correspond with its modern meaning. He suggested the main point is not which linguistic code one uses but the various modes of expression. He used the term 'multilingualism' to point out the differences in expressive modes, such as spoken language, body language, and the language of written letters (or printed characters). However, given his view of literacy, Furukawa's method qualifies as multilingualism for the variety of the modes it incorporates into the context of the language use of hearing-impaired children. Furthermore, Rihei Sakurai suggested that the basis for deaf education in the modern era is as follows:

1   Emphasis on terms and viewpoints of communication
2   The idea that a language is not taught but learned (*Manabareru* in the original Japanese text)
3   Emphasis on the use of hearing ability and early intervention

Sakurai argued against Kawamoto's theory and on behalf of the utterance environment theory, which posits that a deaf child speaks not only by instinct but because of environment.

Literacy of children with hearing impairments

The view that special students would have equality of opportunity for a good education or school participation if they were placed in a mainstream classroom is also difficult to maintain because the situation for each student may well be different (Farrell, 2010). Uenou (2003) interpreted the issue of literacy for children with hearing loss as a problem of inclusion. At first, he criticised the principle of spoken communication and easy integration for misunderstanding the literacy acquisition a hearing-impaired child receives not in schools but from the parents (in most cases the mother). It is often said that the academic achievements of integrated children are considerably low, but academic achievement was also seen as having nothing to do with language ability. The premise of this view is that language ability and academic achievement are different matters. Even if a student has language ability, this may not always become manifest as academic achievement. In fact, what is necessary is not temporary scholastic ability but real language ability, the ability to communicate and express human gentleness in a manner considerate of others. Uenou suggested the concretization of the definition, purpose, and effect of 'academic achievement' as the solution to this 'paradox.'

Achievement in the area of deaf education and integration has not been discussed in this way. Many disabled children in inclusive settings are segregated in the environment of Manabi formed by the other students in the class (Minna) without understanding the purpose and the real effect of Manabi. They devote their time to self-directed study at home in order to catch up with their lessons.

Toshiharu Takeuchi, a director with hearing impairment, tells a similar story of his own experience in his schooldays as a student with impaired hearing. It is important to note that the essential cause of learning difficulties and low achievement is that children who are hard of hearing have been forced to be part of a learning environment in which they have insufficient support for their studies and information processing and the support systems that do exist have not worked well, according to Uenou. Uenou's argument reveals the story behind the failure of Minna ('the silent majority') that has been overlooked despite integrated-and-inclusive's reputation for success. The systematic promotion of inclusion has produced this silent majority. What has, at first glance, been seen as an equalizer is in fact a discrimination device that creates a new differentiation. Many teachers and parents of children with hearing impairment tend to withdraw from the oral method and seek environments for Manabi that teach sign language. Therefore, Japanese sign language is part of literacy education in the Japanese language. Recently, bilingual education has become a focus. At first, children learn the basics of sign language and then proceed to rise to a higher level of competence. However, the differences and gaps between sign language and spoken Japanese continue to cause problems. According to Uenou, the social mission behind promoting the integration of deaf education has been literacy education, especially education in written Japanese.

As the basis for the development through the practice of Manabi, including the attainment of academic skills and perceptions, is the written language, which defines students' identities, but the diverse languages and tools enable the effective practice of Manabi in inclusive education. In the composition guidance portion of language arts, the 'deafness sentence' has been regarded as an inferior and inappropriate sentence that includes errors of convention. For example, when children, basing their sentence structure on sign language, use handwritten words or type on a PC, they write sentences such as, 'It is cleaning in a corridor' or 'What I did at an athletic meet is to run.' These samples apply the pattern of the predicate to words such as 'is' or 'do,' expressed by the same sign. They also rely on the grammar of sign language that deaf students already possess and use to show logic in their meaning. But in Japanese sign language, this is natural for them when communicating and composing their works. Therefore, instead of regarding this writing as 'an error' or inferior, such 'misuse' should be effectively utilized as shared infrastructure for reaching higher levels of understanding of the different grammars of sign language and the Japanese language. In most cases in regular classes, however, such sentences result in the deduction of points.

Language as a barrier/medium

At this point, it is necessary to return to the topic established earlier and to discuss which language forms the culture of schools when certain communities are divided according to language. Tomiaki Yamada pointed out that the 'issue of language' appeared in the 1960s and did not refer to a limited problem; rather, 'a language problem' relates to the political interests of the groups in conflict with each other (Yamada, 2006). It is usual for each group to have different interests, as no language planning or management can be neutral, free from all 'interests,' and politically disvalued. In other words, there are no interests that all community members share and none that cannot be criticised on grounds of justice or the principle of abstraction imposed from a higher level. This claim reflects the 'process of politics' in which a group removes and changes the interests of other groups in order to prioritize its own interests. The relationship between culture and identity is highly complex. The concept of identity lies at the heart of the moral dilemma inherent in the idea of culture. Language and interest as a form of cultural representation found in classroom materials are also crucial in the development of identity (Buzzelli & Johnston, 2002).

Inclusion, in a phrase, is the mainstreaming of the disabled into the robust community of regular schools, which makes it difficult for different groups to relate to one another. In classrooms, the power figure defines learning abilities on the premise of hearing and speaking abilities. However, while many children and teachers accept and correspond to the 'norm' of verbal language use, students in certain categories end up excluded from membership in the learning community because they are not able to use oral language. As Yamada suggested, this shows the difficulty of establishing cooperation in communication. For example, in the Japanese education of the 1960s, the inclusion of disabled people in the robust community was seen as categorically imperative for curing their impairment, and it was thought to be the only way to achieve social rehabilitation and participation. For the disabled and their family members, there seemed to be no hope in these years, except through medical care with the potential to cure the impairment. Far from affirming those with hearing disabilities, a negative view toward the disability and perceptions of the disability as undesirable spread among the general public. Having a disability meant being immediately placed in lower education categories by people who do not pause to think about the principle behind the stigma of deafness, and this situation has contributed to requests for inclusion as a break from segregated education.

Mashiko introduced the general idea of the 'language right' for examining such a problem (Mashiko, 2006). Disability studies seem important in the attempt to solve and improve the conflict between the communities of the deaf and blind and the robust community. The 'care,' 'treatment,' and 'consideration' of the 'good experts' for disabled recipients have been regarded as an obligatory intervention that led to domination. Oral education methods or inner ear operations were often the norm. In this way, for people with difficulty accessing normal spoken Japanese, language serves as a device that constitutes relations of domination and subordination. It forms new divisions between those who can commit to certain activities and causes alienation according to superiority and inferiority in scenes of integration. A deaf school was, in a phrase, the institutionalization of education for disabled children produced by ideas of paternalism, which suppressed sign language as a first language for deaf people and developed the principle of assimilated education, compelling students to engage in spoken language. For example, the education of the disabled has been radically criticised for ghettoizing special education, leading to the push for inclusion with general education and the establishment of a system that adequately cares for students. Nonetheless, this argument does not necessarily apply to deaf education in regard to sign language. In previous eras, most schoolteachers of the deaf were hearing persons who forced their students to imitate the form of their mouths and make utterances under 'the principle of mouth talk,' forbidding the use of sign language. However, the students continued to engage in voluntary sign language training, making the deaf school their primary speech community. It became impossible for people with partial hearing loss that comes with old or middle age to participate in the culture of the deaf community. At that stage, their flexibility would have been lost due to physical changes to their bodies, making it difficult to learn sign language; additionally, few people who have learned language among the hearing can internalize deaf culture, a fact that also alienated those with partial hearing loss from deaf communities. In these cases, the silent majority Minna functions as a barrier to symbiosis and the inclusive culture of education, and the struggle for inclusion has an aspect of assimilation into the Minna.

Manabi for students with special needs: a case of the art project

We face a number of difficult dimensions when exploring Manabi for students with special educational needs. Doing so requires a thorough understanding of the content in order to teach it in multiple ways, drawing on the cultural backgrounds and prior knowledge and experiences of students. This is also informative for exploring the character of Manabi, even though it concerns the area of inclusive and special needs education. The case survey in this section inquires into the notion and character of Manabi in inclusive settings.

The case presented is an ongoing art activity project by regular school students and multiple and severely disabled students. This project has meaning as fieldwork and provides opportunities for reciprocal and collaborative activities with the disabled and non-disabled students.

In this series, a fieldwork survey has been attempted. Junior and senior high school students visited special schools and were active in the same place and with the same theme in the art activities. The focus is on their awareness and recognition of Manabi – including non-verbal instances – of the multiply disabled and the change in university students' views regarding the multiply disabled students' learning and activities through the art activities.

The course of study for special education schools in Japan, the curriculum contents of the subject of 'arts and crafts' (at the primary level) and of the 'arts' (at the secondary level) are regulated and are as shown in Table 5.1.

The table gives all the described contents in the course of study of art in the national curriculum of Japan. The reason for these scanty descriptions is that the curriculum contents are highly dependent on the situations of the students, including the types and severity of disabilities and illness, the accumulation

Inclusiveness in/of Manabi   115

Table 5.1 Contents list for the subject of art in special schools in Japan

Arts and Crafts (Primary)

1st level

1 To have an interest in drawing, creating, decorating, and so on
2 To play with formative arts using familiar materials such as clay, wood, and paper

2nd level

1 To draw, model, and decorate what they see and feel
2 To become familiar with and use materials and tools such as clay, crayons, scissors, and paste

3rd level

1 Thoughtful drawing and creating, as well as decorating and using what students have seen, felt, and imagined
2 Thoughtful use of materials and tools for their purpose
3 Showing their own artworks to one another among friends, and noticing the appeal of shape, colour, and ways of expression of plastic artworks and so on

Art (Secondary: All Levels)

1 Planning (artwork), drawing pictures, making artworks, and decorating them based on their experience and imagination
2 Understanding and using various types of materials and tools
3 Being familiar with the beauty of nature and plastic artworks

---

of knowledge and skills in their daily lives, and their environment. It is then necessary to think of the students' individualities in special educational settings. Teachers should devise appropriate teaching methods and materials for their students' individualized situations. As the students show a wide variety of developmental and health conditions, the common contents in the national curriculum are not applicable to many students. Thus students have few opportunities to learn and think about the school subject for learners with special needs. The SNE students learn about the subject knowledge with non-disabled students in mind and therefore have few chances to learn and inquire about the practice of Manabi.

The project was developed to support learning about art at a special school for the severely disabled and volunteer students from regular schools. In terms of participants, the group now consists of the regular school students and the students at a special school with the collaboration of teachers. A further special school proposed to join us at the point of the exhibition. Students in the regular schools prepared the materials for the workshop with some research on the school beforehand.

The project was originally designed and organized around networking between the special and regular schools in the neighbourhood through arts activities. In the preparation process of the workshop, the concept of Manabi and the meaning of the activities formed by Minna had been noticed. The school with which we collaborated is for students with severe physical impairments and with needs for constant medical observation. This small school is therefore attached to the National Institute of Neurology and Psychiatry, and our workshop has been partly held in the daily caring room in the hospital or sometimes in a bedroom in a ward. Given this opportunity to join the project, components of the regular school students' study were implemented as an extra-curricular program. The mission of this project is to design a network between regular and special schools by endowing them with a specific background in the contents of fine arts, as well as understanding the particular needs of diverse learners (especially severely multiply disabled teens, as in this project) with respect to practicing Manabi. The aim of the project is to immerse regular students in the restricted situation of the impaired students to provide direct experiences with knowledge and skill development.

Process of the workshop

In the workshop in the hospitalized class, one student with multiple impairments and two or three regular school students make up a working group, which then attempts to give concrete shape to and share the younger student's ideas. Special attention has been given to the role of students in both schools in making artworks. Because of the unbalanced number of participants (three regular school students per junior on average, as well as teachers and nurses who participate for health reasons), we are paying attention to how we can promote the disabled students' independence and activeness.

The project suggests the collaboration and practical inquiry that exists between the disciplines, as well as the application of concepts to new situations. This project is committed to providing not only special school students with experience in art but also regular school students with the experience of producing decoration with disabled students and special education teachers.

At the beginning of the project, we recommended that the art students investigate the possibilities and issues of art activities for the disabled and suggested that students in special needs education inquire into the deepening of knowledge and teaching contents of the subject (in this case, art). Later, the project expanded into collaborative activities through the gathering and selecting of materials, choosing the topic (the topic this year is 'sky [with clouds]'), and inquiring into how to address the disabled students (*Koekake*), and so on. Furthermore, the project helps regular students integrate pedagogy and content in the various phases of activities in this project workshop.

A variety of comments can be seen in Table 5.2, and we can also note that they include comments about both the artistic phase and the teaching phase. It is, of course, difficult to divide the activities into two phases, but it is helpful for inquiring into the character of Manabi practice.

Taking an overview of this table, some features of Manabi are revealed through these art activities. The disabled students' disabilities and illnesses

Table 5.2 The contents of Mananda (what was learned) in the activities

Phase	Aspects	Examples of student utterance
Artistic phase	Enjoying the materials	• What do the disabled students like? • What's the meaning of the art experience itself? • Touching unusual materials, which they have few opportunities to do
	Artistic aspects	• Selection of materials (cloth, colours, etc.) • Selection of adhesive bond (ease of use, texture of bond, etc.)
	Creation process	• Students learned from the disabled students through their reactions, what they liked, etc. • A process of visualization was developed from the concept of the sky and clouds.
	The artwork	• How to have disabled students form an image or make sense of the artwork as a whole (Each group made a separate part of the artwork.) • The students' personal preferences for colours (This can be researched in advance, but is that good for us?)
Activities phase	Kinesthetic aspects	• The process of multiply disabled students' body tonus (The art activities would be more effective after reducing their tonus.) • Motion (even if only a little) creates possibilities for a new sense of touch. • Noticing the line of sight as an effective approach for smooth contact.
	Non-verbal communication	• How to recognize that communication has been established and what conditions can be set up • The importance of communication in teaching practice • The importance for regular school students to observe the younger student's eyes (including the line of sight) • Communication style through design and production of the artworks
	Collaboration among students	• (Many art students said they learned about) how to open up to the disabled students and understand their intentions (mainly y/n). • (Many SNE students said they learned about) how to develop the image of an artwork in situations involving limited materials and conditions. • Further expectations for future collaborative learning

present a possibility of restricting their learning potential, and thus it is preferable to arrange for the educational materials to be easy to use. The environment of Manabi, including the environment of learning materials and the environment of human relationships, is an effective condition for escaping alienation from the practice of Manabi for all students.

In special educational settings, since individualized teaching is stressed, it may be possible to prepare materials for individual use, unless the disabled student's learning is not isolated in the classroom context and close human relations exist with friends and teachers. This means that students with special needs are placed in the classroom formed by Minna, and the collaborative activities promote Manabi in the inclusive classrooms.

Through what is reflected in this workshop, kinesthetic perspectives and the attention to non-verbal communication have also been emphasized. Disabilities may impose linguistic limits in the reflection, and therefore teachers' knowledge regarding the context of learning and understanding of the disabilities and restrictions on learning are high requirements in the classroom.

In the arena of teacher education, reflection by the teacher in lesson studies has attracted attention as a need for the professional development of teachers. Ramanaidu et al. (2014) suggests that in music education teacher training, a crucial element in the teacher training programme is lesson planning and that pre-service teachers were helped during the practicum by giving them ideas and holding discussions during the planning stage. Our project also enabled the regular students to have useful opportunities through the planning workshop including preparing the materials, contents, and designing the original works for Manabi, as well as care and treatment for the younger multiply disabled.

The character of art for all learners

Gregoire and Lupinetti (2005) suggest that art is a great equalizer in education, regardless of abilities or disabilities. Because the arts are largely non-verbal and focus on creativity, students can participate in various ways. Gregoire and Lupinetti also insist, 'Fortunately, the arts can reach all types of students.' Consequently, success in school for many students can be supported and facilitated through an arts program that is infused throughout the curriculum. *This may* go as far as to include students with multiple disabilities. The curriculum would be infused with art for multiple disabled students and for students in pre-service teacher training.

Cornett (2003) advocated that integrating the arts into the curriculum would have particular relevance to diverse classrooms. One relevance is that the arts are fundamental to all cultures and time periods and therefore provide a natural view into the social contribution of other cultures. The arts are primary forms of communication because they are based on imagination and cognition. Additionally, the arts may focus on alternative forms of assessment and evaluation (Gregoire & Lupinetti, 2012).

Art includes partly non-verbal activities and is therefore suitable for students with considerable linguistic limitations, but what Gregoire and colleagues suggest would not necessarily be the best place to start a discussion. The experience of creating visual art by communicating with simple verbal language would provide the basis for language development.

While developmental approaches toward content for severely disabled learners have the advantage of tradition and a wealth of excellent examples to adapt from, some educators question their appropriateness and efficacy (Ferguson, 1987). Available data suggest that severely disabled students do not acquire skills in the normal developmental sequence, often because of the complicating factors of sensory, medical, and motor difficulties. Ferguson also stresses that developmental approaches focus on determining content – 'what to teach' – with little concurrent emphasis on instructional techniques and strategies, the 'how to teach.' As regards students' viewpoints, this workshop holds the essence of Manabi for diverse learners. In this case, art functions as a bond for Minna, and the Manabi in art stands upon the activities by Minna.

As for the International Classification of Functioning, Disability and Health (ICF) by WHO, the social function and the degree of 'participation' of the disabled have been stressed. This workshop has aimed not to directly upgrade the physical function of multiply disabled students but to enable the promotion of their 'participation' into Manabi through the collaborative activities of arts and supporting communication by diverse students, even if the younger person is unable to speak. Disabled learners are activated collaboratively around Minna through designing and working. In this case, art activity is effective for Manabi for diverse learners.

Conclusion

Art is essentially said to be concerned with the making and sharing of meanings and stimulates the process of personal growth. Arguably this gives form and expression to an inner drive to externalize images. Perhaps we all have some inner need to communicate, to find forms of expression, and to symbolize or encapsulate our experiences – ways in which we may all find a sense of personal validation. In school we need to ensure that these are achievable by ensuring that children of all abilities develop confidence and appropriate skills. The capacity for all art forms to motivate, to encourage self-esteem, to stimulate the imagination and curiosity, and to encourage children generally to investigate is the source of major outcomes of any learning experience for a child with severe learning difficulties (Carpenter & Hills, 2002).

From a different viewpoint, Imray and Hinchcliffe (2014) argue that a creative curriculum is necessary for those with profound to moderate learning difficulties (PMLD) and disabled students to be directly involved in curriculum development. It is not at all easy to assess whether those with PMLD will benefit in the same way as non-disabled students, simply because the cognitive functioning levels of those with profound learning difficulties may preclude a number of the elements of learning that we might aim for with those with severe learning difficulties. Art is, however, process based, and careful observation of small and subtle changes in those with PMLD will indicate learning taking place over time. Art offers real opportunities for joint ventures, an inclusive curriculum and an addressing of the issues raised in the Quality of Life debate (Lyons & Cassebohm, 2010). Effective participation in reciprocal activities, even if they are constructed with verbal or non-verbal activities, are essential for the practice of Manabi.

One of the major problems surrounding special and inclusive education is treatment compatible with increasing severity, duplicability, and diversity of the disabilities and health conditions of students. In the context of inclusive education, intervention training has been very meaningful with regard to two points. The first is the practical engagement of regular school students in the field of special needs education and treatment. The treatment for multiply disabled students has been accompanied by co-/medical care, and teaching and instruction should be checked on a case-by-case basis in the real-world classroom context. The second is that the small teaching group with diverse students is a condition for Manabi in inclusiveness. This collaborating practice of teachers and other teaching staff has become the basis of the inclusive setting of education. The case indicated that this ongoing project requires further analysis and inquiry, including some theoretical framework. In this chapter, the character of Manabi in inclusive education is shown as a complex assembly of the subject and contents of Manabi, but specifying the features of specialized curriculum contents would be informative in inclusive education for both special and regular school students coming into inclusive education.

The percentage of physically and mentally disabled children engaged in 'education for the disabled' today is very small, compared to the ratio of physically and mentally disabled children educated in many foreign countries, and totals approximately 1.4% of children of school age (2001). About 10–16% are involved in education for physically and mentally disabled children in the UK, and 20% are regarded as children with special educational needs in the United States. In Japan, the ratios of students engaged in education for the physically and mentally disabled to all school-aged children remain low; this applies to those registered in regular classes who are not receiving necessary support.

Disabled children learning in regular schools or regular classrooms, rather than learning in classes or schools for the disabled, often become 'dropouts' or function as 'visitors,' simply because substantial learning is not sufficiently guaranteed. However, this does not justify automatically returning to the premise of segregated education, and there is only some effective integration under present conditions. Uncertainty usually accompanies inclusion in countries without educational reform. On the other hand, reform of the education system and changes to special schools are expected in the future when inclusion is fully accomplished.

Through these discussions, the contour of Minna has been formed. In the Japanese language, we usually use *Minna* as in '*Minna Sou Itteiru*' ('Everyone says so'). In this context, we do not mean that Minna is literally all persons. Rather, Minna indicates all the people with a practical relation to one another. In the context of Manabi, Minna indicates the other students with whom the subject has direct communication and relations that enable her or him to share in collaborative learning. The relation with Minna has to include intimate affection and reciprocity.

In this century, the influence of globalisation may bring long-term strains that must be overcome. Specifically, strained relationships may emerge between mind and material, long- and short-term considerations, competition and equality of opportunity, and human beings' limited ability to digest an expanding and seemingly infinite amount of knowledge. Moreover, there may be strains between global and local, universal and individual, and the traditional and modernised.

Education that promotes the symbiosis of children with disabilities and normal children will not move ahead effectively by adopting simplistic ways of thinking and reductively assuming that those with disabilities only need a place to live together and to learn to overcome obstacles and acquire abilities before being put away. This mindset could again cause the dumping of disabled children in the education system. Further analysis of the reform of the conventional system should aim to polish strategies for progress while also creating education systems to guarantee that those with normal abilities and children with disabilities develop their characters cooperatively together in various situations, steadily engaging in cooperation and collaboration at various levels.

As this examination has shown, the concept of Manabi introduces an important viewpoint when considering the possibilities for the inclusion of disabled children in Japan. Compared to the Western learning theory of group work, such as the situated learning theory, the transition to another work task upon mastering a current task may be discussed, but in this case, the transition between tasks is not emphasized. Rather, most students repeat the same task for months, even after they have mastered it. Teachers prepare the working and learning process that leads from the process to the execution of a task and properly allocate their students to each stage in the work process. Why do they not transition? Their work focuses not only on the mastery and practice of a skill but also on the formation of human relationships among colleagues, giving thought to how people around them would feel and act (慮る), so that students can experience achievement within a communal setting.

We notice two main features of Manabi in this context. The first is the continuity and discontinuity of time. In many Manabi settings, the continuity of time is not highly considered, which is reflective of Japanese culture and the discontinuity of time. The students redo their work many times, even if they master their task, because they meet the here-and-now task in that time, resolving their previous works. Kerschensteiner's Arbeitsschule, for example, which was introduced in Japan in the early twentieth century, was considered to be the practical theory of the role of work as a central subject matter for all students and emphasized not the labour of work but the creation and production of their self-activated works, such as plowing the field, caring for the animals, and making the violin. We can track a series of work of these types of learning.

For students in Manabi settings, however, it is hard to adapt to the continuity of time, which is an aspect of Western culture. According to Numata, the Japanese traditionally deal with time concretely, in a touchy-feely and intuitive manner, and do not rely upon the abstract organization of time, which is in accordance with Western culture, rationally in a transcendent viewpoint like the Western style (Numata, 2002). Kato suggests that one of the concepts of time in Japanese culture is circulated time with the clear segment (Kato, 2007). Manabi and the Japanese sense of time are both concerned with the concentration on now and the present time.

The second factor is the communality of the working groups. The carefully situated allocation of students, the arrangement of tasks, and the selection and separation of stages constitute an environment in which students are members of a Manabi community. The intention of this set-up was for all students to have a unique role in the community and to be able to display their abilities. The establishment of this environment is based on the theory of full participation. In these scenes, the students are absorbed in their work and extend beyond the self (無我の境), so the value of their communal work is more greatly emphasized than the individual's personal work or education.

Tsumori (2002) provides telling clues about Manabi for special needs children. Being a developmental psychologist and a principal of a private special educational school, he finds the features of Manabi and *Sodachi* (育ち, a concept like growing up or development) in each student. He submits the concept of 'multilayered time' in the case of an intellectually disabled student. Multilayered time shows overlapping phases for the children facing the Manabi situation, and the meaning and essence of Manabi are original, even though they participate in the same classes and lessons. As for the students with special educational needs, we sometimes see the teachers' different assumptions of Manabi due to our experience with disabilities and illness, as well as the disabled students' original condition, such as learning disabilities and emotional disturbance. Manabi is based on the different experience of the disabled students' daily lives and learning, the characters of needs and of others, as well as on the learning situation with respect to collecting and collaborating in Minna. Sometimes the selfless care for friends or colleagues leads to reciprocal learning in the inclusive classrooms.

Among the cases in this chapter, literacy and art act as the requisite tools that make it possible for the disabled to learn and join in with Manabi activities and that also act as a factor causing alienation from the learning community in regular classes. Besides, while literacy and art may have various uses for so-called normal children, for a child with hearing loss and other disabilities, their use is local and does not necessarily allow communication outside a specific community. The main argument for inclusion was that it was a way for exceptional children to domesticate themselves within the 'normal' school culture. Given the differences across the described categories from school to school, there are notable contrasts in the service models of support for such learners (Carrington & Elkins, 2005). Similarly, literacy is seen as a normalizing force. Thus, to investigate special education and inclusion, it is necessary to examine the contents of Manabi apart from disability, curability, or medical care.

Bibliography

Barnes, C., & Mercer, G. (2003) *Disability*, Cambridge, Polity Press.
Buzzelli, C. A., & Johnston, B. (2002) *The Moral Dimension of Teaching: Language, Power and Culture in Classroom Interaction*, New York, RoutledgeFalmer.
Carpenter, B., & Hills, P. (2002) "Rescuing the Arts: The Sunmoves Project," *The SLD Experience*, 32, 22–24.
Carrington, S., & Elkins, J. (2005) "Comparison of a Traditional and an Inclusive Secondary School Culture," Rix, J., Katy, S., Nind, M., & Sheehy, K. eds. *Policy and Power in Inclusive Education: Values into Practice*, New York: Routledge.
Cornett, C. E. (2003) *Creating Meaning Through Literature and Arts: An Integration Resource for Classroom Teachers* (2nd ed.), Merrill/Prentice Hall, Upper Saddle River.
Farrell, M. (2010) *Debating Special Education*, New York: Routledge.
Ferguson, D. L. (1987) *Curriculum Decision Making for Students with Severe Handicaps: Policy and Practice*, New York, Teachers College Press.
Giroux, H. (1996) *Fugitive Cultures: Race, Violence, and Youth*, New York: Routledge.
Gregoire, M., & Lupinetti, J. (2012) Supporting Diversity Through the Arts, *Kappa Delta Pi Record*, 41(4), 159–163.
Hori, M. (1994) *Shogaiji Kyoiku no Paradigm Tennkan: Togo Kyouiku heno Riron Kenkyu*, Tokyo: Tsuge Publication.
Imray, P., & Hinchcliffe, V. (2014) *Curricula for Teaching Children and Young People with Severe or Profound and Multiple Learning Difficulties: Practical Strategies for Educational Professionals*, Abington, Routledge.
Kato, S. (2007) *Nihon Bunka niokeru Jikan to Kuukan*, Tokyo: Iwanami Shoten.
Kimura, H., & Ichida, Y. (1995) "Roubunka Senngen," *Gendai Shiso*, 23(2), 354–362.
Lyons, G., & Cassebohm, M. (2010) "Life Satisfaction for Children with Profound Intellectual and Multiple Disabilities," Kober, R. ed. *Enhancing the Quality of Life of People with Intellectual Disabilities: Social Indicators Research Series*, 41, Dordrecht: Springer, 183–204.
Manner, J. C. (2002) "Arts Throughout the Curriculum," *Kappa Delta Pi Record*, 38(1), 17–19.
Mashiko, H. (ed.) (2006) *Kotoba, Kennryoku, and Sabetsu*, Sangensha.
Ministry of Education, Culture, Sports, Science and Technology (2016) "'Team toshiteno Gakkou no Arikata (The Concept of 'The Schools as Teams')," www.mext.go.jp/b_menu/shingi/chukyo/chukyo3/siryo/attach/1365408.htm [accessed 30 August 2018].
Ministry of Education, Culture, Sports, Science and Technology (2018) "Tokubetsu Shien Kyouiku Shiryo (Annual Report for the Special Needs Education), fiscal 2017," www.mext.go.jp/a_menu/shotou/tokubetu/material/1406456.htm [accessed 28 August 2018].
Ministry of Education, Culture, Sports, Science and Technology in Japan (2012) *Tsuujou Gakkyu ni Zaiseki suru Tokubetsu na Kyouikutekishien wo Hitsuyoutosuru Jido Seito ni kansuru Zennkoku Jittai Chousa* (A Nationwide Actual Condition Survey on the Students with Special Educational Needs in Regular Classrooms). https://www.mext.go.jp/a_menu/shotou/tokubetu/material/__icsFiles/afieldfile/2012/12/10/1328729_01.pdf
Ministry of Education, Culture, Sports, Science and Technology in Japan (2009) *Tokubetsu Shien Gakkou Gakushu Shido Youryo* (Course of Study for Schools for Special Needs Education), Tokyo: Kaibundo.

Ministry of Education, Culture, Sports, Science and Technology, Office for Assessment of Academic Ability, Elementary and Secondary Education Bureau (2018) "Improvement o Academic Abilities (Course of Study)," www.mext.go.jp/en/policy/education/elsec/title02/detail02/1373859.htm [accessed 10 September 2018].

Ministry of Education, Culture, Sports, Science and Technology, Office for Special Needs Education, Elementary and Secondary Education Bureau (2018) "Tokubetsu Shien Gakkou no Kyouin no Tokubetsu Shien Gakkou Kyouyu Mennkyojou Hoyuu Joukyoutou Chousa Kekka no Gaiyou (Abstract for the Survey on the Holding Ratio of Teachers' Certification in Special Education Schools' Teachers), fiscal 2017," www.mext.go.jp/a_menu/shotou/tokubetu/__icsFiles/afieldfile/2018/03/26/1402731_1.pdf [accessed 6 August 2018].

Ministry of Internal Affairs and Communications (2017a) "Kyouiku Shokuin Menkyo Hou Kaisei (Educational Personnel Certification Law)," last revised in 2017, http://elaws.e-gov.go.jp/search/elawsSearch/elaws_search/lsg0500/detail?lawId=324AC0000000147

Ministry of Internal Affairs and Communications (2017b) "Gakkou Kyouiku Hou Sekou Kisoku (The Ordinance for Enforcement of the School Education Act)," last revised in 2017, http://elaws.e-gov.go.jp/search/elawsSearch/elaws_search/lsg0500/detail?lawId=322M40000080011&openerCode=1 [accessed 3 September 2018].

Murayama, T. (2017) "Nihon no Tokubetsu Shien Kyouiku Kyouin Yousei no Genjou to Kadai," *Nichi Ei Kyouiku Zasshi*, 3(1), 38–50.

Nakamura, M., & Arakawa, S. (2003) *Shougaiji Kyouiku no Rekishi*, Tokyo: Akashi Shoten.

Numata, H. (2002) *Kyouiku no Jouken: Ninngen, Jikan, and Kotoba*, Sendai: Tohoku Daigaku Shuppannkai.

Oda, Y. (2002) "Choukaku Shougai Kyouiku ni okeru Literacy kan ni kannsuru Kennkyu: Aratanaru Literacy Gainen no Kouchiku ni mukete," *Kokuritsu Tokushu Kyouiku Sogo Kennkyujo Kennkyu Kiyo*, 29.

Oliver, M. (1996) *Understanding Disability: From Theory to Practice*, Macmillan.

Ramanaidu, R. R., Wellington, E. C., Lim. Z. & Hassan, N. R. N. (2014) "Pre-Service Music Teachers' Concerns before a Practicum Stint," *International Education Studies*, 7(8), 35–43.

Sakata, T. (2002) *Gakkou, Hou, Shakai: Kyouiku Mondai no Houteki Kentou*, Tokyo: Gakuji Shuppan.

Sakurai, R. (1964) "Gengo Shido to ha donoyouna koto ka," Rouji no Shinri to Kyoiku Kenkyukai. (not in trade).

Sato, M. (2001) "Kyouiku Kaikaku ni okeru Shin-jiyuushugi no Rhetoric," *Jyokyo*, 11(3), 6–18, Jyokyo Shuppan.

Shibasaki, R. (2000) "Inclusive na Hukushi Shakai e: Shougai no aru Hito ni totte no Jiritsu," *Jinnken to Kyouiku*, 33, 19–33.

Shirakawabe, T. (2019 *Nihonjin ha Naze "Tanomu" noka*, Chikuma Shobo.

Swain, J., & Cook, T. (2005) "In the Name of Inclusion: We All, at the End of the Day. Have the Needs of the Children at Heart," Rix, J., Katy, S., Nind, M., & Sheehy, K. eds. *Policy and Power in Inclusive Education: Values into Practice*, Routledge Falmer.

Takeuchi, T. (1975/1988) *Kotoba ga Hirakareru Toki*, Tokyo: Chikuma Shobo.

Tsumori, M. (2002) "Hoiku no Chi wo Motomete," *The Japanese Journal of Education*, 69(3), 357–369.

Uenou, S. (2003) *Tatta Hitori no Creole: Choukaku Shougaiji Kyouiku ni okeru Genngoron to Shougai Ninnshiki*, Tokyo: Potto Shuppan.

Yamada, T. (2006) "Ethnomethodology kara mita Gengo Mondai," Mashiko, H. ed. *Kotoba/Kenryoku, Sabetsu Gengoken kara mita Jyoho Jakusha no Kaiho*, Tokyo: Sangensha Publishers Inc. 2.

Chapter 6

Practices of Manabi in school

Yasunori Kashiwagi

Introduction

In this last chapter, I would like to introduce the typical practices historically included in Japanese schooling that are representative of Japanese learning, i.e., Manabi. It will be shown that a variety of activities reflect the positive effects of Manabi. If designed correctly, such practices can help children to develop Japanese – and East Asian – 'way' at any place and time.

This chapter will explore how we can support children developing Manabi based on Nothingness theory and Minna theory through typical activities in Japanese schooling: *Nyugaku-shiki* (入学式) and *Sotsugyo-shiki* (卒業式), *Souji* (掃除), *Kyushoku* (給食), *Shiiku activities* (飼育活動), *Undo-kai* (運動会), and *Bukatsu* (部活). All these activities aim to support Japanese learning, namely Manabi, in school.

Activity 1. Nyugaku-shiki and Sotsugyo-shiki: what is the school entrance ceremony?

School in Japan starts with Nyugaku-shiki (the entrance ceremony of Japanese school or kindergarten). When small children enter kindergarten, they experience their first Nyugaku-shiki in the entrance ceremony held there. Elementary school students (5–6 years old) go dressed up and under tension to the centre of the hall where the ceremony is held. As a matter of course, parents accompany their child, but they are seated separately in the entrance ceremony. Parents may watch the children in the ceremony hall. Many fathers bring a video camera and record their children's appearance. The Nyugaku-shiki ceremony lasts for about one hour. Teachers, children, parents, and guests (including local politicians) meet there and together sing the national anthem (君が代, *Kimigayo*) and the school song in the solemn, quiet atmosphere of Nyugaku-shiki. Especially in the case of kindergartners, they are restless because of the non-daily, serious and solemn atmosphere there. Schoolchildren in the first grade of elementary school become silent and sit quietly, and if their 'name' is called by the teacher, they should as new students answer '*Hai!*' in a loud voice. In the quiet hall, no sound other than the child's voice is to be heard. Everyone keeps quiet as if practicing Zen. This ceremony progresses solemnly in silence. The form of the ceremony is similar in junior high school, high school, and university. In addition, when the Japanese join a company in April, the initiation ceremony (入社式, *Nyusha-shiki*) is invariably held like a Nyugaku-shiki.

The main content of Nyugaku-shiki is the school director's or principal's speech. This speech is very important regardless of its pedagogical content. The children become silent, and it is more important that they hear the speech itself than that they understand what is said. Silencing and hearing are very important issues. Every school holds this entrance ceremony, which plays a very important role as an introduction to the silence, doing nothing, or Selflessness needed for their long school lives starting then. Moreover, in forming Minna, which plays an important role in Manabi, this entrance ceremony has a very important meaning. The students will be recognized as members of the school by sharing the same place (場) together, being silent with one another, and experiencing the ceremony in the first stage of their school life. Such recognition may be confirmed in the current students' speech as well.

Nobody has doubts about the existence of such entrance ceremonies in Japan. Several years ago, I explained in a lecture that the Nyugaku-shiki is an authoritarian event with all the appearance of Formalism and Totalitarianism and criticised the ceremony afterwards. However, at that time, no students

Figure 6.1 The entrance ceremony of Japanese primary school

expressed doubts about the ceremony. On the contrary, one student said to me with distrust, 'Why do you deny Nyugaku-shiki so much? We think Nyugaku-shiki is a beautiful time!' Strangely, Nyugaku-shiki is held at both old conservative schools and progressive schools. Not even progressive educators criticise this conservative ceremony. Nyugaku-shiki is widely accepted by all Japanese, and no one seeks to abolish this ceremony, yet nobody can neatly explain its educational meaning. Therefore, it may be said that this entrance ceremony is a good example of the hidden curriculum of Manabi.

Although graduation ceremonies are held at schools in Western countries as well, their atmosphere is different from that of the graduation ceremonies in Japan. Western graduation ceremonies resemble the closing ceremony of the Olympics. Rhythmic music is played, and laughter fills the ceremony. Even slide shows are prepared in advance, and the participants enjoy seeing pictures of their school life in the ceremony. Some graduation ceremonies even have orchestral performances. Moreover, some graduation ceremonies also feature dancing; the students perform a so-called graduation dance or celebratory dance. In traditional Christian schools in the West, the graduation ceremony is held in a solemn church atmosphere like that in Japan, but there is no religious meaning in Sotsugyo-shiki despite its resemblance to graduation ceremonies.

Sotsugyo-shiki, the Japanese graduation ceremony, means the end of Minna, the dismantlement of Minna, and the final farewell to Minna, and teachers and students might tear up during the ceremony. The symbol of Sotsugyo-shiki is tears of farewell. For instance, in the lyrics of a very famous graduation song, *Aogeba Totoshi* (a Japanese version of an old U.S. school song) from 1884, it is sung, 'Now is the time for farewell; good-bye, everyone' (今こそ別れめ いざ さらば). Almost all students cry while singing this song. Now I want to ask: From whom are the graduating students separating during Sotsugyo-shiki? To whom should they say goodbye? The answer is everyone, i.e., Minna. Sotsugo-shiki is for saying farewell to Minna. Similar to Nyugaku-shiki, it is important for students who take part in the ceremony to share silence with Minna. When a student speaks, the other students should be silent. In this silence, the students share the last moment of their school lives with Minna. It is apparent that Japanese schooling starts with silence in the Nyugaku-shiki, then ends with silence in the Sotsugyo-shiki. Likewise, it is also clear that schooling starts with Minna, then ends with Minna.

Activity 2. Souji: the reason why students clean their classroom

One thing that all children should experience in Japanese schooling is *Souji* (掃除), namely 'school compound cleaning' (校内清掃) or 'cleaning activities' (清掃活動). Interestingly, Souji is viewed positively by not only conservative educators but also progressive ones, so it might be impossible to eliminate this activity from the schools. In fact, janitors or custodians are not employed in

Japanese schools. Souji time is included in the daily schedule, so the responsibility of cleaning belongs to the students who study there (Tsujikawa, 2019). This cleaning often occurs after the break after Kyushoku (lunch). Most Japanese find an educational meaning in Souji, and the passion for Souji is very strong among the Japanese. Souji is practised in schooling in Taiwan as well.

Souji is the most familiar and popular activity for children in schooling in Japan. Therefore, this activity is often used in teaching materials as setting a good example. The accompanying box contains a passage taken from the textbook of moral education (道徳) for fourth graders.[1]

A transfer student came from abroad to our classroom. His name is Tom. He speaks Japanese very well because his mother is Japanese. He can talk with his classmates naturally. He caught on like wildfire with the students in our classroom.

But there is only one thing about him that I disapprove of. It is that Tom doesn't do cleaning (Souji) well.

Our class does its best in cleaning, but Tom only wandered around here at cleaning time several days later without doing any cleaning. I got up my courage and said to Tom at my side while cleaning the stairs:

'Let's clean together, with everyone (Minna).'

He often beams, but he gazed blankly (stupefied) at me when I made this suggestion and didn't say anything. I tried to suggest cleaning to him once again, but he said nothing. Involuntary, I said loudly,

'Why don't you clean up!?'

Then Minna (the classmates) around me said,

'Stop it. You seem to be bullying him.'

They stopped me. I said,

'I am not bullying him. This is advice (warning). We need to talk (It is understandable if we talk).'

After that, I started cleaning again, though something didn't sit right with me.

In a short meeting (in the afternoon), I asked him,

'Let me know why don't you clean up. It is natural that we clean the space where we are using.'

He answered,

'It isn't natural. In the school where I had gone to, the grown-up cleaners cleaned up, so I can't understand why we have to clean up.'

'Eh, is there a school that doesn't do cleaning . . .'

I heard the murmured voice to be surprised.

'This is our school here. Don't we clean ourselves . . .'

> 'It's fun to clean with everyone (Minna)!'
> 'But Tom has never cleaned with everyone (Minna) before.'
> . . .
> Our classroom went quiet.
> 'I'd been thinking that grown-up cleaners should clean the school,'
> Tom said. I thought a little bit and said,
> 'There is no such cleaner in our school. If we do not clean it, then this school will be dirty. When the school is clean, it is more pleasant. Tom, let's do cleaning together!'
> Then, toward the entire class,
> 'Let's show Tom the way to clean!'
> So I stepped forward. Tom and Minna nodded and said, 'yes.'
> . . .

As shown in this text, Souji is one of important educational means of recognizing children transferring from foreign countries. In Japanese schooling, 'to not do cleaning' means 'not to belong to the Minna formed in school.' Thus, refusing Souji could cause a student to be excluded by the class. Conversely, the transfer student who just participates in Souji could become a member of Minna and stand at the starting point of Manabi. This is a simple way for students to enter school life in Japan. Tsujikawa explains also that the purpose of Souji is 'to clean because Minna [everyone] use the classroom and corridor in school everyday' (Tsujikawa, 2019).

Because the cleaning activity is an experience considered part of Japanese learning, children may use only a basic cleaning tool, such as a dust cloth or a broom and dustpan. This cleaning activity includes a deeper meaning than merely cleaning skills. The children bring a dust cloth (雑巾) from their own home to polish the floor. The cloth should not be bought but sewn by the parents voluntarily. In the classroom, there are children who enjoy 'dust cloth races' too. When the long hallways are being cleaned, many children take part in this race and enjoy cleaning by competing. In school cleaning, vacuum cleaners are not used, much less robot cleaners. If Japanese meet a child cleaning with a broom, then they are put in mind of the prototype of an exemplary child, for example, *Ikkyu-san* (一休さん), who is one of the most famous of Japanese children's novice monks (僧). Rather than discussing a topic intelligently or having deep dialogues with others, it is more important for Japanese children to learn to sweep in silence. The body (体) and the mind (心) are not distinguished in Japanese learning, as discussed in Chapter 3. It is valued that students learn the silent mind through a silent body. Therefore, the cleaning activity may be called an intrinsic Manabi. In addition to the dust cloth race, children play a balancing game involving the broom. Children stand a big broom on their palm and compete to see how many seconds they can balance it there. It is called broom balancing among students.

Moreover, restroom cleaning is especially important for Manabi. Many teachers and educators admit to a pedagogical meaning in cleaning the restroom (Hirata, 2018). Almost all school toilets in Japan are so-called Japanese-style toilets or Asian toilets, i.e., squat toilets, which are thus easy for them to clean. Children eagerly polish the toilets in the restroom while squatting. Children certainly dislike restroom cleaning, but through the experience of restroom cleaning, they understand that the school is an important place like a home, and they recognize that school exists as the public space of Minna. Children play different games in restroom cleaning like dust cloth races or broom balancing. Children enjoy playing hockey with deck brushes and round soap while cleaning the restroom. In this way, the cleaning activity is performed by the children, who want to play in Souji, and the teacher, who wants to let children clean. These cleaning activities may be called the school culture of Japan.

The name of this cleaning activity is also unique. For example, there are elementary schools that implement this cleaning activity positively as a project called the 'clean big strategy' or 'cleaning project.' There is also the activity of the 'environmental beautification campaign' that shows the connection between cleaning and beautification. Children occasionally leave campus to clean the whole town as part of the environmental beautification campaign. Neighbours also smile while watching the children's cleaning without having doubts about the children's work. Moreover, there are schools where not only the children but also the parents clean as well. Teachers, children, parents, neighbours, and all the local populace find an educational meaning in this activity.

Souji is also applied as a punishment for children. Instead of corporal punishment or admonitions, Souji punishment is often given to students. For example, there is so-called *Inokori Souji* (居残り掃除) in which students who forgot their homework must clean the classroom alone after school as punishment. Cleaning is not merely performed to clean the school space but is also understood as the best method for teaching children guidance. Using Souji as pedagogical guidance may indicate that Manabi is connected intimately with Shugyō, and indeed Souji has contributed to Japanese schooling as a traditional educational process based on Shugyō. Therefore, Souji is ultimately an important method for Japanese learning even after the modern Western education system has overspread all the traditional religion of Japan. As Hirata (2018) pointed out, it is true that the 'consciousness of guidance for group order and bodily control' (集団秩序と身体統制の指導意識) exists in the minds of almost all teachers who urge the students to carry out Souji activities, but it is also true that we can confirm many different learning effects for which we can't provide an explanation with the phrases 'group order' or 'bodily control.' As Tsujikawa (2019) explained, Souji is a good practice for children to learn responsibility in the classroom and to develop their minds.

In the past, Western classical music was used as background music during school cleaning activities, but recently the music of the Beatles or Japanese pop music (J-Pop), as well as rock music (J-Rock), has been frequently used. Many students look forward to listening to such music and dancing during Souji.

Activity 3. Kyushoku: lunch as an educational practice

Kyushoku (給食) means 'school lunch.' 給 means 'to issue something from a public agency,' while 食 means 'food' in general. The Japanese school lunch is also an important educational activity that provides good examples to clarify Manabi. Many schools require students to bring a bento (lunch box), but in many public schools Kyushoku, i.e., school-made lunches, are provided in the dining hall during the schoolday.

Atsuko Satake, the Cafeteria Culture media director, produced an original film to introduce Kyushoku all over the world that she uploaded to YouTube (see www.youtube.com/watch?t=1&v=hL5mKE4e4uU).

The opening of this film displays the following massage: 'The 45-minute lunch period is considered an educational period, the same as math or reading.' This film had received 21 million views as of September 2018 and has been watched by people in all parts of the world.

According to the Japanese course of study (学習指導要領, 2017), i.e., the curriculum guidelines defining the basic standards for education, it is important for schooling 'to attempt the formation of preferable eating habits and to improve interpersonal relationships through eating, placing Kyushoku time at the center of the curriculum' under the section on 'the formation of preferable eating habits based on the perspective of food education' (食育).

Kyushoku is one of the most elaborate practices of Manabi in Japanese schooling. The students nominated for lunch duty must bring the Kyushoku foods from the Kyushoku chamber into the classroom, then prepare the tables for tray service and plate the food for every classmate. Finally, all the classmates have Kyushoku in a group in the classroom. Using the words from the Japanese course of study, Kyushoku aims 'to make the interpersonal relationship better.' It is now possible to say precisely that Kyushoku exists not only for lunch but also for the formation of Minna. Thus, it is true that Kyushoku is not just about eating, and indeed, because Kyushoku is an educational practice, the students clean up after themselves after Kyushoku.

Kyushoku has various menus and a wide variety of foods. Of course, the Kyushoku menu is different every day. Students enjoy eating Japanese food and Chinese food as well as Western food, so these culinary repertoires are also multifarious. The menu for Kyushoku is planned under the professional supervision of nutritionists, so students enjoy having healthy and cultural meals every day.

The students have Kyushoku in the form of *Han* (班), like a group. Basically, they have Kyushoku close to their classmates, but they sometimes can have lunch with someone else they want to eat lunch with. However, teachers should be careful not to leave them alone. If there is bullying in the class, teachers should be especially watchful during lunch. The student in charge of the duty for the day (日直) gives his or her classmates a command to say '*Itadaki masu*,' a greeting before eating, after which students start to have Kyushoku.

Children show a keen interest in the menu every day. As soon as students know the day's Kyushoku menu, their feelings and condition during the day will change accordingly. Students know the taste of junk food and fast food from an early age and thus might not find the school lunch delicious. But it is also a part of food education to encounter ingredients and dishes that cannot be experienced with junk food or fast food.

Parents prepare many different items for the school Kyushoku, such as place mats, drawstring bags, drinking cups, toothbrushes, and chopsticks. As a matter of course, parents wash them every schoolday and do their share of Kyushoku.

Activity 4. Shiiku Katsudo: raising animals and growing plants in school

In almost all Japanese elementary schools, rabbits, hamsters, or chickens are raised by the students and teachers. Rabbits in particular are symbolic for schoolchildren. According to Nakagawa, some sort of animal is raised at about 90% of all elementary schools in Japan (Nakagawa, 2007). Many schools raise oryzias (Japanese rice fish), crawfish, turtles, ducks, and the like. But not only animals are raised. The idea that all students should grow 'morning glories' is very popular in Japan. Moreover, they should continue to record the daily growth of the morning glories during their summer vacations. In addition, tomatoes, loofahs, *gorya*, okra, eggplants (aubergines), green peppers, and *hoozuki* (Chinese or Japanese lanterns, *Physalis alkekengi*) are grown in the school garden.

Shiiku activities, animal- or plant-raising activities as just described, are pursued very actively and have taken deep root in school culture. According to Section 5 of the 'Courses of Study for Elementary School' of MEXT, Shiiku is specified as serving 'to enable pupils to become interested in the habitats of animals and plants and their changes and growth through raising and growing them, to realise that they are living and growing, to be familiar with living things, and to be able to cherish them' (Section 5, Living Environment Studies). In this section, we can find evidence of this activity oriented toward 'interest in changes,' 'realization of living,' or 'familiarity with living things,' and according to Nakagawa (2007), students must learn 'affection,' 'self-esteem,' 'responsibility,' 'a cooperative mind,' 'selfless consideration of others,' 'scientific interests,' and the like. Based on the theory of Manabi, we must focus on a mind of cooperation with Minna, or selfless consideration as Selflessness. All the educational practices in Japan are motivated toward cooperation with Minna and inculcating a selfless consideration of others (Seken).

Additionally, according to the research of Nakajima et al. (2011):

> If the participation of both students and school is high (frequent), and if the guidance in the raising of animals on the part of the school and the educational aims are steady, and counseling by a veterinarian continues, then raising animals in school and attachments to animals have the effect of facilitating adaptation to school or selfless carefulness toward animals and others.

This sentence suggests that the effect of learning 'selfless carefulness toward animals and others' is an aspect of Selflessness.

Children experience raising animals and growing plants selflessly in the process of learning in school. In these practices, Selflessness plays an important role in learning. Additionally, by raising something with the other students, they learn the consciousness of solidarity, i.e., Minna-consciousness. This point of view is also an important element of Shiiku activity.

Activity 5. Undo-kai: the meaning of the wonder sports festival in school

One of the top highlights in the school year from kindergarten to junior high school is the yearly sports day (or sports meeting) called *Undo-kai* (運動会). *Undo* (運動) means 'sports' or 'activities,' and *Kai* (会) means 'meeting' or 'party.' 'It is very popular as one of the school events as well as the company recreation. It is not just sports or competition; it has many benefits such as enhancing the teamwork, and the unity among the organisation' (see http://undokaiya.com/). See Figure 6.2.

Normally, Undo-kai takes place as a struggle between a red team and a white team; in addition, in some cases a yellow team and a blue team are formed. In Undo-kai, red and white caps and red and white headbands are used by students.

JICA (国際協力機構, Japan International Cooperation Agency) has received requests to help put on this Japanese sports event from about 20 countries in the world. Undo-kai is also a typical annual educational event in Japanese schools like Nyugaku-shiki or Sotogyo-shiki.

The duration of the period spent preparing for Undo-kai is remarkable; it lasts about one month until Undo-kai Day. The pre-practice and rehearsal of Undo-kai in kindergarten is particularly hard and punishing not only for older children but also for kindergarteners. In kindergarten Undo-kai, children run, throw balls, sing songs, dance with music (sometimes folk dances), perform skits, and engage in other activities. As kindergarteners begin preparations for Undo-kai one month or more before the event, teachers generally devote a great deal of time and energy to making Undo-kai succeed.

Figure 6.2 50-meter race in kindergarten

Undo-kai is not merely a 'sports festival' and 'sports day.' Winning or losing is not important in Undo-kai, although in some events, participants must compete against one another, such as the 50-meter race or 100-meter race that require competition with other students. A student who wins the race gets a medal for first prize, and similarly for the second- and third-place finishers, as in the Olympics. But besides such personal events as various races and competitions, there are also many events involving group dynamics that derive from Japanese tradition or East Asian culture. The most representative event of all those events is *Kiba-sen* (騎馬戦, 'mock cavalry battle'). This cavalry battle is like the so-called 'chicken war' in Western nations. Undo-kai gradually approaches its climax in Kiba-sen, and in fact this battle takes place in girls' junior or senior high schools as well. Kiba-sen is popular amongst many people regardless of age or gender in Japan. And Pan-Kui-Kyousō (パン食い競争, 'Bun eating race') is also very popular for children. See Figure 6.3.

Another activity that the Japanese have a liking for is *Kumi-taisō* ('the human pyramid'). If you visit a Japanese high school Undo-kai, then you can see 6- or 7-tier human pyramids or even human pyramids with 10 tiers. Traditionally, physical education teachers had students construct human pyramids to improve

Practices of Manabi in school   135

Figure 6.3 Bun eating race – without using their hands!

children's physical abilities. However, Uchida, a sociologist, has criticised this activity based on educational sociology and risk management (Uchida, 2016). This is a lively topic of debate in Japan, as it is unclear whether we should continue to let students play Kumi-taisou or abolish the practice. The principal of one kindergarten has stated that Kumi-taisou involves cooperating with Minna. Children can join with other children to share the joy of achieving one thing with Minna in making this gymnastic formation. Although Kumi-taisou is strongly criticised by those interested in risk management in schools, I think that we will continue to hold this gymnastic formation for children. It is not easy to abolish this event because many teachers and educators still believe in the pure joy of cooperating with Minna and achieving something together. Undo-kai aims to enhance the consciousness of Minna so that all the children become part of a whole that unites everyone. Because of the formation of Minna-consciousness, Kumi-taisou will survive for years to come, even if progressive educators or sociologists criticise the pyramid from the perspective of 'the critique of totalitarianism.'

The cheer battle (応援合戦, *Ouen-Gassen*) that is held at the beginning of Undo-kai is also one of its highlights. Little children yell, applaud, and cheer for their own team. If Japanese hear, 'Fuleee, fuleee, red team, Fule fule red team, fule fule red team!', then they readily imagine the situation of this cheer battle.

Also, the male cheer group leader cheers not only for his own team but also for their opponents at the same time. Many parents look forward to this little cheer battle. If non-Japanese or foreigners watch this battle, then they may imagine a mass game, but those who enjoy this battle most are the students themselves. The Japanese cannot imagine Undo-kai without Ouen-Gassen.

In many events, students play with other students (Minna) in the context of Undo-kai, such as the centipede race, tug of war, three-legged-race, beanbag toss, ball-rolling race, parent–child competition, and eye of the typhoon. Almost none of these events will work without cooperation with the other students. In those events, many educational elements are connected with Manabi, Japanese learning: cooperating with one another, helping one another, uniting as one, and getting in sync with one another. Considering these elements, we should say that Undo-kai is not a mere sports festival.

Activity 6. Bukatsu: why students belong to extracurricular clubs in school

Bukatsu (部活, 學生社團), or *Bukatsudou* (部活動), is the most important familiar activity in all of school life for students. Japanese school life will not work for students without Bukatu. Generally, Bukatsu is club activities after school. *Bu* (部) means 'club' or 'team,' and *Katsudou* (活動) means 'activity' or 'action.' Bukatsu pertains to individual schools, not to public club teams competing outside of school.

Bukatsu activities continue from elementary school to university. Bukatsu is especially important for middle school and high school students. In addition, almost all parents and adults support Bukatsu enthusiastically since it brings to mind their own activities in their younger days. Those who graduate from Bukatsu are called OB (old boy) or OG (old girl); 'OB' and 'OG' also refer to students who belong to the same Bukatsu group. Bukatsu is considered a symbolic aspect of school culture in Japan. It is no exaggeration to say that there is no school without Bukatsu.

It is said that there is no single suitable equivalent for Bukatsu. If translated literally, it would be 'school club activities,' 'team activities,' or 'extracurricular activities.' If translated into German, it might be similar to *Verein*. Whereas *Verein* refers to community activities outside of school, Bukatsu refers to school activities. Those who lead the activities are teachers, who take the lead not merely in teaching but also in Bukatsu activities. In general, Bukatsu starts in the third or fourth grade of elementary school at the earliest. In junior high school and high school, Bukatsu activities reach their highest peak.

According to the course of study provided by MEXT, Bukatsu is defined as acting autonomously and independently, mainly occurring after school under the support (guidance) of teachers, serving as an educational activity, and involving like-minded students interested in the same sports, culture, sciences, or other areas. In accordance with this definition, Bukatsu is basically an autonomous, independent school activity.

Bukatsu is not merely an activity. It gives students their own identity and sense of belonging. Questions like, 'What extracurricular activity (Bukatsu) are you in?' and 'What Bukatsu do you belong to?' are essential questions for good communication skills. Bukatsu is a top concern of all students at all times.

There are roughly two categories of Bukatsu: Bunka-kei (non-athletic clubs) and Taiiku kai-kei (athletic clubs). *Bunka* means 'culture,' and *Taiiku* means 'PE' or 'sports.' It is extremely difficult to translate these two categories. *Taiiku kai-kei* is a common term to express a type of student identity. If you say, 'I'm Taiiku kai-kei,' then all Japanese can immediately form an image of you, and if you say, 'People tell me that I'm Taiiku kai-kei,' this means 'I'm macho both physically and mentally, tough, authoritarian, shy, honestly, faithful, polite, patient, and brave.' The term *Taiiku kai-kei* is a psychological concept used to express personality as well as character.

In addition, clubs (部, *Bu*) give students a greater sense of belongingness than does the classroom. Clubs become students' identity in school, and the solidarity formed in club activities will become Minna-consciousness. To make this consciousness effective, Selflessness is more strictly demanded in clubs than in the classroom. Those who belong to Bukatsu are forced to practise Selflessness and Emptiness because they have to defend the Minna-consciousness. In just this way, the essential elements of Manabi stand out in Bukatsu, which represents Japanese school life for students. Therefore, we must take care of students who quit their club because they have lost their sense of belonging in school and solidarity with Minna (members of the club).

The following clubs are typical examples of Bunka-kei clubs: brass band club, chorus club, fine art club, drama club, cinema club, Japanese flower arrangement club, tea ceremony club, volunteer club, calligraphy club, school broadcasting club, newspaper club, natural science club, parlour (popular) music club, computer club, astronomy club, cooking club, and anime club.

Similarly, the following clubs are typical examples of Taiiku kai-kei clubs: baseball club, soccer club, table tennis club, basketball club, volleyball club, track and field club, wrestling club, sumo wrestling club, judo club, kendo club, archery club, dance club, cheerleading club, swim club, softball club, badminton club, rhythmic gymnastics club, tennis club, handball club, archery club, and skiing club.

There are many choices of extracurricular activities, and the adviser-teacher arranges the individual extracurricular activities.

Each club is important in providing a sense of belonging to all students joining it. Once a student joins a club, Manabi starts to work, and then each and every student learns something concerned with Minna, Nothingness, Selflessness, or Seken. What they learn in Bukatsu is to achieve something with Minna, with the other members of the club, to think rationally, to help one another, to care about one another, to think kindly of one another, to resolve all kind of conflicts with the other members, to discover the meaning of 'all for one, one for all,' and to live together. Given all this, it is no exaggeration that they have a solidarity that is stronger than their bonds with their classmates. In conclusion, Bukatsu is an educational activity whereby students can learn what we suggest in this book.

There have, however, been some criticisms of Bukatsu. One such criticism is that students must learn absolute hierarchical relationships inside school, namely the hierarchical relationship between the teacher in charge of the club (顧問) and its members or the hierarchical relationship between the Senpai (mentor, senior, older students) and the Kohai (junior, younger students).

This absolute authoritarian power relationship appears prominently in Taiiku kai-kei clubs. No matter how much this power relationship is criticised by those who affirm democracy and anti-authoritarian thought, nobody can break down this relationship.

By criticising this hierarchical relationship over the years, the situation in Bukatsu has improved little by little. However, many instances of violence and physical assault continue to occur in schools even today. In addition, many students who belong to Bukatsu (mainly in Taiiku kai-kei) at the university are assaulted by coaches and managers.

As is the case with *Karoshi* (overwork death) from working long hours, the expanded training time that students undergo in order to take part in Bukatsu activities is becoming a serious problem in Japan. The term 'black Bukatsu' (excessively hard club activities that habitually violate school standards) is widespread in Japan, paralleling the 'black company' ('evil company'). The prolongation of extracurricular Bukatsu activities might not only increase teachers' working hours excessively but also lead students to a wrong valuation of labour and work.

An Australian who lives in Japan and whose daughter goes to Japanese public school describes this:

> Australian mother Melissa understands only too well how bukatsu can permeate into every spare waking moment of a teenager's life. Her younger child is a member of the high school dance club and practices not only mornings and evenings, but even at lunchtime most days. 'Generally I think kids doing sport is good, but why can't Japan get the hang of moderation?' asks Melissa. 'Basically they are training them to be great salarymen – work 18-hour days without complaining and without having another life.'[2]

Not only in Bukatsu but also in all the Japanese learning, Manabi, such a negative aspect or dark side may be found. Therefore, there have been several sharp criticisms of Japanese schooling and public education, and it seems not unfounded to argue that Japanese education is profoundly connected with the cause of Karoshi.

However, Bukatsu will continue to exist in the schools. Japanese progressive educators do not completely repudiate the necessity of Bukatsu itself, although they criticise the power structure of Bukatsu; indeed, it seems that, instead of repudiating it, progressive education is generally not interested in Bukatsu. In my view, the absolute abolition (disestablishment) of Bukatsu inside school must be demanded. It would be better to organize local club activities outside school like the *Verein* of Germany, but no one seriously shares my position.

It is too difficult for us to reform Bukatsu because it exists at the heart of schooling in Japan. Through Bukatsu, students can learn everything that Japanese truly want to teach, and consequently Bukatsu will continue to be needed by both teachers and students.

Conclusion

The key ideas to draw out of this last chapter is that Manabi can be performed in many different ways. This chapter has shown some of them. The several activities show how Manabi can be embodied in a physical learning and training. For instance, Undo-Kai and Bukatsu provide a fun and engaging structured program to learn about ways to live together, including Selflessness, Minna, Harmony, Kata and Shugyō. Similarly, many activities are strongly related with Manabi as Japanese learning.

This chapter discussed not only the different ways of Manabi but also how Manabi is represented and realised through the actual everyday activities in school. It explains the different practices of Manabi, as well as how Manabi is exhibited using the key concepts described in this book.

Notes

1 See *Atarashii Doutoku* (2018), Tokyo Shoseki, 28–31.
2 See the following resource: http://openprivatelife.blogspot.com/2014/06/bukatsu-japanese-sports-clubs.html [referred to December 29, 2018]

Bibliography

Hirata, O. (2018) *Korekara no Gakkouseisou*, Tokyo: Ikkei Shobou.
Ministry of Education, Culture, Sports, Science and Technology (2017) *Courses of Study*, Tokyo: Ministry of Education, Culture, Sports, Science and Technology.
Nakagawa, M. (2007) "Research of Humane Education Utilizing Animals in Elementary Schools and Sport-System of Veterinarian," *Bulletin of The Research Center for Child and Adolescent Development and Education*, No. 4, Ochanomizu University, Tokya.
Nakajima, Y., Nakagawa, M., & Muto, T. (2011) "The Impact of Rearing School-owned Animals for One Year on the Psychological Development of Elementary School Children," *Science Council of Japan*, 227–233.
Tsujikawa, K. (2019) *Souji Shidou Kanpeki Manual*, Tokyo: Meiji Tosho.
Uchida, R. (2016) "Gymnastic Formations in Schools: Risk of Injury Associated with Larger and Higher Models," *Japanese Journal of Sports and Health Science*, 38, 13–23.

Conclusion

The aim of this book, which focuses on Manabi and Japanese schooling, is to explore an alternative approach to learning called Manabi that could not entirely be explained by the dominant concept of learning in the age of globalisation. This means that our study has described the actuality of Japanese theory and practices of learning that might have a different perspective from the traditional pedagogies in the West and that will provide progressive thoughts on learning in East Asia. The Manabi concept of learning that we consider in this book is related to an art of learning in which Nothingness, Emptiness, Selflessness, Silencing, and No-mind-ness play crucial roles. Although Manabi has been confirmed in Japanese thought to be deeply influenced by East Asian traditions, it should be understood that the practices of Manabi are seen worldwide wherever we live.

The idea of Manabi is not a turgid notion that we can call a 'new discovery' or 'panacea' but rather the quiet little arts of good learners which have been assumed to be 'insignificant' in the context of an enlightened education in the modern era. Viewed from this perspective, the arts of Manabi have been underestimated, marginalised, or ruled out. In other words, the arts of Manabi – to be quiet (to silence), to stop telling (to stop speaking), not to chat aimlessly, to listen attentively (carefully) to the voice of the others, to stop to do something (to come to a standstill), to harmonise (interface) with other people or things, to go along with one's story (to empathise with the story of other people), to sit quietly, and to speak soulful words, the so-called *Kotodama* (言霊) in Japanese, etc. – have been significantly negated by enlightenment educators or modern pedagogy.

However, those arts of Manabi are necessary for human beings to live together in society and in public spaces. Unquestionably, the people who have learned those arts exist all over the world, and, in fact, we receive many benefits and a zest for living from those persons. Consider the situation when you travel to a foreign country where you cannot understand the language. What kind of person will be the most helpful to you if you have any trouble? Probably the person you need at this time would not be the person who speaks fluently in his or her native language. Certainly, your sense of disconnectedness would be resolved, but you would still have considerable anxiety because you could not understand what that person is saying. You will then look for the person who tries to understand what kind of trouble you are having or what you are feeling. In this sense, we have discussed the arts of living in a more situational and contextual way by focusing on the Japanese approach to learning and schooling.

Therefore, the main purpose of this book is not to explain the social and historical background by introducing cultural anthropology research that studies the thoughts and practices of Eastern/Japanese education. Moreover, our purpose is not to describe the educational activities seen in the Japanese schools by using Western pedagogical or philosophical concepts, as many educational researchers have tried to do in the past. Furthermore, the purpose of this book is not to maintain a demand for 'anti-foundationalism' or 'deconstruction' on the basis of post-structuralism or post-modernism. We also aim neither to confuse non-Japanese readers by using the strange wording of the Japanese language in terms of Orientalism or Feminism nor to exaggerate the excellence of Japanese education and schooling in the context of reactionism, conservatism, or patriotism, which we have strongly to beware of.

In addition, as this book shows, learning as Manabi takes neither an anthropocentric nor an anthropomorphic standpoint. Manabi should not be thought of as anthropomorphic learning because it shows the process of a deliverance from self-centredness towards Minna (Everyone) or Nothingness; concurrently, it is a process of human formation whose philosophy has been developed prominently in East Asia.

Our study of Manabi attempts to remain in the range of educational anthropology based on our lifeworld, and it is vital that we seek a pragmatic and metaphysical point of view. To put it differently, we try to address this issue because the elements learned by Manabi as Nothingness would never be experienced directly despite the fact that those elements occur in and from our ordinary living or daily experiences in the lifeworld. It seems to be almost impossible for us to find Nothingness as an object although we learn Nothingness in our ordinary lives during schooling.

However, this unexperienced character of Manabi does not indicate that it involves an educational impossibility; on the contrary, it involves the possibility of learning in schooling the unexperienced arts of living within our ordinary lives. For instance, children learn Selflessness, No-mind-ness, or aesthetic consciousness through learning experiences including lunchtime and cleaning, namely, that Manabi is a process of learning that transcends the dualism between self and others, mind and body, and subject and object in the sense that these constitute 'unexperienceable things' or 'something not assumed to be experience' in ordinary lives. In this regard, Manabi is a more progressive and emancipative process of learning wherein children can be finally free from an active Self.

Manabi is related not to the concept referred to as educational formation (*Bildung*) that aims for a subjective- and objective-individual Self but to the commutative concept which aims to live together with others or nature (in the world) by drawing away from self-centredness. Therefore, it is not too much to say that Manabi presents a conception of humans who can overcome various kinds of conflict and tensions that we might face today.

For instance, during a lesson in a Japanese classroom, we often see a teacher asking different questions of a group composed of five or six students so that they can discuss issues with one another. However, teachers often face occasions when students do not suggest any opinions on their own. Instead of saying something, they only watch one another very carefully. They then start, little by little, to talk about how they should discuss something in their group. In the discussion, students are careful and discrete, not denying other students' thoughts even if someone offers completely different or opposite opinions to their own ideas. On the contrary, they ask the other students, "Everyone (Minna)! What do you think about this opinion?" or "Is there a different opinion?" They are very prudent and cautious about discussing and competing with one another about their own correctness even if their discussion seems to be superficial. Before expressing their own opinions, they care about their classmates first. Then they listen to the opinions of other classmates. After that, they ponder those opinions and then carefully seek the most fitting word with their group members so as not to offend other students. In Manabi, it is more important for Japanese students to care about/for the other classmates, and thus they often do not display conclusively different or opposite opinions because all of the members in the group care about/for the other members. In this respect, it can be said that both the strong and weak points of Manabi are shown simultaneously.

What we should learn in our time is to never outdebate others, never to overcome discussion with 'enemies' in sports and games, never to accomplish self-realisation, never to obey someone blindly, never to follow an authority compliantly and still less to simply resist authority. What we should learn from Manabi is to halt, to take a step back, to stand there and stop moving, to be silent, and to stop to think as well, namely to unthink, and finally to let go of thinking itself. As a matter of course, resistance movements such as demonstrations and strike actions play an important role in democratic societies. It is meaningful to chant slogans and carry placards. Although educating an active and democratic citizenship is effective in a changing society, it is necessary for us not only to learn to raise our voice in protest but also to build our attitude towards taking a step back and to stand there doing nothing; for example, it may also be possible to learn an attitude of nonresistance or pacifism.

We start with an assumption that there is some kind of deficiency in the educational/philosophical discussions of learning. What is lacking in the prevailing educational discourses globally is an exploration of the meanings of doing nothing. As far as we know, doing nothing has rarely been offered as an educational conception in human history; for instance, conceptions such as 'the ability to do nothing,' 'the ability to be silent,' and 'skills for No-mind-ness' are almost nowhere to be found as educational goals or as the achievements of school practices. What we need to reconsider in the era of globalisation in which democratic ideals are at stake because of various issues, such as enhanced nationalism and expansion of social divisions, is that this makes it difficult in our world to promote mutual understanding by dialogue, which would demand an alternative attitude to learning by doing nothing and thinking in mutual silence through reducing self-centredness. Instead of trying to find quick and simplified solutions that might cause additional conflicts and antagonism, Nothingness, Silencing, and Selflessness would construct the foundation of the communicative dialogues. Manabi, as Nothingness, Silencing, and Selflessness, should not be seen as a denial of dialogical communication but as another way of life through which people from various backgrounds can live together.

In this sense, Manabi occurs in a silence which aims to deepen our mutual communication and go beyond the limitations of the language. It makes it possible for us to think and communicate in a more profound way. The practices of doing nothing and 'teaching without words,' which are learned by Zen, Shugyō, and other disciplines, are not given naturally. Therefore, this would never be acquired without learning from someone in some way. Moreover, it would never be learned intensively and efficiently in a short period of time, and it could not be reduced to a simple pattern; in fact, it is impossible to dissolve Nothingness and to take it apart into its component structures. Nevertheless, it is possible to learn the way of doing nothing through Manabi. Manabi refers not only to the result of a particular educational experience but also to the whole process of opening up a different approach to living as subjectification. Manabi will provide an opportunity to reflect 'good learning' and 'good education' in an era of globalisation. Similarly, it will provide a new image of the conception of humanity: an ethical conception of a human who is a silent, harmonious, quiet, and careful person.

This is why we chose *Beyond Learning in the Era of Globalisation* as a subtitle for this book. Policymakers and educational researchers tend to focus more and more on the importance of learning in an era of globalisation, and its concept of learning is likely to be marketised and standardised in a way that is defined by the 'learnification of education.' The standardised concept of learning is so influential that it is adopted as the main direction of educational reform in many countries. Driven by these concepts of learning, a number of international tests and surveys of academic achievement are introduced in schools. As a result, concepts of learning that have different traditions, backgrounds, and philosophies have been trivialised, unified, and finally marginalised in accordance with the trends in globalisation. Japanese Manabi is the theory and practice of learning that goes beyond self-centredness. What we attempted in this book was to provide and elaborate an alternative conceptualisation of learning: Manabi.

Index

Page numbers in *italics* indicate figures and in **bold** indicate tables on the corresponding pages.

Abe, J. 81
active learning 11, 60
Analects of Confucius, The 81, 17–18
animals and plant, raising of 132–133
art: character of, for all learners 118–119; for special needs students 114–116, **115**, 119–120; workshop process for 116–118, **117**
art, Japanese 13–14, 25–26
Art Nouveau movement 26
asceticism 59, 60
Ashida, E. 81
ATC21 (Assessment and Teaching of 21st Century Skills) 11
authentic education, Manabi as 29–31

Being and Nothingness, Western conception of 48–50
benevolent compassion *see* No-mind-ness
Biesta, G. 12, 22, 23
Bildung ix–x, 81, 30, 41; body and mind in Manabi and 74, 75, 76, 79, 80
body and mind in Manabi: introduction to 69–70; Kata and 70–74, *73*; Shi-tei kankei and 83–85; Shugyō and 74–75; Shuyō and mindfulness in school education and 81–83; Shuyō and principle of cultivation and 77–81; Shuyō concept in modern Japan and 76–77; Yōjō and 75–76
Bonno 59–60
Book of Changes, The 81
Book of Documents, The 81
Book of Five Rings, The 53

Book of Poetry, The 81
Book of Rites, The 81
Book of Tea, The 12, 14, 57
Buber, M. 61
Buddhism 11, 37; Euro-American 66; Mahayana 14; mindfulness and 82–83; Nothingness in 43–44; Prajña school of 14–15; Shugyō and 59–60; three marks of existence in 50–51; Zen 12–15, 27
Bukatsu 136–139
Buraku 16
Bushido 12, 16–17, 70
Bushido: The Soul of Japan 22, 70, 78

Cai Yuanpei 23
Carter, R. E. 49
cast off learning 27–29, *28*
ceremonies, school entrance 125–127, *126*
cherry blossoms 16, 57–58
Christian art 26
Chuang Tzu 20
Chūkun Aikoku 80
clearing, school 40, 127–131
clubs, extracurricular 136–139
comptency-based-curriculum 11
Confucianism 81, 11, 24, 37; Dewey and 22–24; effort principle in 32–33; reinterpretation of education in Japanese 19–22; theories of learning in 17–19
Confucius 17–18
cooperative inquiry 23
Corbin, A. 55
Cornett, C. E. 118
cultivation, Shuyō and principle of 77–81

deaf education in Japan 110–111; literacy of children with hearing impairments and 111–112
deep learning 11, 60
democracy 16–17, 22–23
Democracy and Education 23
Descartes, R. 69, 81
Deshi community 83–85
Dewey, J. 16–17, 28; Confucianism and 22–24; Taoism and 24–27
Doctrine of the Mean, The 81
Doi, T. 100
doing nothing 24–29

ecological worldview 22
Edo period 17–18, 20, 56, 69–70; Minna in 95
education, Japanese: benefits of Manabi in 140–143; cast off learning in 27–29, 28; globalisation and 10–12, 32–34; historical influences on 37–38; Japanese Confucianism in reinterpretation of 19–22; learner-centred education in 22–24; Minna in 89, 94–96; nationalism in 33–34; one- versus two-level house model of 65–66; school events in 33; special needs education in 103–106; in a VUCA world 89–90; *see also* Manabi
Educational System Order 21
effort principle 32–33
Emotionlessness 61
Emptiness *see* Nothingness
Encouragement of Learning, An 21, 39
Ende, M. 56
English language, global use of ix–x
ephemerality 58
Epicurus 47, 55–56
Essays in Zen Buddhism 12
Expressionlessness 61
extracurricular clubs 136–139

filial piety *see* No-mind-ness
Five Classics of Confucianism 81
Foucault, M. 76
Four Books of Confucianism 81, 19
Freud, S. 15
Fromm, E. 15, 48–49
Fueki Ryuukou 64
Fujimura, M. 78
Fukuzawa, Y. 21, 38–39
Furukawa, T. 110–111

Gakusei 21
Gakushu 81, 17
Geneaology of Morals, The 47
German language ix–x, 81, 30, 41
globalisation ix–xi; Manabi and Japanese schooling within 31–34; rethinking learning in age of 10–12
Great Learning, The 81
Gregoire, M. 118

Hanh, T. N. 82
Hannya Shingyo 31
Haplessness 57
Harmony 52–53
Hasunuma, M. 79
hearing impairments and literacy 111–112
Heidegger, M. 27, 47, 63, 76
Heimindo 16–17
Hepburn, J. C. 20
Herrigel, E. 15
Hinchcliffe, V. 119
Hirata, O. 130
Hobsbawm, E. 77–78
Hōjōki 58
Hokusai and Japonisme 25
Hokusai Katsushika 25–26
Hölderlin, F. 27
Husserl, E. 61

I Ching 81
Imai, Y. 41
Imperial Rescript on Education 21
Imray, P. 119
inclusiveness in/of Manabi: art and 114–120, **115**, **117**; conclusions on 120–123; deaf education and 110–111; introduction to 103; language as barrier/medium and 112–114; literacy of children with hearing impairments and 111–112; Minna and 120–121; for profound to moderate learning difficulties (PMLD) 119–120; social change for inclusion in Japanese context and 106–110; special needs education in Japan and 103–106
interactive learning 11, 60
International Association for the Evaluation of Educational Achievement (IEA) 10
International Classification of Functioning, Disability and Health (ICF) 119
Introduction to Zen Buddhism, An 15

Itō, J. 19
Izutsu, T. 27

James, W. 28, 46
Japanese and English Dictionary: With an English and Japanese Index, A 20–21
Japanese language, structure of 92–93
Japan Times, The 39
Jiaoyu 20, 21
Jin 18
Jiyu Minken Undo 21
Jung, C. 15

Kabat-Zinn, J. 82–83
Kaibara, E. 56, 75
Kamo no Chōmei 58
Kant, I. 81
Karaki, J. 80
Kata 70–74, *73*
Keiko 70–72
kendo 71
kindness *see* No-mind-ness
Kinoshita, T. 81
Kiyosawa, M. 80
knowledge, elimination of 26–27
Kobayashi, M. 58
Kokutai 33
Kou 18
Koudo 33
Kuuki 63–64, 100
Kyōiku 20–21
Kyoto Mou A In 110
Kyushoku 131–132

Lao Tzu 18, 20, 24–28
learner-centred education 11, 22–24
learning by doing 24–27
Levinas, E. 22
liberalism 23
Löwith, C. 52, 65
lunch as educational practice 131–132
Lupinetti, J. 118

Mahayana Buddhism 14
Manabi: alternative dimension of learning toward Nothingness and Selflessness in 65–66; as authentic education 29–31; benefits of 140–143; body and mind relationship in (*see* body and mind in Manabi); control element in 66; extracurricular clubs in 136–139; inclusiveness in/of (*see* inclusiveness in/of Manabi); introduction to thought in 12–17; and Japanese schooling within globalisation 31–34; Kata in 70–74, *73*; learner-centred education and 22–24; lunch as educational practice in 131–132; methodological perspective on studying 40–42; Minna in 89, 94–96; Nothingness in 42, 43–50, 96; origins and definition of x–xi, 81–10; question of, underlying learning 38–40; raising animals and growing plants in 132–133; as response to learning in age of globalisation 10–12; school entrance ceremony 125–127, *126*; Seken in 61–65; self-formation and 90–92; Selflessness in 42, 50–54, 96, 132–133; Shi-tei kankei and 83–85; Shugyō in 43, 58–61; Silencing in 42, 54–58; Souji in 40, 127–131; sports festivals in 12, 133–136, *134–135*; structure of 42–43, *43*; theories of learning in Confucianism and Taoism and 17–19; *see also* education, Japanese
Mashiko, H. 113
Matsuo, B. 48–49, 54
meditation 42, 56, 66
Meiji Restoration 19–20, 28, 38, 46, 51, 94
Meirokusha group 21
Mencius 20
Merleau-Ponty, M. 71
meta-stage model of learning 41
methodological perspective on studying Manabi 40–42
MEXT (Ministry of Education, Culture, Sports, Science and Technology, Japan) 103, 132, 136
Mi 90–92
micro-society, Japanese 61–65
Minamoto, R. 71–72
mind-body dualism 28, 69; *see also* body and mind in Manabi
mindfulness 42, 66; Shūyō and 81–83
Minna 89, 94–96; empathy from and unity of 97–99; including people who are not present 99–101; inclusiveness and 120–121; Minna's Classroom and 96–97
Mitsukuri, S. 21
Miyadera, A. 99
Miyamoto, M. 53
Mohsin, S. M. 49
Mori, A. 21
Motoda, N. 21

Mou A Kyojyu Sankosho (A Reference Book for the Instruction of the Blind and the Dumb) 110
Mu-Funbetsu-Chi 46
Munen-Musou 53
Muromachi period 70
Mushin 15, 31, 51

Nakagawa, M. 132
Nakajima, T. 33, 133
Nakamura, M. 20, 76–77, 78
Naoki, S. 93
nationalism 33–34
Natsume, S. 28, 58
Neo-Confucianism 17, 75, 76
Nietzsche, F. 47–48
Nihon Shoki 89
Nishi, A. 21
Nishida, K. 28, 46
Nishihira, T. 73–74
Nitobe, I. 16–17, 22, 50, 51, 78
No-mind-ness 15, 27, 33
Nothingness 28, 30–31, 33, 34, 42, 43–50, 96; alternative dimension of learning toward Selflessness and 65–66; as authoritarian Selflessness 52; in Japanese school curricula 49–50; Minna and 101; Shugyō and 43, 58–61; Western concepts of 47–50
No Thought-No Concept 53–54
nous 63–64
Numata, H. 95
Nyugaku-shiki 125–127, *126*

Oda, Y. 110
Ogyū, S. 19
Okakura, K. 12–14, 57
Okubo, T. 14
one- versus two-level house 65–66
Organisation for Economic Co-operation and Development (OECD) 10, 11, 12, 32, 39
Ota, T. 20
other minds 61–62

plants and animals, raising of 132–133
politeness 16
Prajña school of Buddhism 14–15
Principal Doctrines 47
proactive learning 11, 60
Programme for International Student Assessment (PISA) 10, 11, 12, 32, 39, 99

project-based learning 11
purposeless *see* No-mind-ness

quitting learning 24–29

Ramanaidu, R. R. 118
Ranger, T. 77–78
religious nationalism 33–34
Ren 18, 19, 28, 31, 32
Rinsho 81
Rousseau, J.-J. 95

Saigusa, H. 75
Saito, T. 71, 100
Sakurai, R. 111
Salamanca Declaration 107, 109
Sartre, J.-P. 47–48
Sasaki, S. 60
Sato, M. 29, 91
Satori 14, 49
Sawayanagi, M. 80
school cleaning practice 40, 127–131
school entrance ceremony 125–127, *126*
school lunch 131–132
schools as teams 106
Schopenhauer, A. 81
Segawa, D. 78
Seken 61–65, 93
self, Japanese 93–94; *see also* Seken
self-activation 41
self-actualisation 42
self-control 59
self-formation 90–92
Self-Help 20, 76
self-improvement 24–25
Selflessness 42, 50–54, 96, 132–133; alternative dimension of learning toward Nothingness and 65–66
selfless self 61–65
self-realisation, Western conception of 52
Shiiku Katsudo 132–133
Shimazaki, T. 95
Shimazono, S. 33
Shingari 90
Shinran 44–45
Shirakawabe, T. 103
Shi-tei kankei 60; Manabi and 83–85
Shugyō 43, 58–61; defining 74–75
Shuhari 72
Shuowen Jiezi 20
Shushigaku 17

Shūyō: mindfulness in school education and 81–83; principle of cultivation and 77–81
Shūyō concept, in modern Japan 76–77
Silencing 42, 54–58; Western conception of 55–56
Smiles, S. 20
social change for inclusion in Japanese context 106–110
Socrates 50
Sodoku 81, 19
Somei Yoshino 57–58
Sotsugyo-shiki 125–127, *126*
Souji 40, 127–131
special needs education in Japan 103–106; art project case study on 114–116, **115**
Spirit of the Educator, The 80
spiritualism 80
sports festivals 12, 133–136, *134–135*
Spring and Autumn Annals, The 81
structure of Manabi 42–43, *43*
style 71
Suzuki, D.T. 12, 14–15, 46, 52–53

Taisho democracy 16
Tajima, H. 20, 21
Takeuchi, T. 111–112
Takizawa, T. 75
Tan, S. 23
Tanaka, F. 21
Tannisho 45
Tanomu 103
Tao/Taoism 81, 11, 12–13, 17, 37, 90; Dewey and 24–27; knowing 93; quitting learning in 24–29; theories of learning in 17–19; truth in 30
teaching without words 27–29, *28*
Teaism 12–14, 22–23; Silencing and 57
Terakoya 70
Tokkatsu 12
translation ix, 20–21

Trends in International Mathematics and Science Study (TIMSS) 10, 32
truth 30
Tsujimoto, M. 17, 19, 95
Tsuneyoshi, R. 32–33, 95
Tucker, J. 19

Uchida, T. 84
Ueda, S. 96, 111–112
Uenou, S. 111
Ukiyo-e 25–26
Undo-kai 12, 133–136, *134–135*
Unno, T. 59

vacuum *see* Nothingness
Volatility, Uncertainty, Complexity, and Ambiguity (VUCA) 89–90

Wakimoto, H. 49
Washida, K. 90
Watsuji, T. 92
Wordsworth, W. 28
Works of Mencius, The 81
World Health Organization (WHO) 119

Xiao 18, 19, 31
Xue 17, 22, 32
Xuexi 17

Yamada, T. 112, 113
Yoga 42, 60, 66
Yōjō 75–76
Yoshino, S. 16

Zeami 51
Zen and Japanese Culture 12, 53
Zen Buddhism 12–15, 27; Euro-Americans and 66; Silencing in 42
zest for living 11
Zhu Xi 19

Printed in the United States
by Baker & Taylor Publisher Services